How to make an impact

FT Prentice Hall
FINANCIAL TIMES

In an increasingly competitive world, it's quality of thinking that gives you the edge – an idea that opens new doors, a technique that solves a problem, or an insight that simply makes sense of it all. The more you know, the smarter and faster you can go.

That's why we work with the best minds in business and finance to bring cutting-edge thinking and best learning practice to a global market.

Under a range of leading imprints, including *Financial Times Prentice Hall*, we create world-class print publications and electronic products bringing our readers knowledge, skills and understanding, which can be applied whether studying or at work.

To find out more about our Pearson Education publications, or tell us about the books you'd like to find, you can visit us at
www.pearsoned.co.uk

How to make an impact

Influence, inform and impress with your reports, presentations and business documents

Jon Moon

Prentice Hall
FINANCIAL TIMES

An imprint of **Pearson Education**
Harlow, England • London • New York • Boston • San Francisco • Toronto • Sydney • Singapore • Hong Kong
Tokyo • Seoul • Taipei • New Delhi • Cape Town • Madrid • Mexico City • Amsterdam • Munich • Paris • Milan

PEARSON EDUCATION LIMITED

Edinburgh Gate
Harlow CM20 2JE
Tel: +44 (0)1279 623623
Fax: +44 (0)1279 431059
Website: www.pearsoned.co.uk

First published in Great Britain in 2008

ISBN: 978-0-273-71332-6

British Library Cataloguing-in-Publication Data
A catalogue record for this book is available from the British Library

Library of Congress Cataloging-in-Publication Data
A catalog record for this book is available from the Library of Congress

10 9 8 7 6
11 10

Typeset in 9.5pt Din by 30
Printed and bound in Great Britain by Ashford Colour Press, Gosport, Hants

Brief contents

Acknowledgements xi

Introduction xiii

1 Bullet points ('WiT') 1

2 Graphs 41

3 Tables 85

4 Making comparisons 127

5 Slides 151

6 Numbers 177

7 Document design 193

8 Variances, KPIs and 'flashes' 231

9 Organisation charts 249

10 Next steps 261

Appendix: Computing 265

Bibliography 275

Index 277

Contents

Acknowledgements xi

Introduction xiii

The benefits of clarity and impact xiii
Why so much information is poor xiv
What you will get from this book xvi
Some other pointers about the book xvii
How to save time implementing these ideas xix
Final thoughts xix

1   Bullet points ('WiT') 1

The problems with bullet points 2
The answer – 'WiT' 3
Turning a bullet point list into 'WiT' 6
How 'WiT' helps ensure completeness 12
How 'WiT' is great for slides too 14
How 'WiT' helps cut out words 15
How 'WiT' reassures readers 18
How 'WiT' ensures consistent writing 19
When to 'WiT': repeating patterns, brief sections 21
How 'WiT' can develop a line of argument 23
How 'WiT' can do headings *and* subheadings 26
Can you have too much 'WiT'? 30
When bullet points are acceptable 32
Final thoughts and recap 35

2   Graphs 41

When to do graphs: myths and reality checks 42
Tips for smart graphs 48
Graphs that compare (i.e. not time series) 55

Time-series graphs 63
More than one data set – popular graphs to avoid 69
Tips for graphs in presentations 73
Other ideas for business graphs 74
So what exactly makes a 'good' graph? 77
Final thoughts and recap 79

3   Tables 85
The Big Five Changes 87
Big Change 1: Remove unnecessary gridlines 88
Big Change 2: Avoid too much emphasis 91
Big Change 3: Sort out the row and column order 92
Big Change 4: Make compact 100
Big Change 5: Give a lead-in title 104
Common mistakes with tables 108
Should data be in rows or columns? 117
The big final redo 120
Final thoughts and recap 123

4   Making comparisons 127
A table of ticks and crosses 128
A two-by-two grid 133
A cluster chart 137
Covering the bases 140
A decision tree 143
Final thoughts and recap 147

5   Slides 151
How to get your message remembered 152
Other better alternatives to bullet points 158
Getting the audience to listen, not read slides 163
'But the bullets are my script . . .' 165
Better bullet points 166
When to bend 'rules' for slides 171
How to do a great handout 172
Final thoughts and recap 173

6   Numbers 177
Why numbers confuse 178
Why people don't round 180
How to round – variable rounding 181
Dealing with objections to variable rounding 184

When not to round 186
How to show numbers in text 188
Problems showing percentages 188
Why numbers need friends 190
Final thoughts and recap 191

7 Document design 193
Which fonts to use when 196
Quick and effective typographical tips, part 1 197
Introducing the four principles 198
Principle 1: Contrast 199
Principle 2: Repetition 200
Principle 3: Alignment 201
Principle 4: Proximity 204
Applying the principles: slides, CVs, meeting notes 205
Ideas for your documents 210
Quick and effective typographical tips, part 2 215
Avoiding mistakes with colour 220
In-house design templates 225
Final thoughts and recap 226

8 Variances, KPIs and 'flashes' 231
Variance analysis 232
The one-page KPI and 'flashes' 240
Easier-to-understand balance sheets 245
Final thoughts and recap 247

9 Organisation charts 249
The conventional organisation chart 250
A better way to show the structure 252
The technology bit 257
Final thoughts and recap 258

10 Next steps 261

Appendix: Computing 265
Plotting some of the graphs in this book 266
Excel versus Word and linking between them 268
Showing numbers in Excel 270

Bibliography 275
Index 277

Acknowledgements

I got a lot of help writing this book. It covers a wide range of topics and is relevant to many different types of practitioner – sales, marketing, finance, HR, executives, and so on. Because of this I've called in many favours and sent draft chapters to lots of people for their insight. So at the risk of my sounding like a long Oscar acceptance speech, I am incredibly grateful to Catherine Galvin, Joanna Green, Paul Greenhill, Izabella Grzyb, Chris Jones, Anders Kvan, Jonquil Lowe, Richard Moon (my brother), Ed Percival, Robin Williams, John Scriven and Claire Thomson. They all gave their time and knowledge unstintingly and helped refine this book by an embarrassingly large amount.

My publisher, Liz Gooster, was a constant source of ideas and support and helped keep me on the straight and narrow with the lightest of touches.

Also, Robin Wade gave me great help on the legalities of publishing deals and Judith Castle (my sister) helped me with a regular writing retreat away from distractions.

I owe a great intellectual debt to those authors who originally inspired me and made me realise these topics are more than just 'common sense'. The first was Edward Tufte and his books *The Visual Display of Quantitative Information* and *Envisioning Information*. Then there is Professor A.S.C. Ehrenberg's *A Primer in Data Reduction* which had 12 great pages on constructing tables and showing numbers; his ideas kickstarted many of the tips and methodologies that I developed for Chapters 3 and 6 ('Tables' and 'Numbers'). Finally, in *The Non-Designer's Design Book*, Robin Williams set out the four design principles I mention in the chapter on document design. She was also kind enough to review that chapter.

I am also grateful to JLT Group plc where I worked for ten years in a role that was varied enough to try new ideas (fraud studies, competitor analysis, acquisitions, strategy studies and more). And it was varied enough to see how others showed information – I saw work from many different continents, companies and industries.

Finally, there is my wife Joan. She has been a constant sounding board for new ideas. She has reviewed chapters. She has kept my feet on the ground when I get over-confident – and, much more often, she has picked me up when doubts creep in. She has coped magnificently whenever I retreated into my study to blast out a few more pages. I owe her a huge holiday.

To everyone that helped, thank you for your time, support and wisdom.

Introduction

Information is not power.
Clarity and impact is.

- ➢ The benefits of clarity and impact
- ➢ Why so much information is poor
- ➢ What you will get from this book
- ➢ Some other pointers about the book
- ➢ How to save time implementing these ideas

Confusion, it's just utter, utter confusion.
Tony Hancock, *The Rebel*

The benefits of clarity and impact

I once did a note for a confused CEO. His company had done several months' due diligence to see whether to buy a group of companies, yet he was struggling to see whether to do a deal and on what terms. The problem wasn't too little information – during the due diligence, he'd received lots of weighty reports. And the problem wasn't insufficient 'executive summaries' – he'd received lots of those too. The problem was: he'd received information that was poorly presented, poorly structured and poorly written. It didn't inform.

The CEO asked me to review the information and fixed a time for us to meet. However, it coincided with my son's School Sports Day, so I gave him my apologies and instead sent a three-page note of my thoughts. The thoughts weren't technical. They weren't new either. They'd all been seen in previous reports and notes. But they were clear.

And because I'd used many of the principles in this book, the note didn't just have clarity, it had *impact*.

It clarified and galvanised. Within two days, he'd called off, then drastically renegotiated the deal – and I saw my son win the Hoop and Hat race. Clear information saved the company a *lot* (millions of pounds) and saved me enough time to go to Sports Day.

It shows that neither one-page notes nor 100-page packs were enough. What was needed was information that had clarity and impact.

Clear work *gets results*. Your documents and analyses get read; they are more inviting for readers. People understand and absorb your points faster. You'll help them reach better decisions more quickly.

Also, your business proposals are more likely to succeed – decision-makers look more favourably on proposals they can quickly understand. Clear information shows clear thinking, and clear thinking impresses.

Why so much information is poor

Every day, so many of us grapple with unclear information. We wade through uninviting documents crammed with impenetrable bullet points, graphs and tables.

It wastes so much time, and also leads to bad decisions. I've heard that managers post-rationalise their decisions, that they reach them based on intuition and then look selectively at the information to support their hunch. I'm not surprised. They have to resort to intuition simply because they can't make head nor tail of the information they get sent.

When we're confused, we often don't even admit it. Just as in *The Emperor's New Clothes*, we don't want to seem stupid. We rationalise away our confusion. We blame ourselves: 'I'm no good with numbers.' Other times we blame the topic: 'It's a big complex subject, it takes time to understand.'

Or we say: 'Miggins, this topic that you did a note on, it's quite complex . . . can you pop over to my desk and talk me through it?' But if information is clear, it stands up on its own. I've investigated complex frauds yet didn't have to 'talk through' my reports. Many business journals and newspapers write about complex issues, and I've never had to invite a journalist to my home to 'talk me through' an article.

Also, people don't realise just how much clearer their information could be. Before 1932, the London Tube map was a literal representation of where trains went and everyone thought it was fine. Not Mr Harry Beck, though. He straightened twisting lines, magnified central London and shrunk outer London. His map was launched to public acclaim and highlighted just how average earlier maps had been. It has since become one of the world's most iconic images.

So it is with much business information – until something better comes along, management aren't aware they are being short-changed with poor information.

To add to the problem, many people think that showing information is common sense. Got a lot of numbers? Then do a pie chart – we learnt about them at primary school. The only difference is we now use computers, not crayons. Got a complex point to make? It's easy – just carve the text into brief sections, each preceded with a little black dot known as a 'bullet point'. Computers really do fool us into thinking our documents are well written and our presentations interesting and informative.

And people think that because showing information is just common sense, they needn't spend time learning how to do it. They spend lots on a new system to produce management information, yet spend nothing learning how best to show the information. When I trained as a chartered accountant and MBA, not once did anyone teach me anything in this book. That's quite a statement.

When people try to improve, they misguidedly sign up for Advanced PowerPoint, Excel or Word courses and learn how to do groovy swinging-in bullet points, zany 3-D graphs and fancy fonts. Yet these courses tell us what things we *can* do but not whether we *should* do them – we can't make informed choices. They not only miss the point, they make it worse. They encourage style to triumph over content. Don't worry about clarity, learn instead how to be stylish. If your work is funky, people might not notice it's confusing.

This is a shame because we've got brilliantly powerful software on our desks. Now, more than ever before, all of us can produce beautifully clear work that has incredible impact – at least, we could if only we knew what we *should* be doing.

Some people realise that computers aren't the answer, and instead sign up for writing courses. Yet as we will see, often the best way to show information is not to improve words but to get rid of them altogether and show it a different way instead.

Some people believe one-page notes solve the problem of bad reports. Granted, a confusing one-page note wastes less time than a confusing ten-page report – but it's still confusing. Many CVs are just one or two pages but most don't show the information clearly.

Some people think that it's a communicating problem. They surmise that everything would be fine if people thought more about their objectives and messages. But knowing these won't get you far if you don't know how best to convey them clearly.

Finally, there is one last reason why the problem prevails: people don't know where to find the answers.

This book provides the answers – and as we see in the next section, it provides more, much more.

What you will get from this book

This book will inform and inspire. After reading it, you will do reports and slides that are clearer than you thought possible. Also, they will be more inviting – the book has simple design tips to make work look *sharp*.

But it's more than that. Next time you're pondering what to put in that note, report or slide, you'll be in *control*. Because you know you're doing the right thing, you'll feel more confident, and that confidence will shine through in your work.

Chapter 1 will change for ever how you view bullet points. It's my signature dish, something I call 'WiT' – 'Words in Tables'. Bullet points simply don't give impact to your work. 'WiT' does. It gives *incredible* impact. It visually lifts ideas from slides and reports. It is also how to do a dramatically improved CV.

This book will also change for ever how you view **graphs**. If you think that a graph should be memorable and make instant sense, hold that thought, then read Chapter 2.

Tables get a bad press in business, but that's because many people do bad tables, not because tables are bad. Chapter 3 gives the principles and tips for fantastic tables that communicate your points clearly and concisely.

Many reports, notes and slides make comparisons between alternatives, e.g. outsourcing or staying in-house, but are bad at *showing* the pros and cons of them. Decision-makers struggle to have informed discussions about the alternatives. Chapter 4 on **making comparisons** changes that.

If you are tired of bullet points on slides, Chapter 5 is the answer. It gives ideas and inspiration for **slides**, ones that will better help you meet your objectives.

Chapter 6 looks at how to **show numbers** so they clarify, not confuse.

If you've ever wasted time tinkering unsuccessfully on a computer to make your work look good ('Let's try some bold there and upper case here'), read Chapter 7 on **document design**. Learn quick, simple tips to do reports and slides that really impress.

If you prepare **KPIs, variance analysis** and 'flash' figures – or even if you just review them – Chapter 8 shows some brilliant layouts you will want to adopt and adapt. If you thought your variance analysis was as good as it could be, think again.

Chapter 9 is how to do a much better **organisation chart**. I once used it to show 250 reporting units on a single A3 sheet of paper. Try doing that the conventional way in PowerPoint.

Chapter 10 is on **next steps** (just four pages), then there are some **computing** tips in the Appendix. This book is about *what* to do, not how to do it on a computer, and most tips are easy to do in Word, Excel or PowerPoint. Nevertheless, this appendix gives computing tips for some ideas in this book.

Throughout the book you'll see how to improve even reasonable-looking work. Many of the 'before' and 'after' redos are based on real work I've seen and which aren't too awful, yet the 'after' is significantly better.

By the end, you'll be ready to play Info Bingo. If you've heard of Buzzword Bingo, you can guess roughly what it is. Visit www.jmoon.co.uk and click on 'Downloads' for a single sheet of A4. Then either hand it out at the next presentation or tuck it into the front cover of the next information pack you hand out.

Some other pointers about the book

You are unlikely to have seen a business book like this. How many business books have you seen with whole chapters on alternatives to bullet points or better organisation charts or making comparisons(!) or document design?

And because it's different, here are some pointers about what to expect – the good news and bad news (well, more like minor qualifiers actually):

Its ideas are easy to understand	*But* you will need your brain in gear more for some bits. In particular, the chapters on 'tables' and 'graphs' have a lot of detailed ideas to absorb.
It's good sense	*But* please don't dismiss it as common sense. If the tips were common sense, we would all be following them. Few people do.
Collectively, its tips will improve your work hugely	*But* individually, many will only make a small difference. This book is a few big ideas and hundreds of small ones.
It will improve most of your documents	*But* it won't help annual reports much. A lot of their layout is prescribed by accountants and cannot be changed. As for format, business expects a particular style for annual reports, regardless of its rights or wrongs. That's why most annual reports contain presentational gimmicks and charts which hinder clarity, not help it. Chapter 2 explains more.

It will help readers understand your points more quickly	*But* it won't help readers that refuse to engage. Some people just don't make an effort to read something even if it is simple and clear. When people are confused, sometimes it's their fault, not the information's. Also, think of your audience and their personal preferences. I once worked for someone who hated decision trees, so even if a decision tree was ideal for what I was doing, I wouldn't do one.
It covers most things in reports and slides	*But* it doesn't cover everything, e.g. flowcharts and other useful but rarer ways to clarify, such as isobars and scattergrams. Also, it doesn't have specific sections on writing or communicating. I did write chapters on each, but there wasn't room for them. Anyway, both topics are well trodden paths — there's numerous books on them already, should you wish to find out more.

Finally, note the following:

- *Some tips turn up more than once in the book*. None of the topics is completely stand-alone. Four chapters are relevant if doing bullet points on a slide. So if a particular tip is both brief and relates to more than one chapter, it turns up several times, once in each relevant chapter. If not brief, I cross-refer between chapters (e.g. 'see Chapter 4 for more').

- *I am not a sports fan*, but occasionally I look at how information is shown outside work and refer to football league tables quite a few times. Just so there is no doubt, I don't even follow football, but many people are familiar with sports league tables so they aren't a bad way for me to make a point.

- *I can't speak Latin, but there's quite a bit of it in this book*. Often, I want you to focus on the physical layout of text without being distracted by its exact words. So I've dropped in some Latin, something often done by designers when dummying up their work. I have no idea what it means.

- *All the graphs, tables and page and slide mock-ups in this book are exactly as originally prepared in Excel, Word or Powerpoint*. None have been tarted up by a fancy designer on their Apple Mac.

How to save time implementing these ideas

After having read this book, you may wish to redo your templates or apply some of the ideas to a note you are doing. In which case, visit www.pearson-books.com/impact or www.jmoon.co.uk/downloads; they have examples from this book that you can download. If you're trying to get a table or graph or whatever to look like one in this book, check the websites – it might be there, along with annotations and explanations. If it is, download it and adopt and adapt. Getting reports and slides ready on time is tough enough already. Hopefully, these downloads will help you more quickly benefit from the ideas in this book.

As it is, some of this book improves your work *and* saves time. If unsure how best to do something, you experiment – and often still fail to get it right. If you *know* how to do something, you go straight to the answer. You quickly get it right, rather than slowly get it wrong. Also, when preparing big documents, much time is wasted chasing people for information they forgot to include in the first draft. As you'll see, there's a neat by-product to some ideas in this book – they help you get complete answers first time.

If I'm honest, though, other ideas will create extra work. But the extra time is often a fraction of the time spent up until then. Maybe you're working on a client pitch or a big investment proposal. Whatever it is, you've already spent a long time getting the words and numbers to the final stage, and the extra time created by the ideas in this book is a drop in the ocean. It's such a waste to do all that work, only then to present it badly.

But with a bit of extra effort, it could have been so much clearer and had so much more impact. Yes, it is quicker to click robotically on the Excel Graph Wizard, but to do something that has impact often can take a little bit longer.

Final thoughts

It doesn't matter whether you are in sales, marketing, strategy, communications, finance, IT, HR, compliance or on the board – every part of business wants to present information in a way that influences, informs, impresses and has impact. They all want to get results.

This topic is relevant for all levels of seniority in business. I have given my courses and talks to executive boards at group conferences and away-days, to secretaries, to MBA classes at business schools, to senior civil servants. It's not just for those that prepare the information or decide what goes into the reports and slides, it's also for those that review them all. If that's you, you'll realise how you can demand so much more from those that send you bad reports and show you bad slides. You no longer need to waste hours on unclear work.

The glib cliché is 'information is power'. So, people deduce, if they've got the information, then that's enough, they reckon they've got the power. But they haven't if that information is confusing and has no impact.

I would like to rephrase the cliché and say *'impact is power'*. Information without impact is useless – and clarity is how to give impact to your information. Don't strive for information. Strive for impact and clarity.

Finally, I will borrow a phrase from a great book I mention later. It's by Robin Williams – the female designer, not the actor. She says: 'I guarantee you will never look at a page in the same way.' You might not like or agree with everything in this book (I hope you like and agree with most) but one thing is certain: after reading it, I guarantee you will never look at a table, bullet point, slide, graph, note, report or information pack in the same way.

Chapter **1**

Bullet points ('WiT')

'WiT': the seriously better alternative to many bullet points

> Why bullet points often don't work
> An alternative way to give real impact to your findings and comments: 'WiT'
> How 'WiT' helps readers and writers
> 'Before' and 'after' – slides, notes, reports, client pitches, KPIs, CVs, and so on
> When bullet points are acceptable

For the naïve, bullet lists may create the appearance of hard-headed organised thought.
Professor Edward Tufte, *The Cognitive Style of PowerPoint* (page 16)

This chapter is on 'WiT', which stands for 'Words in Tables'. If I were a chef, it would be my signature dish. On my courses, it's everyone's favourite bit, the mantra they take away at the end. 'WiT' is simple yet effective. It's seriously good, seriously underused and gives immediate impact to your reports and slides. It's what they never teach you on report-writing or presentation courses.

And it is a dramatically better alternative to many of the bullet points we see today. Talking of which, let's quickly see why bullet points often don't work.

The problems with bullet points

What do you do if you have a particularly complex piece of analysis to communicate, either in a report or on a slide? In the old days, you would have a good hard think and work out an effective way of doing it. But nowadays, we can avoid all that hard thinking, computers have given us the answer – we write our complex analysis down in words, then divide our words into bullet points. Or rather:

- We write our complex analysis down in words.
- Then divide our words into bullet points.

These little black dots seem to be the panacea for all our communication problems. Got a slide to do? Bullet points will do nicely. Got a series of isolated findings to write about in a report? I know – show the findings as bullet points. Got a linear series of arguments that take the reader from (a) through to (f) and then on to a conclusion? Here's an idea – list each step of the argument as a bullet point. Got to analyse a series of pros and cons for different alternatives (go in-house, outsource or do a joint venture)? Hey, guess what? List the pros and cons as bullet points.

And yes, bullet points have had their moments. When they first took off in the mid 1980s, they did create a new and welcome break to an intimidating page of dense text. Back then, they were a novelty, an innovative typographical artefact. Given how ubiquitous they are today, it seems the novelty hasn't worn off.

As well as making the page more inviting, bullets also help make text easier to grasp – or at least in theory they do. Bullets divide the analysis into a series of smaller points, so – in theory – each should be easier to grasp. It's like the kid's joke: How do you eat an elephant? Answer: One chunk at a time. The bullet points allow us to digest complex analysis one chunk at a time.

So that's the theory and history of why bullets help. But if we look at current-day reality, it's a different story. Often bullet points don't help, they actually hinder because they suffer from four massive shortcomings:

They are seriously overused	Many people get weary, even depressed, when they see bullet points. Their hearts sink when faced with another report or presentation crammed with them.
They don't break up dull text, they *are* dull text	Computers have moved on a lot since the bullet point arrived. To break up a page of text, we can now add graphs, tables, cartoons. We can create columns or simply align the text down only the right half of the page. As for bullets, they are so overused, they no longer break up dull text. They *are* dull text.
They often result in incomplete analysis	We will explore this one in detail soon. For now, just reflect on how bullet point lists have no underlying structure, nothing that imposes a discipline or validation on the writing. The points are simply a list of what the author remembers to blast down. If the author's forgotten to include a particular point, he or she is just as likely not to notice the oversight – and readers probably won't either.
They are not easy to refer back to	Assume you had 15 bullet points on a page and each bullet consisted of two sentences on a different European country. Usually, you would have quite a hunt on your hands if you wanted to find the bullet on, say, Spain. Bullets don't make it easy to find things.

Many bullet points fail to influence, inform or impress. They are unmemorable, often incomplete, visually unappealing and difficult to refer back to in discussion. And because we see bullet points *everywhere*, they have long lost whatever impact they once might have had.

The answer – 'WiT'

If you're wondering what 'WiT' is and can't wait to see it in action, you already have – see above. I didn't do bullet points to explain why bullet points were bad. I put the 'Words in a Table', and the first of many benefits is obvious: the key points are easier to refer back to than if in a list of bullet points – they aren't hidden deep in text but stand proud and are easy to see in the left column of the table.

Let's do another example, but this time let's show both the 'before' and 'after'. Figures 1.1 and 1.2 are two ways to show a page from a monthly update report. The page gives brief updates on the IT systems, personnel and client wins and losses. The detailed commentary is in Latin – I want you to focus on the structure of the page, not the detailed comments.

FIGURE 1.1

IT systems
Projects more than £30k

Lorem ipsum dolor sit amet, consectetuer adipiscing elit, sed diam nonummy nibh euismod tincidunt ut laoreet dolore magna aliquam erat volutpat. Ut wisi enim ad minim veniam

Personnel
Changes in the month, salaries more than £30k

Lorem ipsum dolor sit amet, consectetuer adipiscing elit, sed diam nonummy nibh euismod tincidunt ut laoreet dolore magna aliquam erat volutpat. Ut wisi enim ad minim veniam

Wins
Wins in the month more than £20k

Lorem ipsum dolor sit amet, consectetuer adipiscing elit, sed diam nonummy nibh euismod tincidunt ut laoreet dolore magna aliquam erat volutpat. Ut wisi enim ad minim veniam

Losses
Losses in the month more than £20k

Lorem ipsum dolor sit amet, consectetuer adipiscing elit, sed diam nonummy nibh euismod tincidunt ut laoreet dolore magna aliquam erat volutpat. Ut wisi enim ad minim veniam

FIGURE 1.2

IT systems Projects more than £30k	Lorem ipsum dolor sit amet, consectetuer adipiscing elit, sed diam nonummy nibh euismod tincidunt ut laoreet dolore magna aliquam erat volutpat. Ut wisi enim ad minim veniam
Personnel Changes in the month, salaries more than £30k	Lorem ipsum dolor sit amet, consectetuer adipiscing elit, sed diam nonummy nibh euismod tincidunt ut laoreet dolore magna aliquam erat volutpat. Ut wisi enim ad minim veniam
Wins Wins in the month more than £20k	Lorem ipsum dolor sit amet, consectetuer adipiscing elit, sed diam nonummy nibh euismod tincidunt ut laoreet dolore magna aliquam erat volutpat. Ut wisi enim ad minim veniam
Losses Losses in the month more than £20k	Lorem ipsum dolor sit amet, consectetuer adipiscing elit, sed diam nonummy nibh euismod tincidunt ut laoreet dolore magna aliquam erat volutpat. Ut wisi enim ad minim veniam

Figure 1.1 is a linear sequential layout down the page. It is visually uninspiring, and its layout doesn't help people navigate around the page to find particular points. Short bits of text stretch all the way across the page, so readers' eyes have to flick back and forth unnecessarily. All in all, the page looks a bit basic, a bit *amateurish*.

Figure 1.2 shows the page redone as 'WiT'. *Nothing* else has changed, but the difference is dramatic. It is much more visually appealing. Even though both pages have the same number of words, Figure 1.2 creates white space more effectively. It's easier to navigate around. It's easier to read, since the text is in columns (and columns are easier to read). It looks more designed, more *professional*. All those benefits have come simply from putting the 'Words in a Table'. Notice that Figure 1.1 didn't have bullet points – 'WiT' improves documents that don't even have them.

And that is 'WiT'. Simple, really.

The rest of this chapter looks at the 'why and when' of 'WiT'. It shows when 'WiT' helps – for presenting a series of arguments that build on each other, for presenting a list of findings, for comparing alternatives, and so on. It shows the wide range of documents that would benefit from 'WiT' – slides, notes, client pitches, reports, key performance indicators and more. It explains the different benefits of 'WiT'. We've already mentioned some, but we will see several more.

Also, for those that don't just use bullets but sub-bullets and sub-sub-bullets, we see how 'WiT' can do that as well (and do it *beautifully*). Then we see when you needn't do 'WiT'. For example, why aren't these last two paragraphs in 'WiT'?

But hang on, I hear you say, why the fuss? This isn't new. Yes, some of you will have seen documents or slides where there were words in tables – maybe you've prepared some yourself. But it's done very rarely – study other documents and slides and check out just how little it's done. And when it is done, it's an arbitrary, intuitive and almost experimental act, done without a full understanding of when to do it and without an awareness of the benefits it brings. Without this awareness, people don't do 'WiT' as often as they should.

That will now change. You will learn the two conditions when you can use 'WiT'. Armed with these, you will use 'WiT' consciously, not randomly, and you will give your work *real* impact.

Why editing often addresses the wrong problem

People are usually too busy tweaking words to think about changing the *physical* layout of draft documents and slides. They realise something isn't quite right, but then tackle the wrong problem. They believe that, if the words don't work well, the answer is to choose different words. So they *tinker*, making small changes here and there. They try to change emphasis by adding or changing an adjective – 'we are very concerned' becomes 'we are extremely concerned'. Then someone else comes along and feels that that is coming on a bit strong and tones it down slightly to 'mostly we are extremely concerned'. So it goes on.

But often these tweakings miss the point – changing the words doesn't improve their overall *format* and *structure* and so won't make much difference to the document's clarity. Format is about document design (font sizes, alignment, etc.) and is in Chapter 7. And this chapter is about structure. Sort both of these out and the words sort themselves out much more easily.

Turning a bullet point list into 'WiT'

Rather than going straight to another 'before' and 'after', let's get there over a few steps (and 'WiT' isn't until step 6). Each step will illustrate something that helps. By starting at the beginning it will reinforce just how far we've progressed when we reach the end. Figure 1.3 is a typical bullet point list of findings from studying a company. Its layout probably looks familiar.

The list is a mix of the quantitative and qualitative. Some points are financial, e.g. the property is worth £3m more than the balance sheet says. Some are quantified but aren't financial, e.g. staff turnover is 30%. Some are qualitative, e.g. the company has been cleared of mis-selling. Because of this, we can't shoehorn the findings into a simple numerical table.

But we can still improve it. In Figure 1.4, we've put a conclusion at the start, we've grouped the points and we've put the list in columns. Each is discussed in more detail below. If you've read books or attended courses on report writing, you can probably quickly skim through steps 1 to 2, though start paying attention again from step 3, because it gets different from then on.

FIGURE 1.3

Findings of interest were as follows:

- There has been a problem with staff turnover – 30% of staff left last year, up 10% from the prior year. Many leavers were from "Global Solutions" department.
- Last month, Regulators formally announced the company has been cleared of the mis-selling accusations that hung over it for the last 2 years.
- Its computer system is inadequate and needs replacing at a cost of £2m. This will also add £500k a year extra to running costs.
- Its pension deficit has worsened in the year from £10m to £30m. The company is increasing contributions by £7m a year to remedy.
- Its new business initiative has been a success and income is up 20% on last year. Every department has increased income by at least 12%.
- Because of its lack of hedging, the dollar weakness will hit profit by £3m next year. It has recently recruited a new Treasurer.
- The market value of their Leeds site is worth £3m more than shown on its balance sheet
- It's finished clinical trials on the major new drug and Medical Authorities have indicated it should approve it next week.

FIGURE 1.4

There were mixed findings, but overall the company seems in good shape:

Good findings

- Its new business initiative has been a success and income is up 20% on last year. Every department has increased income by at least 12%.
- It's finished clinical trials on the major new drug and Medical Authorities have indicated it should approve it next week.
- Last month, Regulators formally announced the company has been cleared of the mis-selling accusations that hung over it for the last 2 years.
- The market value of their Leeds site is worth £3m more than shown on its balance sheet

Bad findings

- Its pension deficit has worsened in the year from £10m to £30m. The company is increasing contributions by £7m a year to remedy.
- Because of its lack of hedging, the dollar weakness will hit profit by £3m next year. It has recently recruited a new Treasurer.
- There has been a problem with staff turnover – 30% of staff left last year, up 10% from the prior year. Many leavers were from "Global Solutions" department.
- Its computer system is inadequate and needs replacing at a cost of £2m. This will also add £500k a year extra to running costs.

Step 1: Put the conclusion at the start ('start at the end') Write a conclusion or summary and put it first. In the redone example (Figure 1.4), the conclusion says: 'There were mixed findings, but overall the company seems in good shape.' This gives readers context with which to grasp and judge the findings that follow. As they read each bullet, they mentally compare it with the overall finding: 'Yes, that one is good news – and that one is not good, but not that important . . . yup, I see where the author is coming from.'

Compare this to the previous version which didn't give a summary. It just led into the bullet points with the comment 'Findings of interest were as follows', so readers are forced to work out the summary themselves. What readers do next is both laborious and all too common. They read the points once, reach the end and realise they haven't quite grasped what they probably are meant to grasp – overall, is it good or bad news? So they might then get out their pencil and go over the points again, this time putting a tick against good findings and a cross against bad ones. They might even put a double tick against particularly good points or a double cross against particularly bad ones. Then having done that, they would add up the ticks and crosses to get a feel for whether it's good or bad overall.

No wonder so many readers struggle to grasp the points that reports and slides try to make.

Newspapers summarise well. By the time you reach the end of the first paragraph, you know the overall story and have the context. The rest of the article is simply putting flesh on the bones. It is a very effective way of writing clearly.

So start with the summary – it gives readers context. Sorting the bullet points helps give further context. We look at this next.

Why we don't start at the end

Starting at the end is the opposite of what we were taught to do at school and college. We were told to start with our objectives, then outline our methodology, then give the analysis, then – and only then – reach the conclusion.

Well, that's fine for school and college where the person marking your work already knows the answer and is merely seeing how close you got to it. *In business though, your audience only know the answer when you tell them.* And they prefer you to tell them sooner rather than later so they then have context to judge your analysis that follows.

As an example, assume your report lists the seven items that have hit costs this year. Assume the first one you mention is the new compliance procedures that cost the company £2m. If you haven't yet told readers by how much costs changed overall, they have no context to judge that £2m figure. Is it £2m out of a £3m total increase in costs? Or £2m out of a £103m total increase? They don't know what to make of it – and won't know until they get to the end of the list and find out the total change in costs.

And this leads into the second reason why many people struggle to start at the end – it is how we draft the document. We write down the seven items, then get out the calculator, add them up and write the last line of our report: 'The total costs went up £15m.' The conclusion is at the end because we didn't write it until the end – and that's where it stays.

Correct this with a simple bit of cut and pasting in your documents. Use the mouse to highlight your conclusion, then pick it up and put it down at the start of the report. Then tweak the odd word to accommodate its new position in life. That's all it takes to make your report much better.

Step 2: Segment, order, maybe strip out Look back at the original list of bullet points (Figure 1.3). They don't seem to be in any particular order – but actually they are. They are in the most popular order of all, the haphazard order in which they were first written.

Never leave like them that. Segment them. Order them. Edit them and strip a few out. Maybe do all three. (I feel another 'WiT' coming . . . yup, here it is.)

Segment	Segment your thoughts into good and bad, or important and unimportant, or recurring and non-recurring, or local and global, or whatever.
Order	Put them in some order. Avoid simply alphabetical. If you've grouped them into good and bad, put the good ones in descending order of 'goodness'. Then tell readers you have ordered them; if you don't, they will waste valuable brain space trying to put the bullets in some sort of discernible order so that they can better understand them, little realising that you've already done it for them.
Maybe strip out	Do you need to show all your bullets in the main bit of the report? If there are, say, 15 good and 15 bad findings, some are probably less important than others, and these will lessen the impact of the findings that really do matter.
	Relegate the less important points to a secondary table ('Further below is a table of less important findings which I include for completeness and information'). Or put them in an appendix and tell readers where to find them.
	Maybe you don't wish to relegate any to the appendix, for fear they won't get read. In which case, it is even more important to segment and order them.

To recap, so far we've started with the conclusion and then segmented the points. Both these steps are fairly well known. Step 3 onwards gets more unusual. (As an aside, I haven't reordered any of our good and bad findings, nor stripped any out. That's because I want the final 'before' and 'after' to be as comparable as possible.)

Step 3: Put in columns In the redone example (Figure 1.4), the good findings are in one column, the bad findings in another. People find it easier to read columns of words rather than text that spreads all the way across a sheet of A4. After all, newspapers are in columns (see page 198).

The list of points is already significantly better. But there is still much more we can do. In Figure 1.5 we see the result of steps 4 and 5: 'Start each paragraph at the end' and 'Give the start of each bullet some typographical contrast'.

FIGURE 1.5

There were mixed findings, but overall the company seems in good shape:

Good findings

- **New business drive successful**: income is up 20%, and every department is up at least 12%.

- **Major drug to be approved**: clinical trials have finished, and the Medical Authorities have indicated they should approve it next week.

- **Cleared of mis-selling**: last month, the Regulators formally announced the end of the 2-year review.

- **Property £3m undervalued**: the Leeds site has a market value £3m more than stated on the balance sheet.

Bad findings

- **A £30m pension deficit**: it's worsened in the year from £10m to £30m. The company is increasing contributions by £7m a year to remedy.

- **£3m 'forex' hit next year**: the company didn't hedge its dollar exposure. It has recently recruited a new Treasurer.

- **30% staff turnover**, up from 10% last year. Many leavers were from "Global Solutions" department.

- **£2m needed on IT**: the systems need replacing. This will also add £500k a year to running costs.

Step 4: Start each paragraph at the end Just as we started with the overview for the page as a whole ('overall in good shape'), we can do likewise for each individual bullet point. The first point now starts with the phrase 'New business drive successful' and this helps people skim-read. Readers that are familiar with the new business drive needn't read any further than this subheading and can skip to the second point. It also helps readers find a comment when referring back to the report. If the board is discussing the findings, readers can easily flick through the report and find a particular point ('Here, see – remember the new business drive has pushed income up 20%'). If the findings are embedded deep within wordy paragraphs, it's more of a struggle to find the point.

Step 5: Give the start of each bullet some typographical contrast Each point's lead-in is now in Arial Black, a typeface that has much more impact than doing Arial in bold. Doing this makes the page look less visually the same and dull. It gives the lead-in more prominence, making it easier for readers to find information.

Now we're ready for the big change: get rid of the bullets and put the words in a table – 'WiT'.

Step 6: Put the words in a table ('WiT') In step 5, we gave some typographical contrast to the opening bit of each bullet and it made a bit of a difference – but we can do more. Previously, we laid out the first bullet as follows:

- **New business drive successful**:
  income is up 20%, and every
  department is up at least 12%.

To make the opening bit stand out even more we could show it in a separate column and give it its own uninterrupted vertical space:

New business drive successful	Income is up 20%, and every department is up at least 12%.

(The 'WiT' is a table one row high by two columns wide.)

And if we do the same for all points, the information is as Figure 1.6.

FIGURE 1.6

There were mixed findings, but overall the company seems in good shape:

Good findings

New business drive successful	Income is up 20%, and every department is up at least 12%.
Major drug to be approved	Clinical trials have finished, and the Medical Authorities have indicated they should approve it next week.
Cleared of mis-selling	Last month, the Regulators formally announced the end of the 2-year review.
Property £3m undervalued	The Leeds site has a market value £3m more than stated on the balance sheet.

Bad findings

£30m pension deficit	Up from £10m last year. The company is putting in an extra £7m a year to remedy.
£3m 'forex' hit next year	The company didn't hedge its dollar exposure. It has recently recruited a new Treasurer.
30% staff turnover	Up from 10% last year. Many leavers were from "Global Solutions" department.
£2m needed on IT	The systems need replacing. This will also add £500k a year to running costs.

Now we have clear information. Compare it to the linear, sequential, unordered outpouring of bullet points in Figure 1.3. This layout has visual interest, white space and summaries. Hey, it even looks *sharp*. Readers can navigate around easily to find or refer back to particular points of interest. 'WiT' forces words into columns and we find it easier to read text in columns. These are the benefits we've seen so far from putting 'Words in Tables'.

Let's recap what we've done to the bullet points. We put the overall conclusion at the start, we segmented between good and bad, we put in columns, we started each paragraph at the end, we gave the start of each bullet some typographical contrast. Then we put 'Words in Tables'. And the difference is dramatic.

The rest of this chapter looks at 'WiT' in all its fantastic and beautiful forms and we will see several more of its benefits. It will put 'WiT' firmly in your business toolkit, ready to give impact and immediacy to your notes, slides, reports and packs.

Next we study a client proposal and see how 'WiT' helps ensure your analysis is *complete*.

How 'WiT' helps ensure completeness

Figure 1.7 shows a typical page from a report that is pitching for business. It says why you should be chosen in preference to your competitors. The comments probably resonate with those that write or read client pitches, because similar comments are made the world over. Similar layouts are adopted too – the ubiquitous bullet point list. It's all a bit uninspiring.

Here we have nine bullet points, which is quite a number for readers to grasp. If we could segment them, it would greatly help readers make sense of them.

But how to segment? Try this: segment by importance – some comments are important and make a difference, and some are vacuous and a waste of space. The vacuous ones are 'We recruit the best staff', 'Our clients are King' and 'We deliver innovative solutions'. Who would ever say they don't recruit the best staff, or that they don't put clients first? (Some might say they don't deliver innovative solutions, but they wouldn't be in this particular beauty parade.) These statements fail the 'not' test. If no one would ever say they don't recruit the best staff, what's the point in saying you do, why waste space saying it?

So I'm going to strip them out. If you have to or really want to keep them, at least relegate them to a secondary list under the main list.

That leaves six of the original nine bullet points, so let's do 'WiT' with them (Figure 1.8). Here we've done a table of features and benefits, a standard and useful way of selling a company or product. But if we put the six bullet points into a 'features and benefits' table, we have a problem. For four out of the six bullet points, we didn't talk about the benefit to the client. We only

FIGURE 1.7

Why choose us?

- We have been serving clients for over 150 years
- We recruit the best staff
- Our clever web system gives you 24/7 service
- Being the biggest, we get the best deals from the market for you
- Our clients are King – we put them first
- Your case is presented not by salesmen but by one of your account executives. Result: a better deal for you
- We deliver innovative solutions
- Our parent is a Multinational Inc, the third biggest conglomerate in the world
- We won the Employer of Choice award last year

mentioned the feature. OK, we have a strong parent company, but so what? What's the advantage to the client of this?

This is another benefit of 'WiT'. Tables impose a discipline on writing, one that helps ensure the information is *complete*. If something is missing, it's much more obvious – there's a blank cell in the table. 'WiT' not only helps those that read the report, it helps those that write it. Compare this to bullet points which are often a random list of whatever authors can remember to comment on. If they don't remember to comment on something, it's not in the list. And often readers won't spot the omission either, because bullet point lists rarely have a structure that helps highlight the omission. Getting complete information will be a recurring benefit to 'WiT'.

Returning to the client proposal (Figure 1.9), I have put some Latin text into the missing cells – I don't have the heart to work out why being 150 years old is a benefit, and even if I did, you'd probably disagree and it would just be a distraction from the point I am making. And that point is: we now have a complete table. Also, readers can skim around, finding summary points or detail with ease. This table is far better than the linear listing of bullet points we started with.

FIGURE 1.8

Why choose us?

Feature	Benefit
The biggest	You get the best deal from our market leverage
Clever web system	You get 24/7 access
A strong parent	?????
Employer of Choice	?????
150 years' experience	?????
Account execs, not salesmen	?????

FIGURE 1.9

Why choose us?

Feature	Benefit
The biggest	You get the best deal from our market leverage
Clever web system	You get 24/7 access
A strong parent	Ut wisi enim ad minim veniam, quis nostrud
Employer of Choice	Suscipit lobortis nisl ut aliquip ex ea commodo
150 years' experience	Accumsan et iusto odio dignissim qui blandit
Account execs, not salesmen	Azril delenit augue duis dolore te feugait zzril

These improvements make it easier for readers to choose you instead of the competition. Every decision-maker has a manager to answer to, and that manager will stroll into the decision-maker's office and ask: 'I gather you went for Jones Limited. Why's that?' If your company's features and benefits are hidden deep within bullet points, the decision-maker will struggle to find them. The manager will be hovering around while the decision-maker scans the bullet points trying to find something to say. Eventually half a reason will emerge: 'Ah-ha, got it, here it is – they have a strong parent.'

It won't inspire confidence in the decision. And if the manager then says 'OK – but why's that a benefit, though?', the decision-maker will struggle again.

'WiT' makes it easy for the decision-maker to say to the manager quickly and efficiently: 'I like that they are the biggest – it means we get the best deal. Also, they have a strong parent – the benefit of that is . . .'. Much cleaner, crisper and authoritative. 'WiT' helps decision-makers be your advocate, it helps them find and repeat your messages on your behalf to their people.

So 'WiT' helps ensure your analysis is complete. However, we haven't finished with the client pitch. Next we see it again, but this time on slides – and 'WiT' is great for them too.

How 'WiT' is great for slides too

We've got the same words as before, but now in landscape format. It could be part of a handout on people's desks or up on the screen as a slide. Here, in Figure 1.10, assume it's a slide. If you've ever sat through sales pitches by suppliers, its layout probably looks depressingly familiar – to show how

FIGURE 1.10

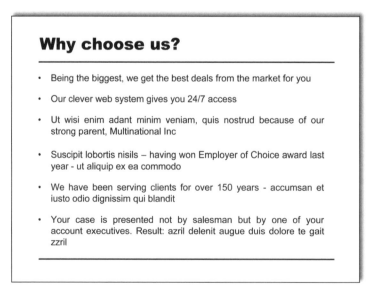

FIGURE 1.11

Why choose us?

Feature	Benefit
The biggest	You get the best deal from our market leverage
A clever web system	You get 24/7 access
A strong parent	Ut wisi enim adant minim veniam, quis nostrud
Employer of Choice	Suscipit lobortis nisils ut aliquip ex ea commodo
150 years' experience	Accumsan et iusto odio dignissim qui blandit
Account execs, not salesmen	Azril delenit augue duis dolore te gait zzril

different they are, companies show slides that look just like everyone else's. How bizarre.

The bullet points don't communicate well – visually uninteresting with no white space, important details embedded deep in wordy sentences, difficult to refer back to.

Time to do the slide as 'WiT'. And yet again, the difference is dramatic (Figure 1.11). It's much more inviting; the points visually lift from the page.

'WiT' is seriously good for presentation slides. (In common with many examples I give in this chapter, the redo doesn't have the 'conclusion at the start'. That's because I want you to focus on putting 'words in tables' and not be distracted by a summary you might not agree with.)

The next example is a progress report on plans made at the start of the year. It illustrates yet another new benefit to 'WiT' – it helps cut out words.

How 'WIT' helps cut out words

Figure 1.12 shows a page from a 'key performance indicator' (KPI) pack, it gives an update on the year's plans. The plans made at the start of the year are listed on the top half of the page, and the progress against those plans is listed on the bottom half.

The layout makes it difficult to compare 'Plan' and 'Action to date'; they are not physically close to each other. The layout also makes the document

FIGURE 1.12

Plan

- Put new IT system into Bristol and Bath in the summer
- Recruit 200 more salesmen by May
- Undertake compliance training for all run-off units by end of year
- Do market research on customer perceptions of us
- Open new office in Singapore
- Sell off unwanted business in Norway and Australia
- Relocate Group finance to Milton Keynes

Action to date

- Group finance to move next month
- Singapore office to open in September
- Unwanted business in Norway now sold; in negotiations on Australian disposal
- Tenders being received from market research company
- 150 salesmen recruited so far – should hit May target
- Compliance training programme for run-off currently being designed

---

unnecessarily wordy. Look at the 'Plan' to sell unwanted business in Norway and Australia (top half of the page, sixth bullet point).

As for the related 'Action to date', it's further down – the third bullet point in the bottom half of the page (third? Why not sixth?). It says 'Norway now sold; in negotiations on Australia'. Except it doesn't say it that succinctly, it uses eleven words instead of seven – it says 'Unwanted business in Norway now sold; in negotiations on Australian disposal'.

These extra words are to remind readers that the businesses were unwanted – and readers need reminding because of the physical separation between the plan and action to date.

Four extra words don't sound much but if you can remove words like this throughout the document, it collectively makes a big difference. The document is much easier to read, much less flabby.

FIGURE 1.13

Area	Plan	Action to date
IT	Put new IT system into Bristol and Bath in the summer	Ready to roll in Summer
Recruitment	Recruit 200 more salesmen by May	150 so far – on target for 200 by May
Compliance	Undertake compliance training for all run-off units by end of year	Training programme being designed
Market research	Do market research on customer perceptions of us	Tenders being received from market research company
Singapore	Open new office in Singapore	To open in September
Divestments	Sell off unwanted business in Norway and Australia	Norway now sold; in negotiations on Australia
Relocation	Relocate Group finance to Milton Keynes	To move next month

Figure 1.13 shows the words as 'WiT'. Note its left column. It is a further aid to help readers navigate around the report – one or two words to describe the topic that is being commented on.

Also, guess what we find when we did 'WiT'? The information wasn't complete, there was an empty cell in the table. The original page mentioned seven plans, yet only gave updates on six of them – we hadn't given an update on the new IT system. Yet this omission was not apparent because of the way in which the information was originally presented. I know it's not apparent because I have given this example on my courses numerous times, and no one spots this omission until I point it out.

If you think this would never happen, this is a real example. A client's KPI reports gave updates on plans, and laid them out down the page, not in a table – and some updates were missing.

What order should the table be in? We haven't put it in any obvious order, and we should have. Maybe we could sort the list between projects that are going well and projects that are going badly. Maybe we could have a third category: projects which aren't due to start just yet. If the market research project is not due to start for another six months, it is neither going well nor badly. The best order depends on your objectives or those of the audience.

Whatever we do, we should not leave it in alphabetical order or the order in which it was first written. Also, we should ensure readers know the order.

Two final points. Firstly, take care if thinking of using 'Red, Amber, Green' traffic lights to signal how well items are progressing. The section on page 223 explains why.

Secondly, 'WiT' doesn't just improve bullet points, it improves narrative too, such as this narrative version of the KPI bullet points:

We started the year with well-defined key strategic action points. First was to put in a new computer system in Bristol and Bath over the summer. Next we looked to recruit 200 more salesman by May . . . [until all seven plans have been listed].

Now let's see how we've progressed. First, we are pleased to say that we are on track with the Group finance relocation to Milton Keynes — it is due to move next month.

Needless to say, 'WiT' does wonders for this narrative. It visually lifts points from wordy paragraphs and makes it easy to skim and refer back to them. *Also, it cuts out even more words than were cut from the bullet point list.*

So 'WiT' stops you *writing* unnecessary words. Next we see another benefit: 'WiT' reassures readers and stops them *reading* unnecessary words.

How 'WIT' reassures readers

Figure 1.14 shows a typical note that describes the contents of a report. The note is to help readers see the structure of the report and navigate around. But readers struggle to navigate the note, let alone the report. Section numbers, titles and contents are hidden within the bullet points. Also, readers feel obliged to read it all *just in case* – after all, there might be something unusual or important hidden within it (e.g. 'Section 3 is from the Internet'). Readers have to read the note in full.

FIGURE 1.14

The report consists of the following:

- Section 1 is the executive summary which looks at the recommendations, next steps and areas to clarify
- The scope, methodology and limitations are in section 2
- The options, along with the cost-benefits, are the analysis in section 3
- The Appendix is section 4 and is all the detailed supporting schedules

If you do 'WiT', however, the usual benefits apply (Figure 1.15) and there's more. The table *reassures* readers more than bullet points. A table has a rigid structure and is less likely to have something unusual in it – this table is simply: column 1 = numbers, column 2 = titles, column 3 = content. Simple. If the writer wished to flag something unusual to readers, he or she would probably do a note on it either above or beneath the table but not within it – unusual items don't fit well within the structure of a table.

FIGURE 1.15

1	**Executive summary**	Recommendations, next steps, areas to clarify
2	**Introduction**	Scope, methodology, limitations
3	**Analysis**	The options, including cost-benefit analysis
4	**Appendix**	The detailed supporting schedules

And if any readers *still* felt they had to check there was nothing unusual, they need scan only the third column. And because the note is a 'WiT', readers won't take long to scan it, since there aren't many words in the third column.

So 'WiT' helps reassure readers. But there's more. Next we see how it helps ensure the analysis is *consistent*. After that, we run out of benefits and start to draw the threads together.

How 'WIT' ensures consistent writing

Most CVs show a career history in reverse date order like the part of a CV shown in Figure 1.16. The layout is a repeating pattern of rows – date, position, company, achievements, then again, date, position, company, achievements, and so on.

Figure 1.16 might look familiar but it isn't effective. Firstly, it's visually unappealing. More importantly, it makes readers hunt to find information. To see the achievements, readers' eyes flick down the page, skipping over stuff they don't want: ' "Date" – nope. "Position" – nope. "Company" –

FIGURE 1.16

Date: '06 - now
Position: Group Marketing Director
Full plc director with 40 staff, reporting to plc CEO
Company: LJZ Group plc - FMCG group, income £3bn
Achievements: agam conceptam mel cu, eum et por ro recteque interesset. Ea fugit ullum assentior duo.
Ex ius idque corrumpit democritum, ad sit ponderum.

Date: '04 - '06
Position: Marketing Director with 20 staff and reporting to MD
Company: ITS Solutions Ltd - IT software distributor with lincome £500m and a subsidiary of ITS plc
Achievements: agam conceptam mel cu, eum et por ro recteque interesset. Ea fugit ullum assentior duo.
Ex ius idque corrumpit democritum, ad sit ponderum.

Date: '02 - '04
Position: Group Marketing Manager with 10 staff and reporting to Group Sales director
Company: Cableco Ltd – privately owned industrial cabling company with £300m income
Achievements: agam conceptam mel cu, eum et por ro recteque interesset. Ea fugit ullum assentior duo.
Ex ius idque corrumpit democritum, ad sit ponderum.

nope. Ah, at last – "Achievements"'. After reading the first set of achievements, the hunt starts afresh as readers look for the second set, again
skipping over stuff they don't want. And to see positions held over the
years, it's the same painful procedure.

In Figure 1.17 we've done it as a 'WiT'. Achievements are now easy to
see – just scan down the right column. Want to see positions held? Scan
the second column. Want to see what was happening in 2003? Scan the
third row. Readers can navigate around easily and find the information they
want. Also, it's got more effective white space. It has *impact*.

But there is a new benefit too – 'WiT' helps ensure *consistent* writing.
Imagine the author of the CV is a bit flaky in his or her thinking and accidentally writes as an achievement 'Ran the Marketing Department for two
years', even though it's a responsibility, not an achievement. In a traditional CV, this error might go unnoticed because of the stop–start staccato
way readers are forced to read the achievements – read an achievement,
then hunt down a few rows to find the next, read another, then hunt down a
few more rows, read another, and so on.

When the CV is in 'WiT' and all achievements are in a column, the error
would stand out. Comparable items are much easier to compare because
they can be read in one quick uninterrupted sweep of the eye, and inconsistencies stand out much more. If readers scanned the achievements,
they'd spot the anomaly – 'Ran the Marketing Department' just wouldn't
chime properly alongside the other genuine achievements.

FIGURE 1.17

Year	Position	Company	Achievements
'06 - now	**Group Marketing Director** Full plc director reporting to plc CEO 40 staff	**LJZ Group plc** FMCG group Income £3bn	Agam conceptam mel cu, eum et por ro recteque interesset. Ea fugit ullum assentior duo. Ex ius idque corrumpit democritum, ad sit ponderum.
'04 - '06	**Marketing Director** Reporting to MD 20 staff	**ITS Solutions Ltd** IT software distributor lincome £500m Subsidiary of ITS plc	Agam conceptam mel cu, eum et por ro recteque interesset. Ea fugit ullum assentior duo. Ex ius idque corrumpit democritum, ad sit ponderum.
'02 - '04	**Group Marketing Manager** Reporting to Group Sales director 10 staff	**Cableco Ltd** Industrial cabling £300m income Privately owned	Agam conceptam mel cu, eum et por ro recteque interesset. Ea fugit ullum assentior duo. Ex ius idque corrumpit democritum, ad sit ponderum.

So we have the final benefit of 'WiT' – it helps ensure consistent writing. Let's summarise the benefits. Needless to say, I've shown them as 'WiT':

It helps the writing	It helps ensure the writing is complete and consistent. It helps cluster items and sharpens the thinking (see below). It cuts out words.
It helps the reading	It makes the page more inviting with better white space. It's easier to scan and skip sections. It's easier to refer back to. It forces words into columns and columns are easier to read. Its rigid structure reassures readers.

'WiT' really does sharpen the writing. When I first wrote the above list of benefits, I just blasted them down in narrative. Then, given what I was writing about, I decided to show them as 'WiT' – and it really forced me to think. I realised that some benefits help the writing, others help the reading, so I clustered them and edited them until I got to the table above. Much better.

Next we see the two conditions when you can do 'WiT'.

When to 'WiT': repeating patterns, brief sections

There is a common theme running through many of these examples: the text has a *repeating pattern*. The CV had 'Date', 'Position', 'Company', 'Achievements'. The client pitch had 'Features' and 'Benefits'. The KPI had 'Area', 'Plan', 'Action to date'. The index had 'Section', 'Title', 'What it covers'. In each case, the text repeated the same captions.

Look out for this. If your text repeats similar captions, it would probably be better as 'WiT'. Recently, a client looked at a dense page of text that gave historical background on a competitor. It had a repeating pattern – one long paragraph gave details about acquisitions the company had made in the 1960s. The next two paragraphs talked about the 1970s when the company developed new products. Finally, there were details about diversification in the 1980s. The repeating pattern was 'Date', 'Overview', 'Detail', and the text was crying out to be in a table. It would be easier to navigate around. It would have white space. It would be easier to refer back to. It would force words into columns that are easier to read. Also, if readers already knew about the new products in the 1970s, they could skip that detail, confident that nothing of relevance would be missed.

However, there is more. Even if there is no repeating pattern to the text, still do 'WiT' if there are sections or comments that are *brief*. The 'good findings, bad findings' example didn't have a repeating pattern, it was just a list of brief isolated comments. The first was about new business, the second about the new drug. OK, we sorted them into good and bad findings, but that is a grouping of like items, not a repeating pattern to the underlying text. All the same, 'WiT' worked brilliantly for these bullet points (Figure 1.18).

FIGURE 1.18

There were mixed findings, but overall the company seems in good shape:

Good findings		Bad findings	
New business drive successful	Income is up 20%, and every department is up at least 12%.	**£30m pension deficit**	Up from £10m last year. The company is putting in an extra £7m a year to remedy.
Major drug to be approved	Clinical trials have finished, and the Medical Authorities have indicated they should approve it next week.	**£3m 'forex' hit next year**	The company didn't hedge its dollar exposure. It has recently recruited a new Treasurer.
Cleared of mis-selling	Last month, the Regulators formally announced the end of the 2-year review.	**30% staff turnover**	Up from 10% last year. Many leavers were from "Global Solutions" department.
Property £3m undervalued	The Leeds site has a market value £3m more than stated on the balance sheet.	**£2m needed on IT**	The systems need replacing. This will also add £500k a year to running costs.

Earlier we showed part of a monthly update as a 'WiT' (Figure 1.19). There wasn't a repeating pattern to the text, other than (arguably) section, then detail. But there were *brief* sections: a section on IT, then a few words

FIGURE 1.19

IT systems Projects more than £30k	Lorem ipsum dolor sit amet, consectetuer adipiscing elit, sed diam nonummy nibh euismod tincidunt ut laoreet dolore magna aliquam erat volutpat. Ut wisi enim ad minim veniam
Personnel Changes in the month, salaries more than £30k	Lorem ipsum dolor sit amet, consectetuer adipiscing elit, sed diam nonummy nibh euismod tincidunt ut laoreet dolore magna aliquam erat volutpat. Ut wisi enim ad minim veniam
Wins Wins in the month more than £20k	Lorem ipsum dolor sit amet, consectetuer adipiscing elit, sed diam nonummy nibh euismod tincidunt ut laoreet dolore magna aliquam erat volutpat. Ut wisi enim ad minim veniam
Losses Losses in the month more than £20k	Lorem ipsum dolor sit amet, consectetuer adipiscing elit, sed diam nonummy nibh euismod tincidunt ut laoreet dolore magna aliquam erat volutpat. Ut wisi enim ad minim veniam

on it; a section on personnel, then a few words on it, and so on. Which means it is ideal for 'WiT'.

And with brief sections, 'WiT' *really* does help cut out words. Within the monthly update, the original layout stretched the text out across the page (refer back to Figure 1.1) and each section looks a bit *insignificant* with just three lines of comment (sometimes the comments might be only two lines of text). Many authors would be tempted to flesh out the commentary to four or five lines so it didn't look so *barren*. But when we did 'WiT', it became five lines anyway and hence looks less insubstantial. Also, with 'WiT', you have less space to write comments, so you choose words more carefully.

Minutes of meetings are great for 'WiT' – they meet both criteria: brief sections and a repeating pattern (section number, heading, detail, who to action). I show a 'before' and 'after' of a client meeting note on pages 208–209.

Now you know when to use 'WiT', keep your eyes peeled: you will spot repeating patterns or brief sections in every report, note, slide presentation and information pack. And you now know you can 'WiT' them all.

Next we look at a slightly different application for 'WiT', one that needs a bit more introduction than normal. Until now, each row of 'WiT' has been distinct from other rows – with the good and bad findings, each good finding was different and unique from other good findings. One was about a new drug, another was about the end to some litigation. In the monthly update, one section was on IT, another on personnel. Again, they are distinct and different.

But the rows don't have to be distinct, they can follow on from each other. Next we use 'WiT' to powerfully present a sequential series of arguments that take the reader from (a) to (c) and then to a conclusion.

How 'WIT' can develop a line of argument

Assume a retail group is thinking how to improve the performance of its store in a particular town. Figure 1.20 shows a page from a report on the store. The 'WiT' outlines a sequential line of argument running down the page. The left column of the 'WiT' is each conjecture in the argument, and the right column contains the detailed comments that support them (albeit in Latin in this example).

The page powerfully argues why the store is a bit stuck. Each row of the table looks at a different part of the argument, and as readers progress down the page, the argument progresses too. The first row starts with the first thought: 'Locals prefer other shops' products'. The second row then moves to the follow-on thought: 'Even if they didn't, we are in a poor location'. The third row gives the final thought: 'We can't relocate because of

FIGURE 1.20

Locals prefer other shops' products	Lorem ipsum est gloriatur expetendis an. Congue contentiones consequuntur et eos, autem vocibus in nam. Agam conceptam mel cu, eum et porro recteque interesset. Ex ius idque corrumpit democritum, ad sit ponderum sensibus.
Even if they didn't, we are in a poor location	Eu sit cetero appareat accusata. Per et dicam tempor praesent, eripuit nonummy volumus cu sea. Per tantas altera praesent in, nam assum recteque disputationi ut. Mea ne elit iusto. Id corpora salutatus usu, eirmod animal eu est. No natum eripuit lobortis sit, vel lucilius expetendis cu, ei possit persequeris mel.
We can't relocate because of Planning Restrictions	Eum luptatum contentiones cu, eu mei fabellas mediocritatem. Vivendo antiopam nec te, malis ullum epicuri pro cu. Graeco virtute detracto sit ei, mea sonet dicant et.

Planning Restrictions'. (At this point, the conclusion is probably 'close the store', but it doesn't say that at the top of 'WiT' because, again, I don't want you distracted by the summary point.)

Visually, the important bits stand out – readers can scan the left column and see the summary points progress logically down the page, and the detail is there on the right if needed. 'WiT' gives clarity, impact and immediacy to the train of argument.

So we've seen how 'WiT' is great not only for isolated points but also for narrative that builds and develops down a page. It's great for bullet points and continuous text too. Take your dauntingly dense page of continuous text and turn each paragraph into a row of 'WIT' with its key point in the left column and the detail on the right. This not only helps the reader but helps the writer too. It really does sharpen the thinking.

Meanwhile, let's study the layout. Notice that the text in the left column is right aligned and looks good. Also, this layout looks *really* good if you have text above and below it on the page that you align similarly, like the one in Figure 1.21.

It's worth taking three paragraphs to study the page layout. The text at the top (just underneath the thick rule at the top) is the introductory prose. Even though it isn't part of the 'WiT', we've aligned it both left and right with the text in the right of the 'WiT'. We've also similarly aligned the concluding comments at the bottom of the page underneath the 'WiT'. All this

FIGURE 1.21

The findings of our research

We appear to be ad novum omnesque vel, ad altera petentium pro. Intellegat consectetuer ei vis, etiam audire mel te. Iudico semper prompta has id, libris postea iracundia ea sit, et quo aperiam salutandi. Mel eu epicurei constituto. Ne nam eros doming legimus, sit in quando altera. Menandri periculis vix no. Doctus consequat rationibus eos id.

Locals prefer other shops' products Lorem ipsum est gloriatur expetendis an. Congue contentiones consequuntur et eos, autem vocibus in nam. Agam conceptam mel cu, eum et sum et porro recteque interesset. Ex ius idque corrumpit et ante democritum, ad sit ponderum sensibus.

Even if they didn't, we are in a poor location Eu sit cetero appareat accusata. Per et dicam tempor praesent, eripuit nonummy volumus cu sea. Per tantas altera praesent in, nam assum recteque dis putationi ut.

Mea ne elit iusto. Id corpora salutatus usu, eirmod animal eu est. No natum eripuit lobortis sit, vel luc ilius expetendis cu, ei possit persequeris mel.

We can't relocate because of Planning Restrictions Eum luptatum contentiones cu, eu mei fabellas mediocritatem. Vivendo antiopam nec te, malis ullum epicuri pro cu. Graeco virtute detracto sit ei, mea sonet dicant et.

It seems that sit cetero appareat accusata. Per et dicam tempor praesent, eripuit nonummy volumus cu sea. choro blandit consectetuer ad. Summo copiosae mea ex, doctus eleifend in sea. Vel in prompta singulis eloquentiam, viderer mediocrem incorrupte ne his, audiam nonummy sed in. Mel at erant decore, mea id sum vitae postulant neces sitatibus.For more on the exercise, see page 43.

Page 25 of 43

---

makes the page look neat and aligned and also helps the comments in the left column of the 'WiT' to really stand out. It is an immensely effective way of presenting findings. (It is not too dissimilar to 'pull quotes' which we look at on page 211.)

Notice how the left column gives conclusions, not just descriptions of the right columns. If the top left cell had said 'Do locals prefer other shops' products?', readers would have to read the right column to find the answer. Because the left column gives the conclusion, skim-readers see the answer immediately. Great 'WiT' is when the left column summarises the right column, not just describes it.

Finally, see the page number at the bottom: it is typographically similar to the top of the page, i.e. a thick rule, in Arial Black font, right aligned. It helps keep readers on the page. Let me explain. Often when reading, people reach the end of the text at the bottom of the page and their eyes just wander off – they've nowhere else to go. If that's what you want, fine. But sometimes you want them to *linger* a bit longer – maybe the page has tables of numbers, and you don't want readers to lazily skim over them, reach the bottom, then turn the page. In which case have something at the bottom that's typographically distinct and similar to something at the top. Readers' eyes hit the bottom bit, then bounce back to the top and lo, readers are kept on the page. It's a well-known typographical trick. Look out for this in magazine adverts, business cards and so on.

What if you want not just bullet points, but sub-bullet points, and sub-sub-bullet points? Don't worry, 'WiT' can still more than cope, and, as will be seen next, it delivers *beautifully*.

How 'WIT' can do headings *and* subheadings

Figure 1.22 shows a proposal from me to a client. The top half of the page tells the client what I am to deliver, and the bottom half lists the parts of the project.

There are then three main parts to the top half of the page: I am to (1) redo documents (2) in Microsoft packages (3) by the end of November. However, the bottom half – the project steps – is more complicated.

As before, there are three main parts: (1) before we start, (2) before the first draft, and (3) after the first draft. But within 'before we start', there are three steps too – three sub-parts. We now have another hierarchy.

Many documents show this hierarchy by the use of different-shaped bullet points. Here, we've shown the hierarchy with a black circle, a white circle, and a dash. As a typographical tool, though, these different bullet points are rather useless. The page is not easy to navigate around and skim-read. Visually it is dull, not helped by the unimaginative use of fonts (all the same size, with just a bit of upper case and bold to try to create distinctions). Also, all the indenting and further indenting makes the page look inelegant, amateurish. (Please don't dismiss these sub-sub-bullets as an exaggerated parody. Stuff like this appears everyday at work.)

With 'WiT' (Figure 1.23), it looks much more professional. We've divided the top and bottom half of the page by using a much bigger font to say 'What I am to deliver' and 'The project steps'. The two-part structure of the document is immediately obvious (much more so than in Figure 1.22 that just uses bullet points).

FIGURE 1.22

WHAT I AM TO DELIVER

- **Redo the documents**

  o   I am to redo and consolidate the ABC and DEC documents, the Checklist and the XYZ Information Pack. I am to make them easier to understand.

- **Do it in routine Microsoft packages**

  o   I am to do some sort of handout, the exact format of which we will discuss as the exercise progresses. I will produce my 'redo' in Word, Excel or PowerPoint.

- **First draft by 30 November**

  o   I understand you want something by the end of the year. Given my existing work commitments, I should be able to have delivered a reasonably final version for your first review by 30 November.

THE PROJECT STEPS

- **Before we start**

  o   *Please confirm costs are OK*

        −   Please confirm your agreement to the rates and estimated times. And please confirm your agreement to putting a note on the bottom: "designed by Jon Moon, www.jmoon.co.uk".

  o   *Please email soft copies*

        −   Please email a soft copy of the three documents in a form which allows me to copy and paste.

  o   *Please send me checklists*

        −   Please send me the checklist – you mentioned you had one. And if you have any from other companies, they would be useful too.

- **Before the first draft**

  o   Part way through the exercise, I will have some queries that I'd like to talk through. Can we pencil in a 2-hour meeting in a few days? The following times would be good: Wednesday 15, Thursday 16.

- **After the first draft**

  o   We need to discuss it and amend as appropriate, then circulate to managers for them to review and give feedback on.

We then do 'WiT' for the three parts of each half. See the bottom half of the page – the three parts are 'Before we start', 'Before the first draft' and 'After the first draft'. Then in the first of these three, we use different typography to signal the difference between a part ('Before we start') and a sub-part (e.g. 'Please confirm costs are OK'). In the left column, we've put sub-parts in Arial, not Arial Black, and we've used italics.

FIGURE 1.23

What I am to deliver

Redo the publications	I am to redo and consolidate the ABC and DEC documents, the Checklist and the XYZ Information Pack. I am to make them easier to understand.
Do it in routine Microsoft packages	I am to do some sort of handout, the exact format of which we will discuss as the exercise progresses. I will produce my 'redo' in Word, Excel or PowerPoint.
First draft by 30 November	I understand you want something by the end of the year. Given existing work commitments, I should be able to have delivered a reasonably final version for your first review by 30 November.

The project steps

Before we start

Please confirm costs are OK	Please confirm your agreement to the rates and estimated times. And please confirm your agreement to putting a note on the bottom: "designed by Jon Moon etc".
Please email soft copies	Please email a soft copy of the three documents in a form which allows me to copy and paste.
Please send me checklists	Please send me the checklist – you mentioned you had one. And if you have any from other companies, they would be useful too.

Before the first draft	Part way through the exercise, I will have some queries that I'd like to talk through. Can we pencil in a 2-hour meeting in a few days? The following times would be good: Wednesday 15, Thursday 16
After the first draft	We need to discuss it and amend as appropriate, then circulate to managers for them to review and feedback.

'WiT' doesn't just cope with these levels of hierarchy, it excels at them. It shows them *beautifully*. And it's got all the usual benefits of 'WiT'. The page has impact.

What if we want yet another level of hierarchy? An obvious answer is: do you really need that many? Maybe there is some other way to communicate – both author and reader would struggle to conceptualise too many levels of hierarchy.

But this is ducking the question. Assume that, within 'Please email soft copies', you want to talk about the three documents you need emailing to you. Those three documents create another level of hierarchy – or at least they do in today's bullet point-obsessed world. People show it like Figure 1.24 (from now on, the mock-ups only show the first two sub-parts of the project steps).

It is getting surreal – a heading, a bullet, a hollow bullet, a dash, a tick. For the three documents, why not just put the title of each document in italics and show it as a separate paragraph? See Figure 1.25. Readers can

FIGURE 1.24

THE PROJECT STEPS

- **Before we start**

  o   *Please confirm costs are OK*

  -   Please confirm your agreement to the rates and estimated times. And please confirm your agreement to putting a note on the bottom: "designed by Jon Moon etc.

  o   *Please email soft copies*

  -   Please email a soft copy of the three documents in a form which allows me to copy and paste:

  ✓   The Annual Report: please send the 2004 version, not the latest version

  ✓   The Management Accounts: please send the Word document and the Excel spreadsheets that link to it

  ✓   The checklist: please also send the previous version that covered the overseas offices too

FIGURE 1.25

The project steps

Before we start

Please confirm costs are OK   Please confirm your agreement to the rates and estimated times. And please confirm your agreement to putting a note on the bottom: "designed by Jon Moon etc".

Please email soft copies   Please email a soft copy of the three documents in a form which allows me to copy and paste:

Annual Report: please send me the 2004 version, not the latest version.

Management Accounts: please send the Word document and the Excel spreadsheets that link to it.

The checklist: please also send the previous version that covered the overseas offices too.

easily refer to the note to see which documents to send, and the page retains its strong alignment and looks sharp.

And if you want the list of documents to have a typographical cue, then I know something you could try – a bullet point (Figure 1.26). You didn't expect that, did you? Soon we will look at when bullet points are acceptable and this is one such occasion. Also, here they are made even more acceptable because of the italicised opening words and the less visually intrusive dash (rather than the more popular black dot).

FIGURE 1.26

The project steps	

Before we start

Please confirm costs are OK	Please confirm your agreement to the rates and estimated times. And please confirm your agreement to putting a note on the bottom: "designed by Jon Moon etc".
Please email soft copies	Please email a soft copy of the three documents in a form which allows me to copy and paste:

- *Annual Report*: please send me the 2004 version, not the latest version.
- *Management Accounts*: please send the Word document and the Excel spreadsheets that link to it.
- *The checklist*: please also send the previous version that covered the overseas offices too.

So 'WiT' is great, but can you have too much of a good thing? We answer this one next.

Can you have too much 'WiT'?

The short answer is: it depends on the document. The long answer is as follows:

Presentation slides can have too much	Imagine 25 slides on the trot, all done as 'WiT'. The audience would struggle – they might even cry out for a bullet point. With presentations, you need to ring the changes. Chapter 5 gives ideas how.

Business reports rarely can have too much	There are many reasons why business reports really need 'WiT'. Often, they aren't written that brilliantly and their layout is not that great, especially if done for an internal audience (client reports get spruced up more). Also, their readers are usually short of time and want to refer back to the report when discussing it. 'WiT' helps *all* these problems (and more). I have done 100-page reports all in 'WiT' and it's been fine.
Emails need help to have any	With emails, you need to make an effort to create 'WiT', because it's not easy to do it on the face of the email. If I want to say something that is more than just very simple, I do the note in Word then attach it to the email. In Word, I can do 'WiT', and format the page better. Unfortunately, a Blackberry somewhat puts a spanner in the works. I have not worked out how to do 'WiT' that can be read on the screen of a Blackberry. Also, Blackberry users aren't keen on attachments.

Next we show mercy on bullet points and see when they are acceptable.

Why isn't this book entirely in 'WiT'?

If I've written 100-page reports almost entirely in 'WiT', why didn't I do more of this book that way? Two reasons why: I didn't need to and I didn't want to. Let me explain.

'WiT' helps readers refer back to points, helps ensure ideas are complete and helps break up dense pages of text. But for much of this book, I didn't need help on any of these. For instance, when I previously listed reasons why you should read about 'WiT', I couldn't imagine you'd ever want to refer back to the list. Also, it doesn't matter if the list isn't complete. Finally, the page didn't look dense and intimidating – the book designer has done a great job.

So I didn't *need* 'WiT' – and I didn't *want* 'WiT' either, because tables can have a clinical feel. For this book, I wanted a more breezy style, one that ebbs and flows with the narrative.

However, the clinical feel of 'WiT' is exactly why I've done long reports that way. One was a market research report where many people made very impassioned comments. I did the entire report in 'WiT' because its clinical feel helped tone down the emotional levels and give an air of objectivity and neutrality to the report. Also, I didn't struggle to compose all those short phrases needed to join together bits of prose ('and next we move on to another key point'). They aren't needed in 'WiT'.

When bullet points are acceptable

A lot of bullet points aren't any good, eh? Given how popular they are, it's quite a message – and I say it unrelentingly.

Here's where I pull back from the precipice. Below we see when bullet points are acceptable. Also see page 166 for how to do them properly. Finally, notice that there are bullet points below. I explain why soon.

In general, bullet points are acceptable if:

–   you use them in moderation;

–   you use them to denote only a single hierarchy, not multiple ones;

–   you don't expect too much from them (they *don't* visually lift points).

Each of these reasons applied in Figure 1.26 which had bullets to show the three documents to send.

In practice, you can use bullets as follows:

> They can be acceptable if each point is brief and if there is no repeating pattern. For example, in Figure 1.27 each bullet point is less than a full row of text, so readers can scan down and see the key points more easily than if written in a paragraph. Also, because there's only three points and because each is brief, we don't need to start at the end for each bullet nor make the start of each typographically different, e.g. '• *Interest rates*: . . .'. (For a reminder of these ideas, see page 10, steps 4 and 5.)

FIGURE 1.27

We've assumed the following:
- Interest rates remain at 5%.
- Sterling is 50p to the dollar.
- Prices stabilise at £1.40 per kilo.

However, if there is a repeating pattern within the rows of text, don't do bullet points – use 'WiT' even if each point is less than a full row of text. Confused? Let me illustrate. You wish to list your company's offices – city and country. Figure 1.28 uses bullets, and the country names aren't aligned well, which makes it more difficult for readers to scan them. Figure 1.29 is 'WiT'. Country names are aligned, so scanning is easier.

FIGURE 1.28

- Tokyo, Japan
- Oslo, Norway
- Christ Church, New Zealand
- Lagos, Nigeria
- Basle, Switzerland
- San Francisco, USA

FIGURE 1.29

Tokyo	Japan
Oslo	Norway
Christ Church	New Zealand
Lagos	Nigeria
Basle	Switzerland
San Francisco	USA

➤ Secondly, the occasional bullet point list can help break up a page of dense text if nothing else offers itself up. Usually something does, though, e.g. 'WiT' or some decent document design, so this second reason rarely applies.

➤ Thirdly, if you're not fussed about readers quickly seeing the key points, bullets are just about acceptable in small doses – and this is my somewhat limp justification for using them here. But it's not that convincing – why do something average (show information in bullet points) when you can do something well (show it in 'WiT')?

➤ The fourth occasion is the usual escape clause: remember your audience – some of them might like bullet points, even after you've told them the joys of 'WiT'. Take care, though, because there will be others in the audience that don't like bullets.

➤ Finally, use bullets if they are part of the design template you must follow . . . That's why this book has bullet points at the start of each chapter (albeit they are arrows, not black dots).

Before we reach the chapter summary, here's one last question: does 'WiT' dumb down? After all, many people think bullet points dumb down. And yes, people will still shoehorn simplistic dumb comments into 'WiT' just as they do with bullet points. Which is why 'WiT' is like a razor blade. After the collapse of Barings Bank in 1995, James Morgan in the *Financial Times* (4 March 1995) said:

A derivative is like a razor. You can use it to shave yourself and make yourself attractive for your girlfriend. You can slit her throat with it. Or you can use it to commit suicide.

Well put, even if a bit scary.

So it is with 'WiT'. It can make your work attractive, intelligent and elegant. Arguably, 'WiT's better layout and greater impact also encourages people to engage with information more intelligently. But in the wrong hands, 'WiT' can still do damage. If this isn't that positive, many things in life are like this – from cars to food to exercise. But not bullet points. Far too often, they do damage – and I challenge anyone to say they are elegant.

A final thought: when not to have lines between 'WiT' rows

Every 'WiT' we've seen has faint horizontal lines between rows. The lines look smart and help create a distinction between different parts of the 'WiT'.

However, avoid horizontal lines if your 'WiT' rows are numerous and unusually narrow. This is often applies to reference documents (you will see in Chapter 7 that such documents need narrower rows of text). And one of my course handouts is an example of such a document – it is an A4 pamphlet printed double-sided on card and then folded twice so it will tuck into a top pocket. And because it's folded twice, its columns are narrow. Figures 1.30 and 1.31 show one of the columns. In Figure 1.30 the lines are a bit intrusive because there are so many of them. Figure 1.31 doesn't have the lines – and because the rows are so narrow, it doesn't need them. It's clearer and cleaner.

FIGURE 1.30

	Document design
	Design by numbers
Four	Remember the four design principles: contrast, repetition, alignment, proximity (with thanks to Robin Williams)
10 to 12	Avoid wide rows of text, the eye gets weary reading across them. Have about 70 characters for narrative (10 to 12 words) or 40 to 50 for reference documents (e.g. this handout)
	Avoiding mistakes with formats
Underlining	Avoid, it merges letters and slows reading
Italic	Avoid for continuous text, it's difficult to read, especially in a small font
Arial vs Times New Roman	Serifs such as Times New Roman are readable and good for continuous text. Sans Serifs such as Arial are legible and good for slides, headings, etc
Capitals	Avoid all upper case in continuous text, it slows reading speed
Random upper Case	Avoid, it changes Meanings and is Odd to Read. Remember The Third World Tour...
	Slides
	Avoiding bullet points on slides
An image	Find one that reinforces and internalises, e.g. Moses holding back waves, not naff clipart
A quote	"Van Gogh wasn't good at marketing"
An acronym	See the four design principles...
Something BIG	Don't hide important bits in bullet points
A random layout	Lay words haphazardly around the slide
'WiT'	It visually lifts ideas from slides

FIGURE 1.31

	Document design
	Design by numbers
Four	Remember the four design principles: contrast, repetition, alignment, proximity (with thanks to Robin Williams)
10 to 12	Avoid wide rows of text, the eye gets weary reading across them. Have about 70 characters for narrative (10 to 12 words) or 40 to 50 for reference documents (e.g. this handout)
	Avoiding mistakes with formats
Underlining	Avoid, it merges letters and slows reading
Italic	Avoid for continuous text, it's difficult to read, especially in a small font
Arial vs Times New Roman	Serifs such as Times New Roman are readable and good for continuous text. Sans Serifs such as Arial are legible and good for slides, headings, etc
Capitals	Avoid all upper case in continuous text, it slows reading speed
Random upper Case	Avoid, it changes Meanings and is Odd to Read. Remember The Third World Tour...
	Slides
	Avoiding bullet points on slides
An image	Find one that reinforces and internalises, e.g. Moses holding back waves, not naff clipart
A quote	"Van Gogh wasn't good at marketing"
An acronym	See the four design principles...
Something BIG	Don't hide important bits in bullet points
A random layout	Lay words haphazardly around the slide
'WiT'	It visually lifts ideas from slides

Now let's summarise the chapter.

Final thoughts and recap

We've seen lots of 'before' and 'after' examples. Here's a reminder of how 'WiT' dramatically improves so many different documents.

The monthly update

<table>
<tr>
<td>

IT systems
Projects more than £30k

Lorem ipsum dolor sit amet, consectetuer adipiscing elit, sed diam nonummy nibh euismod tincidunt ut laoreet dolore magna aliquam erat volutpat. Ut wisi enim ad minim veniam

Personnel
Changes in the month, salaries more than £30k

Lorem ipsum dolor sit amet, consectetuer adipiscing elit, sed diam nonummy nibh euismod tincidunt ut laoreet dolore magna aliquam erat volutpat. Ut wisi enim ad minim veniam

Wins
Wins in the month more than £20k

Lorem ipsum dolor sit amet, consectetuer adipiscing elit, sed diam nonummy nibh euismod tincidunt ut laoreet dolore magna aliquam erat volutpat. Ut wisi enim ad minim veniam

Losses
Losses in the month more than £20k

Lorem ipsum dolor sit amet, consectetuer adipiscing elit, sed diam nonummy nibh euismod tincidunt ut laoreet dolore magna aliquam erat volutpat. Ut wisi enim ad minim veniam

</td>
<td>

IT systems Projects more than £30k	Lorem ipsum dolor sit amet, consectetuer adipiscing elit, sed diam nonummy nibh euismod tincidunt ut laoreet dolore magna aliquam erat volutpat. Ut wisi enim ad minim veniam
Personnel Changes in the month, salaries more than £30k	Lorem ipsum dolor sit amet, consectetuer adipiscing elit, sed diam nonummy nibh euismod tincidunt ut laoreet dolore magna aliquam erat volutpat. Ut wisi enim ad minim veniam
Wins Wins in the month more than £20k	Lorem ipsum dolor sit amet, consectetuer adipiscing elit, sed diam nonummy nibh euismod tincidunt ut laoreet dolore magna aliquam erat volutpat. Ut wisi enim ad minim veniam
Losses Losses in the month more than £20k	Lorem ipsum dolor sit amet, consectetuer adipiscing elit, sed diam nonummy nibh euismod tincidunt ut laoreet dolore magna aliquam erat volutpat. Ut wisi enim ad minim veniam

</td>
</tr>
</table>

Findings that were of interest

<table>
<tr>
<td>

Findings of interest were as follows:

- There has been a problem with staff turnover – 30% of staff left last year, up 10% from the prior year. Many leavers were from "Global Solutions" department.
- Last month, Regulators formally announced the company has been cleared of the mis-selling accusations that hung over it for the last 2 years.
- Its computer system is inadequate and needs replacing at a cost of £2m. This will also add £500k a year extra to running costs.
- Its pension deficit has worsened in the year from £10m to £30m. The company is increasing contributions by £7m a year to remedy.
- Its new business initiative has been a success and income is up 20% on last year. Every department has increased income by at least 12%.
- Because of its lack of hedging, the dollar weakness will hit profit by £3m next year. It has recently recruited a new Treasurer.
- The market value of their Leeds site is worth £3m more than shown on its balance sheet
- It's finished clinical trials on the major new drug and Medical Authorities have indicated it should approve it next week.

</td>
<td>

There were mixed findings, but overall the company seems in good shape:

Good findings		**Bad findings**	
New business drive successful	Income is up 20%, and every department is up at least 12%.	£30m pension deficit	Up from £10m last year. The company is putting in an extra £7m a year to remedy.
Major drug to be approved	Clinical trials have finished, and the Medical Authorities have indicated they should approve it next week.	£3m 'forex' hit next year	The company didn't hedge its dollar exposure. It has recently recruited a new Treasurer.
Cleared of mis-selling	Last month, the Regulators formally announced the end of the 2-year review.	30% staff turnover	Up from 10% last year. Many leavers were from "Global Solutions" department.
Property £3m undervalued	The Leeds site has a market value £3m more than stated on the balance sheet.	£2m needed on IT	The systems need replacing. This will also add £500k a year to running costs.

</td>
</tr>
</table>

The client pitch

Why choose us?

- We have been serving clients for over 150 years
- We recruit the best staff
- Our clever web system gives you 24/7 service
- Being the biggest, we get the best deals from the market for you
- Our clients are King – we put them first
- Your case is presented not by salesmen but by one of your account executives. Result: a better deal for you
- We deliver innovative solutions
- Our parent is a Multinational Inc, the third biggest conglomerate in the world
- We won the Employer of Choice award last year

Why choose us?

Feature	Benefit
The biggest	You get the best deal from our market leverage
Clever web system	You get 24/7 access
A strong parent	Ut wisi enim ad minim veniam, quis nostrud
Employer of Choice	Suscipit lobortis nisl ut aliquip ex ea commodo
150 years' experience	Accumsan et iusto odio dignissim qui blandit
Account execs, not salesmen	Azril delenit augue duis dolore te feugait zzril

The client pitch – in PowerPoint

Why choose us?

- Being the biggest, we get the best deals from the market for you
- Our clever web system gives you 24/7 access
- Ut wisi enim adant minim veniam, quis nostrud because of our strong parent, Multinational Inc
- Suscipit lobortis nisils – having won Employer of Choice award last year - ut aliquip ex ea commodo
- We have been serving clients for over 150 years - accumsan et iusto odio dignissim qui blandit
- Your case is presented not by salesman but by one of your account executives. Result: azril delenit augue duis dolore te gait zzril

Why choose us?

Feature	Benefit
The biggest	You get the best deal from our market leverage
A clever web system	You get 24/7 access
A strong parent	Ut wisi enim adant minim veniam, quis nostrud
Employer of Choice	Suscipit lobortis nisils ut aliquip ex ea commodo
150 years' experience	Accumsan et iusto odio dignissim qui blandit
Account execs, not salesmen	Azril delenit augue duis dolore te gait zzril

Updates on the year-start plans

Plan

- Put new IT system into Bristol and Bath in the summer
- Recruit 200 more salesmen by May
- Undertake compliance training for all run-off units by end of year
- Do market research on customer perceptions of us
- Open new office in Singapore
- Sell off unwanted business in Norway and Australia
- Relocate Group finance to Milton Keynes

Action to date

- Group finance to move next month
- Singapore office to open in September
- Unwanted business in Norway now sold; in negotiations on Australian disposal
- Tenders being received from market research company
- 150 salesmen recruited so far – should hit May target
- Compliance training programme for run-off currently being designed

Area	Plan	Action to date
IT	Put new IT system into Bristol and Bath in the summer	Ready to roll in Summer
Recruitment	Recruit 200 more salesmen by May	150 so far – on target for 200 by May
Compliance	Undertake compliance training for all run-off units by end of year	Training programme being designed
Market research	Do market research on customer perceptions of us	Tenders being received from market research company
Singapore	Open new office in Singapore	To open in September
Divestments	Sell off unwanted business in Norway and Australia	Norway now sold; in negotiations on Australia
Relocation	Relocate Group finance to Milton Keynes	To move next month

The report index

The report consists of the following:

- Section 1 is the executive summary which looks at the recommendations, next steps and areas to clarify
- The scope, methodology and limitations are in section 2
- The options, along with the cost-benefits, are the analysis in section 3
- The Appendix is section 4 and is all the detailed supporting schedules

1	Executive summary	Recommendations, next steps, areas to clarify
2	Introduction	Scope, methodology, limitations
3	Analysis	The options, including cost-benefit analysis
4	Appendix	The detailed supporting schedules

A sequential line of argument

Locals prefer other shops' products	Lorem ipsum est gloriatur expetendis an. Congue contentiones consequuntur et eos, autem vocibus in nam. Agam conceptam mel cu, eum et porro recteque interesset. Ex ius idque corrumpit democritum, ad sit ponderum sensibus.
Even if they didn't, we are in a poor location	Eu sit cetero appareat accusata. Per et dicam tempor praesent, eripuit nonummy volumus cu sea. Per tantas altera praesent in, nam assum recteque disputationi ut.
	Mea ne elit iusto. Id corpora salutatus usu, eirmod animal eu est. No natum eripuit lobortis sit, vel lucilius expetendis cu, ei possit persequeris mel.
We can't relocate because of Planning Restrictions	Eum luptatum contentiones cu, eu mei fabellas mediocritatem. Vivendo antiopam nec te, malis ullum epicuri pro cu. Graeco virtute detracto sit ei, mea sonet dicant et.

If a lot of hierarchies

WHAT I AM TO DELIVER

- **Redo the documents**
  - I am to redo and consolidate the ABC and DEC documents, the Checklist and the XYZ Information Pack. I am to make them easier to understand.
- **Do it in routine Microsoft packages**
  - I am to do some sort of handout, the exact format of which we will discuss as the exercise progresses. I will produce my 'redo' in Word, Excel or PowerPoint.
- **First draft by 30 November**
  - I understand you want something by the end of the year. Given my existing work commitments, I should be able to have delivered a reasonably final version for your first review by 30 November.

THE PROJECT STEPS

- **Before we start**
  - *Please confirm costs are OK*
    - Please confirm your agreement to the rates and estimated times. And please confirm your agreement to putting a note on the bottom: 'designed by Jon Moon'. www.jmoon.co.uk'.
  - *Please email soft copies*
    - Please email a soft copy of the three documents in a form which allows me to copy and paste.
  - *Please send me checklists*
    - Please send me the checklist – you mentioned you had one. And if you have any from other companies, they would be useful too.
- **Before the first draft**
  - Part way through the exercise, I will have some queries that I'd like to talk through. Can we pencil in a 2-hour meeting in a few days? The following times would be good: Wednesday 15, Thursday 16.
- **After the first draft**
  - We need to discuss it and amend as appropriate, then circulate to managers for them to review and give feedback on.

What I am to deliver

Redo the publications	I am to redo and consolidate the ABC and DEC documents, the Checklist and the XYZ Information Pack. I am to make them easier to understand.
Do it in routine Microsoft packages	I am to do some sort of handout, the exact format of which we will discuss as the exercise progresses. I will produce my 'redo' in Word, Excel or PowerPoint.
First draft by 30 November	I understand you want something by the end of the year. Given existing work commitments, I should be able to have delivered a reasonably final version for your first review by 30 November.

The project steps

Before we start	
Please confirm costs are OK	Please confirm your agreement to the rates and estimated times. And please confirm your agreement to putting a note on the bottom: 'designed by Jon Moon etc'
Please email soft copies	Please email a soft copy of the three documents in a form which allows me to copy and paste.
Please send me checklists	Please send me the checklist – you mentioned you had one. And if you have any from other companies, they would be useful too.
Before the first draft	Part way through the exercise, I will have some queries that I'd like to talk through. Can we pencil in a 2-hour meeting in a few days? The following times would be good: Wednesday 15, Thursday 16
After the first draft	We need to discuss it and amend as appropriate, then circulate to managers for them to review and feedback.

37

The CV (Visit www.jmoon.co.uk for a template)

In the 1980s, bullet points were neat and new, but now they aren't the force they used to be. 'WiT' will often be much better; it gives documents immediate impact. Only use bullet points when it's valid to use them and don't do them a disservice by using them as follows:

- Badly.

Recap

The benefits of 'WiT'

It helps the writing	It helps ensure the writing is complete and consistent. It helps cluster items and sharpens the thinking. It cuts out words.
It helps the reading	It makes the page more inviting with better white space. It's easier to scan and skip sections. It's easier to refer back to. It forces words into columns and columns are easier to read. Its rigid structure reassures readers.

When you can 'WiT'

Look for 'repeating patterns' or 'brief sections'	*Repeating patterns*: If the same words keep cropping up in the text, do 'WiT' (e.g. like the CV).

Brief sections: Rather than have two rows of text stretching across a page, try 'WiT'. Remember the monthly update.

Or simply use 'WiT' to give impact to your narrative. Take your page of text and turn each paragraph into a row of 'WiT' with its key point in the left column and detail in the right.

'WiT' for particular formats

Slides avoid too much 'WiT'	'WiT' is great for slides but don't overuse – 25 'WiT' slides on the trot is a bit much. Ring the changes.
Business reports do lots of 'WiT'	You'd really struggle to have too much 'WiT' in a business report. 'WiT' till you drop.
Emails put in attachments	Except for the most basic email, do it in Word and send as an attachment – that way, you can do 'WiT'.

Constructing your 'WiT'

'WiT' does *beautiful* hierarchies	This table has three hierarchies: a section called *Constructing your 'WiT'*, then an overview comment in the left column, and finally the detail on the right.
Cluster and order within your 'WiT'	Group them between good and bad, important and unimportant or whatever. Order them within their grouping.
If possible, *summarise* in the left column	Use the left column to *summarise* the right column, not describe what it covers. Do 'WiT' so readers can skim the left column and grasp the points being made. Also, try right aligning the comments in the left column and do them in a typeface like Arial Black.

Chapter **2**

Graphs

Why many business graphs fail –
and how to ensure yours don't

> The myths and realities of graphs – when they
  work and when they don't
> Tips for decent graphs – how to do graphs that
  look smart
> Which graph to do when
> Graphs and your KPI pack
> Popular graphs you should avoid
> Showing graphs in presentations – some tips

Nobody wished to let others know he saw nothing, for then he
would have been unfit for his office or too stupid. Never emperor's
clothes were more admired.
  'But he has nothing on at all,' said a little child at last.

The Emperor's New Clothes

A good graph is incredibly effective, but too many graphs in business aren't good. Often, the author should have shown a different graph, a table or just explained the numbers in words ('income is up 10%'). And even if the graph is the right way to show the information, too often the author makes it ugly and uninviting.

This chapter resolves these problems. It looks at popular business graphs – when to do them, how to format them so they look smart, and which to do when. It also looks at popular business graphs that are almost utterly useless – and there's quite a few of them. We briefly see some unusual business graphs that you could try one day. Finally, there are tips for graphs in presentations. By the end, you will never look at a graph the same way again, and your readers might actually start looking at your graphs too.

One thing I don't do is introduce the different types of graph. You know there are column charts, line graphs, pie charts and so on, you stare at them almost every day. So let's dive straight into the first section – when to do graphs. It's eye-popping, counter-intuitive stuff.

When to do graphs: myths and reality checks

Because we've all seen graphs that bring numbers to life, that have won hearts and minds, many of us attribute graphs with magical powers. We believe they *simplify*. We believe they paint *a thousand words*. We believe they give a good general *impression*. We believe they give more *insight* than tables. We believe they are *memorable*.

With graphs, we *believe*.

The table below subjects these beliefs to a few reality checks.

Many graphs *don't* **simplify** **FIGURE 2.1** 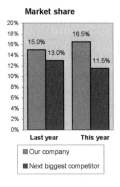	The sort of graph in Figure 2.1 sometimes appears on staff noticeboards or in emails, maybe as part of the end-of-year note from the CEO. Before reading on, first try to work out what it is saying . . . Got it yet? You probably eventually gathered that 'This year, our company took 1.5% market share from our next biggest rival'. I bet it took several seconds to work it out. Why was it such a struggle? After all, it doesn't look complex: it's only got two columns for this year and two for last year. But people need to *acclimatise* themselves to a new graph – and it takes time. Consider what you did to

understand this one – your eyes went from the legend to the columns to the *x*-axis to the *y*-axis. You had to do mental arithmetic, making comparisons between companies and across years – it places quite a strain on short-term memory ('So they are bigger than us – or is it the other way round?'). When you finally work out what you think is the point of the story, you still aren't sure if you've got the maths right or even got the story right.

People think graphs simplify complex points. But here the graph did a great job of complicating a simple point.

Graphs *don't* always paint a thousand words

It took several seconds to work out from the graph that 'This year, our company took 1.5% market share from our next biggest rival'. How many seconds did it take you to understand it when you read it just now in the last sentence? No time at all – your understanding was instant. The words do the maths and comparisons for the readers and give the message the CEO wants. The words don't just help the graph, they replace it.

People think graphs paint a thousand words. In this case, it badly painted just 13 words.

Graphs do give a general impression, but often readers want more

Graphs don't always give more insight than tables

Graphs can give more insight than a table of numbers, they can highlight simple patterns and give a general impression – we'll see some great examples later. But people then assume all graphs are good at giving a general impression. They aren't. Good graphs can, bad graphs don't.

Anyway, in business, readers often want more than a general impression, they want the detailed numbers. Those doing graphs recognise this, but instead of ditching graphs for something better, they adorn their graphs with numbers (Figure 2.2). Readers then just look at the numbers, not the slices or columns. They are given a badly laid-out table.

FIGURE 2.2

2007 income: £350m

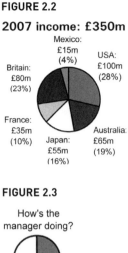

Mexico:
£15m
(4%)
USA:
£100m
(28%)
Britain:
£80m
(23%)
France:
£35m
(10%)
Japan:
£55m
(16%)
Australia:
£65m
(19%)

FIGURE 2.3

How's the
manager doing?

☐ Won
☐ Drawn
☐ Lost

FIGURE 2.4

2007 income

	£m	%
USA	100	28%
Britain	80	23%
Australia	65	19%
Japan	55	16%
France	35	10%
Mexico	15	4%
Total	350	100%

And when readers finally understand the badly laid-out table, they fool themselves into believing the chart helped. When people say they saw a pie chart that gave insight, what *exactly* gave the insight? Was it the numbers around the outside, numbers that perhaps gave new insight into, say, market concentration? Or was it the pretty slices in the middle?

People also apply different standards at work than outside work. When people see a pie chart at work, they nod sagely and say 'It gives a good general impression of distribution'. But if the same people wanted their newspaper to show how their team has done since the new manager arrived four years ago, they'd want a nice table of total wins, draws and losses. If the newspaper instead did a pie chart of wins, draws and losses, they wouldn't nod sagely and say 'Well, it gives a good general impression of results' (Figure 2.3). They'd think the sports editor had lost the plot and would buy a different newspaper, one that gave information, not pretty pictures.

If people want detailed numbers, do a table (Figure 2.4).

Many graphs aren't memorable Of all the charts you've seen, how many can you remember? Not many, I bet. Many graphs aren't memorable.

Our reality checks have shown that many myths are, well, just myths. But there are counterarguments too. Firstly, many graphs aren't memorable and don't simplify because they are bad graphs, not because graphs are bad. Secondly, *not all graphs have to be memorable and make instant sense* – don't assume you only do a graph if it is memorable, simple and instantly understood. Let's do two reality checks on our reality checks.

A graph *needn't* make instant sense

FIGURE 2.5

EIGHTS 2006

MEN	WED THU FRI SAT
I MAGDALEN	
ORIEL	
PEMBROKE	
BALLIOL	
CHRIST CHURCH	
EXETER	
NEW COLLEGE	
S.E.H.	
ST CATHERINE'S	
HERTFORD	
UNIVERSITY	
WADHAM	
II QUEEN'S	
LINCOLN	
KEBLE	
TRINITY	
JESUS	
ST JOHN'S	
WORCESTER	
BRASENOSE	
MERTON	
ST PETER'S	
ST ANNE'S	
MANSFIELD	
III L.M.H.	
WOLFSON	
PEMBROKE II	
LINACRE	
CHRIST CHURCH II	
MAGDALEN II	
CORPUS CHRISTI	
ST HUGH'S	
SOMERVILLE	
KEBLE II	
S.E.H. II	
ORIEL II	
IV UNIVERSITY II	
NEW COLLEGE II	
WORCESTER II	
EXETER II	
ST CATHERINE'S II	
QUEEN'S II	
LINCOLN II	
ST BENET'S HALL	
WADHAM II	
ST JOHN'S II	
OSLER–GREEN	
ST ANTONY'S	
V BALLIOL II	
BRASENOSE II	
PEMBROKE III	
MERTON II	
HERTFORD II	
JESUS II	
LINACRE II	
TRINITY II	
ST PETER'S II	
MAGDALEN III	
ST ANNE'S II	
JESUS III	
VI PEMBROKE IV	
CHRIST CHURCH III	
QUEEN'S III	
WADHAM III	
WOLFSON II	
UNIVERSITY III	
JESUS IV	
REGENT'S PARK	
L.M.H. II	
NEW COLLEGE III	
EXETER III	
PEMBROKE V	
VII ST JOHN'S III	
TRINITY III	
CHRIST CHURCH IV	
WORCESTER III	
ST ANTONY'S II	
CORPUS CHRISTI II	
WADHAM IV	
QUEEN'S IV	
ST HUGH'S II	
ST CATHERINE'S III	
S.E.H. III	
MANSFIELD II	
MAGDALEN IV	

A graph needs to be better than the *next best alternative* for showing the information and *clear* enough to be understood sufficiently quickly to meet your audience's *expectations* and attention spans. Phew. Did you get that?

If there is a lot of data or it is complex, you and your audience may both realise you won't get it across in just three seconds – sometimes everyone needs to devote a bit more time to grasp it properly. Figure 2.5 shows how 85 rowing crews did over four days of events in the 2006 rowing competition at Oxford University, known as 'Eights'. If you've never seen it before, it may be a bit confusing at first. But it's far better than any alternative and readers quickly become familiar with it and appreciate its clarity. And if I'd shown the chart from 1981, you'd clearly see how badly my crew, Christ Church 3rds, did that year.

Compare this chart to the graph that showed market share up 1.5%. It didn't make instant sense *and* was far worse than a simple alternative – just saying it in words.

However, even if the graph is better than the next best alternative, don't do it if it is still awful. Try something else, maybe setting your sights lower. Show less, simplify the data. For instance, if it's a confusing criss-crossed graph of income over the last six years for seven divisions, don't show all the data for all years. Instead just show the movement in the last year. Or show the overall movement over the last six years. Ask yourself why you are showing the graph in the first place – what is the point you are making? Then work out how best to make that point.

A graph *needn't* be memorable

A graph might not be memorable but can still be brilliant at showing the detail. The Oxford University rowing chart isn't memorable – I defy anyone to look at it and then successfully recall its broad patterns. But it's brilliant at showing detailed results for each boat.

Let's bring this all together, given how much we've ebbed and flowed. Good graphs can be dramatic and memorable, showing broad patterns and trends. But graphs take time to grasp; they aren't as intuitive as people assume. People often use a graph for the wrong job. So before doing a graph, ask yourself these questions first:

Would words be better?	If you were to do a lead-in title for the graph, would the title and graph help each other? People remember shapes and patterns even more if the pattern is summarised in words too. Or is the graph no longer needed? If the words merely clarify a confusing graph, the graph hinders, not helps.
Would a table be better?	Are people interested in detailed numbers? In which case, would they prefer a well-laid-out table instead?
Is the graph better than the next best alternative?	Your graphs needn't be memorable nor make instant sense. But are they better than the next best alternative *and* clear enough to be understood sufficiently quickly to meet your audience's expectations and attention spans?
What are you saying?	If words, tables or graphs do not work, simplify the data. Don't try to show it all, show selected bits. What exactly is the point you are trying to make?

Obviously, these beg the question: what do we mean by 'better'? How do we decide if something is 'better than words' or 'better than the next best alternative'? We'll tie this down later, after we've seen a few more graphs.

Finally, even though graphs needn't make instant sense, don't use this as an excuse for typographical laziness when constructing them. *Don't make people spend more time trying to understand your graphs than you spent doing them.*

The Oxford University rowing chart took a few seconds to understand but at least someone had worked on it to make it clean and clear. Compare this to Figure 2.6 which shows staff utilisation by country operations for the last five months. The person doing it simply highlighted the data in Excel then pressed the default line graph. Excel can do fantastic-looking graphs, but you have to work to get them – the default versions aren't good. And this one is particularly awful. It has visually intrusive shading and gridlines that

FIGURE 2.6

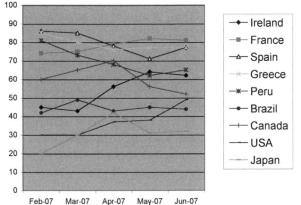

Staff utilisation (%)

dominate thin plot lines. The legend means readers have to flick back and forth to see what each line is. And the data doesn't make a neat plot – the lines are mixed up like a Jackson Pollock painting. People resent wasting time grappling with something the author hasn't bothered to do properly.

Which nicely leads us to the next section – how to format your graphs so they look smart.

'My manager likes graphs, I have to do them'

Above, we saw how people do graphs because they believe graphs have magical powers. There is, of course, another common reason why graphs get done – the boss wants them. Often, managers say they prefer them ('I'm a big-picture person, show me the graph'). But do they prefer graphs? At home, many managers pore over sports league tables in newspapers, then stroll into work and say 'I don't like tables'. But they obviously do; they just don't like tables at work – and that's because of several problems.

Tables at work are bad	Managers get given bad tables at work, but don't realise just how much they can be improved. So when faced with a bad table, they decide they must be 'graph' people. Unfortunately, this attitude then gets aped down the organisation – to behave like a big-picture senior manager, tell your staff that the 'trend is your friend' and ask them to do you graphs. *So* redo the tables. Chapter 3 shows how to do great tables.

▶

Tables at work are dull	You've redone the table properly and your manager *still* doesn't like it (yet you know he or she likes sports tables). And that's because the manager is too busy or lazy to engage with tables at work. Many people view business graphs as a nice distraction – their hearts lift when they see one breaking up a dense page of text in a report. Staring at graphs is easy, people are spared the intellectual strain of facing up to any insight or analysis. *So* the challenge now is to get your manager to intellectually engage with your work. Maybe bump into the manager by the water cooler and slip in an arresting opening. It's all a bit unsatisfactory, though.
Tables at work have jargon	Maybe managers don't like all those accounting terms in the table. Doing graphs won't help – they will still have to face the jargon even if it's in a graph. *So* somehow get them to go on a 'Finance for Non-Finance Managers' course. Maybe even give them a glossary of terms.
Tables at work have numbers	Finally, maybe the manager doesn't like sports tables either and is actually innumerate. Which isn't acceptable – to be in charge of a cost or profit centre, people need the skills to do the job. *So* somehow get them to go on a 'numeracy' course. Or give the job to someone who has the skills to do it.

In managers' defence, not only do people like seeing graphs, but many people like doing them too. It's creative, they don't have to think too hard when doing it, it beats doing real work and computers make it fun. Often they genuinely believe their graphs give insight. It's not surprising that when faced with a load of numbers, people often have an irresistible urge to plot graphs. Clarity seems to be the last thing on everyone's mind. Given this, it's a surprise that *any* business graphs are good.

Tips for smart graphs

Even if it's the 'right' graph for the information, many graphs fail simply because they look so horrible (Figure 2.7). Good design won't make a bad graph good, though it might make it seem good – many people incorrectly assume 'pretty' means 'informative'. But poor design can easily make a good graph bad.

FIGURE 2.7

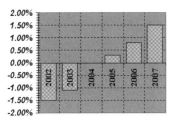

Read these tips to ensure your graphs look smart. Some tips mention Excel because it's the graphing package that many people use.

Doing the plot

Avoid 3-D

FIGURE 2.8

FIGURE 2.9

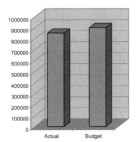

FIGURE 2.10

Often, people seem embarrassed about how dull their graph looks, it's just three simple numbers. So they liven it up with 3-D – which hinders clarity. In Figure 2.8, America and Asia are both 25%, but Asia looks bigger because you see the front of its slice.

And is the budget column above or beneath 900,000 in Figure 2.9? The column stands slightly proud of the background, so it's difficult to tell. Often, 3-D columns and pies take up half a page each just to show two or three numbers incredibly badly.

Finally, newspapers often do 'pictograms' – and these *really* distort. To show that sofa sales doubled from year 1 to year 3, we've shown a sofa doubling in height in Figure 2.10. But the growth seems much bigger – the sofa is also twice as wide and twice as deep. Sofa sales seemingly went up eight-fold.

Keep shading and gridlines typographically discrete

Shading can look bad when printed or copied. And gridlines are usually not needed; graphs are mostly to show shapes and patterns, not detailed numbers. So dispense with shading and gridlines unless there is a good reason to include them, in which case keep them both faint and unintrusive. Study the big London Underground posters – you only notice they have grids on them when looking for a particular station in the index. When the index says the station is 'B2', you only then spot the grids.

However, always have gridlines for log graphs to signal that the *y*-axis is not an arithmetic progression. 'Isobar' graphs need gridlines too. (If you don't use or know about log graphs or isobar charts, don't worry – just move on to the next point below.) With isobar graphs, readers really are interested in the numbers, and the graph is to help readers work out the outcome value that fits their assumptions. See Figure 2.11 – if you think the best price to charge for your new product is £20, and if you think market penetration will be just under 12%, the graph shows profit should be about £20m. See point A. Without gridlines, it would be trickier for readers to work this out. Also, see the text box later (p. 54) for more on the gridlines in the isobar graph.

FIGURE 2.11

Market penetration achieved (%)

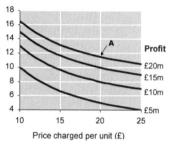

Price charged per unit (£)

Avoid black borders

We will see later that column charts aren't the greatest of graphs. If you do them, at least make them look decent. Avoid the black border that Excel offers you, it's visually dominating and unnecessary (Figure 2.12). Figure 2.13 is better. Study the column charts in *The Economist*, which are clean and clear.

FIGURE 2.12

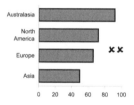

FIGURE 2.13

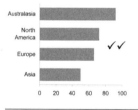

Doing labels, words, axes

Label the graph directly, not with a legend

A legend sits by a chart and tells readers what each slice or column relates to – but it creates problems. Many reports are printed on black and white printers or copied on black and white copiers. Also, 5–10% of people are colour blind. In which case, any colour cross-references are lost.

Also, legends set up a puzzle for readers to decode. To see how each division is doing, readers' eyes have to flick back and forth between legend and graph (Figure 2.14). It places a strain on short-term memory.

FIGURE 2.14

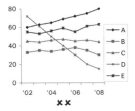

A legend is a default option in Excel. Always reject it and label the slices, lines, columns or dots directly (Figure 2.15). Avoid charts that rely on colour to interpret them. Avoid garish colours too, go for soft colours (soft brown, soft green, etc.).

FIGURE 2.15

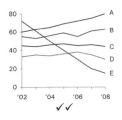

Also, reject the data markers that Excel offers you (the little triangles, squares, circles, etc., that sit on the lines).

Avoid too many tick marks and keep them 'outside'

Tick marks are the little dashes that go on the axes. If you have too many, your graph looks unnecessarily cluttered. Excel offers you tick marks that are inside, outside or cross the axes, as well as 'major' and 'minor' ones (double click on an axis to see 'format axis', then choose 'patterns'). In Figure 2.16, the x-axis has only *major* ticks and they cross the axis. The y-axis has *minor* ticks too and they are *outside* the axis.

FIGURE 2.16

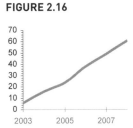

Neither is right. Choose *major* (or even *none* – see next tip). And keep *outside* so they visually detract less from the plot.

Note also that the x-axis is in a grey shade. This helps de-emphasize the axes and also creates a bit of visual interest. I've also done the plot in grey too. Again, it's more visually interesting than if it had simply been in black.

Have titles and labels reading left to right

Don't have labels that are sideways, they force readers to twist their heads to read them (Figure 2.17). If struggling to squeeze long labels into a small space on the *x*-axis under each column, turn the chart round so you have room to label each column with words that read left to right.

Notice that Figure 2.18 doesn't have tick marks on the axis that shows the country names. Neither graph needs such tick marks.

Also, arguably Figure 2.18 doesn't need a line for its *y*-axis. The graph would be clear without it.

FIGURE 2.17

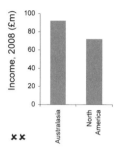

✗ ✗

FIGURE 2.18

Income, 2008 (£m)

✓ ✓

Use a sans serif typeface for labels and titles

For example, Arial. Avoid serif typefaces (e.g. Times New Roman). Chapter 7 explains why – see pages 196–7 on 'readable' versus 'legible'.

Keep labels few and brief

If a time-series graph covers many years (e.g. 1985 to 2000), label, say, every second year on the *x*-axis rather than every year, it looks less visually cluttered. Also, show the years as '85, '87, '89, etc., not 1985, 1987, 1989, etc.

If the *y*-axis shows values, don't label it as 100,000,000, then 200,000,000, then 300,000,000, and so on. Label it as 100, 200, 300 and have '£m' at the top. Shorter numbers get to the brain quicker and also stop labels visually competing with the plot.

Put negative numbers in brackets

Don't show negatives in red or with a leading minus sign. Brackets are less likely to be misread by readers. Also, the opening and closing of the bracket helps reinforce the 'negativeness' of the number.

Give a lead-in title, then a literal title

(I haven't done lead-in titles for all graphs in this chapter, but that's because each illustrates a point. I want you to focus on that point and not on whether you agree with my interpretation of the graph.)

Give a title that brings across the overall message of the graph, don't leave readers to work it out themselves. Don't make the title too long, and don't try to talk through everything in the graph ('A is up, B is the same, etc.'). Rather, say something that helps readers grasp the patterns.

And under the lead-in title, give the literal title too. See *The Economist*, it does this.

Chapter 3 looks at lead-in titles for tables and most comments apply to graphs too. One in particular is worth highlighting: 'give a title that is easily supported' by the chart. People do a column chart that shows the income for six divisions, then say: 'Group income up 7%'. Yet the chart doesn't show group income, it only shows division income. If the increase in group income is the most important point you are making, why do a chart that doesn't even show that point?

Sizing and positioning

Put graphs adjacent to the text to which they relate

Many reports relegate graphs to an appendix ('for an analysis of income by division, see Appendix 10, page 25'). It interrupts the flow of your document. Newspapers don't do this ('There was a by-election last night – for the results, see pages 10 to 12 where we have put all the tables, graphs and charts for today's paper').

See page 68 for more on keeping graphs and text near to each other in management information packs.

Keep graphs small and compact, they look better for it

Avoid big sprawling graphs that take up a whole page. If given such a graph, readers will hold the piece of paper at arm's length in order to understand it. Study the newspapers, they often have small, neat graphs.

We've now seen when to use graphs and how to make them look smart. Now we look at which graph to use when. The next section looks at graphs that *compare items*, e.g. 2007 income for six divisions (as opposed to graphs that plot figures *over time*, e.g. income for the last six years).

The isobar graph – white gridlines on light-grey shading?

The isobar graph in Figure 2.11 had a white grid on a light-grey background shading. But I said that shading wasn't needed, didn't I? Well, this white-on-light-grey is often how magazines do their gridlines and shading, and there are several reasons why it's acceptable (as long as the shading really is light). Firstly, white grids visually compete far less with the plotlines than black grids. Secondly, magazines have a good print quality, so shading doesn't look murky and smudged. Lastly, magazines do graphs that are small and compact, not big and sprawling, so the background shading is not overpowering. It's like walking into a room that's got a flash of bold colour or walking into a room painted entirely in that colour. Small graphs get away with things that big graphs can't.

More unusual typographical oddities to avoid

Avoid empty columns where the column width is similar to the gap between the columns (Figure 2.19) – readers can't quite see if they are looking at a column or a gap between columns. It's like the elephant – how many legs does it have?

FIGURE 2.19

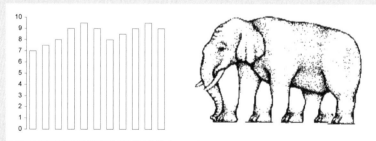

Avoid all the funky black and white hatches and dots that Excel offers you (Figure 2.20), they shimmer like a TV newsreader's check jacket. And how many dots are there in the diagram on the right?

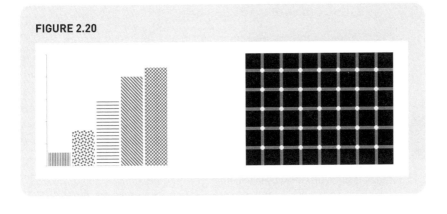

FIGURE 2.20

Graphs that compare (i.e. not time series)

There are three parts to this section. We look at graphs that compare just *one* data set, then a *few* data sets, then a *lot* of data sets. In English, this means we'll look at pie and column charts (Figures 2.21 and 2.22), then clustered column charts (Figure 2.23), then reports and presentations that have lots of different column charts (Figure 2.24). We'll see which work and which don't. (Here's a sneak preview of the answer – three out of four are bad, and the fourth is 'less unacceptable'.)

FIGURE 2.21

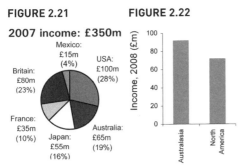

2007 income: £350m

Mexico: £15m (4%)
USA: £100m (28%)
Britain: £80m (23%)
France: £35m (10%)
Japan: £55m (16%)
Australia: £65m (19%)

FIGURE 2.22

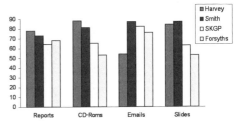

FIGURE 2.23

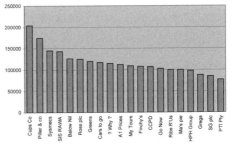

FIGURE 2.24

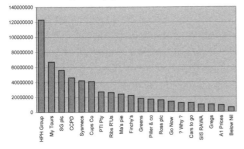

Just one data set

FIGURE 2.25

2007 income: £350m

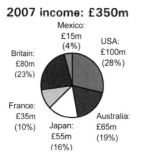

FIGURE 2.26

2007 income

	£m	%
USA	100	28%
Britain	80	23%
Australia	65	19%
Japan	55	16%
France	35	10%
Mexico	15	4%
Total	350	100%

People often do pie charts to show a single set of data. Figure 2.25 shows a pie chart of income by territory for 2007, and it looks pretty neat. But as we said earlier, it's just a badly laid-out table. Look at the chart and tell me the income from the USA and the share of income from Britain. Yes, it's £100m and 23%. Did any of the pretty slices help you answer the questions? Or were you just looking at the numbers around the outside? Also, the eye has to do a strange circular motion to find information. Do a table instead (Figure 2.26).

Some pie charts show so much, they end up like a bicycle wheel (Figure 2.27). Preposterous. And some take a lot of space to show three numbers badly – or sometimes even only two (Figure 2.28).

Also, pie charts can't cope with negative numbers. If plotting profit by division, what if one division made a loss or was a cost centre? I once saw a pie chart try – for the loss-making division, there was a little triangle sitting all alone underneath the pie chart like a little piece of cheese. Very weird. Very wrong.

FIGURE 2.27

FIGURE 2.28

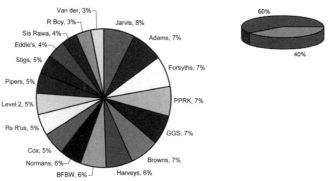

People also do column charts for this sort of information. They do columns to compare staff turnover by business unit, or IT spend by department, or, in the case of Figures 2.29 and 2.30, another set of income by territory. (They show the same data in two ways: Figure 2.29 is in descending order of income, Figure 2.30 in alphabetical order.) But do these column charts help? Let's study Figure 2.29.

It doesn't highlight any trends. OK, it slopes down, but that isn't a trend because it's not a time series. And it doesn't give any great overview, except at a 'high' level ('Look, the columns get smaller – gosh'). It's no

FIGURE 2.29

FIGURE 2.30

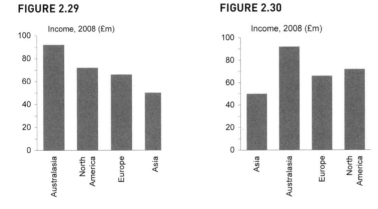

good at detail, a table would show it better. And the graph doesn't make the detail any more memorable, not, that is, unless you somehow memorise the order of the territories – Australasia is biggest, then North America, then Europe, then Asia. Finally, it doesn't particularly have impact nor give any great insight that a table couldn't.

To summarise, the column chart doesn't highlight, isn't good at detail, isn't memorable, doesn't have impact and doesn't give insight. I think that says it all.

Had we shown the bars horizontally instead of vertically (Figure 2.31) it would be *marginally* better – at least readers wouldn't be twisting their heads to read the labels.

I suppose this column chart is *less unacceptable* than a pie chart – at least it doesn't make readers' eyes do a circular motion to read the labels. It doesn't do much harm to include it in a presentation, and it provides pretty colours without hindering clarity too much. (Am I damning this chart with faint praise?)

Don't bother doing it for reports, though.

Arguably there is a time when column charts are useful if comparing items. If one or two items are materially different from the rest, columns communicate that with reasonable impact, more so than a table of numbers could – see Figure 2.32.

Also, as we see later, column charts are acceptable for a time-series set of data, since they can help highlight a trend (e.g. income for the last six years). That's because 2006 is after 2005 and 2005 is after 2004, and so on. There is an arithmetic logic to the *x*-axis that helps readers attach significance to the pattern of columns. Compare this to the columns by territory in

FIGURE 2.31

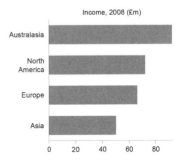

FIGURE 2.32

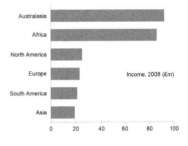

Figures 2.29 and 2.30 – readers can only attach significance to the pattern if they are able to remember what each individual column represents.

To conclude, many charts that compare a single set of data are pointless (remember, we aren't talking about time-series graphs). Readers are usually interested in the numbers, so a well-laid-out table would be better.

What about more than one data set though? The next section looks at how to chart them.

A few sets of data (not time series)

A company has researched customers' views on the reports, CD-Roms, emails and slides done by four different companies (Harvey, Smith, SKGP, Forsyths). A high score means customers liked them, a low score means they didn't. There are now four loads of four data – how can this be shown? A common way is the clustered column chart shown in Figure 2.33.

FIGURE 2.33

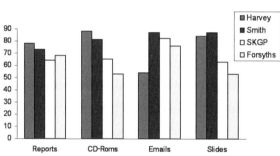

Instead, try the graphic in Figure 2.34 (the Appendix describes how I did it in Excel). Each company's score is indicated by the position of its logo – the first column gives scores for reports, and, as seen, Harvey scored about 78%, Smith about 73%, and so on.

Also, to help differences in scores stand out more, the chart now starts at 50, not 0 – and we've put the bottom left number '50' in a box to help

FIGURE 2.34

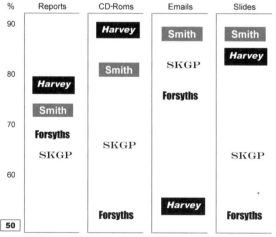

highlight this to readers. If readers realise the chart starts at 50 only after close scrutiny, they might incorrectly think we'd done it not for clarity but for deception and spin.

There are several benefits to this layout. Firstly, there is no need for a legend. Also, each category is now in an order – study emails. In the clustered column chart, the columns go up then down, whilst in the 'logo' chart, the logos are in strict descending order.

Next, there is less clutter, so readers aren't visually fighting their way through a jungle of columns, *they aren't staring at faceless anonymous blocks*. Also, because it no longer looks like a typical number-cruncher's graph, non-accountants will engage with it more. They are looking at something that is distinctive, easy to understand and probably familiar to them too – company logos. It's *accessible*.

And it's easier for readers to see patterns by company. For example, look at Harvey: it is mostly near the top save for emails where it did poorly. And readers can more easily see patterns by type of communication, e.g. the scores for reports are closely grouped whereas the scores for slides are more spread out. Compare this to the clustered column chart: readers could spot these patterns if they looked hard enough, but they won't, they'll lazily skim over it. The anonymous blocks don't engage readers, they don't invite scrutiny.

If detailed numbers are needed, a table would be better (Figure 2.35), but it doesn't show patterns well. Also, all columns are in the order of the first column (reports), so it's not easy to see rankings within the other three columns.

We can overcome this by having four tables, each in descending order (Figure 2.36). This saves readers from mentally reordering data for columns that aren't in strict descending order. It's better than the single table, but still doesn't give the patterns as easily as the 'logo' chart.

The 'logo' chart in effect plotted the labels. It's a powerful way of showing detail and distribution. Next is another example of it in action, this time on data reported by UNICEF.

At the start of 2007, UNICEF issued a report comparing the lives of youths across 21 countries. Newspapers quoted the report, showing

FIGURE 2.35

All in %	Reports	CD-Roms	Emails	Slides
Harvey	78	88	54	84
Smith	73	81	87	87
Forsyths	68	53	76	53
SKGP	64	65	82	63

FIGURE 2.36

All in %	Reports		CD-Roms		Emails		Slides
Harvey	78	Harvey	88	Smith	87	Smith	87
Smith	73	Smith	81	SKGP	82	Harvey	84
Forsyths	68	SKGP	65	Forsyths	76	SKGP	63
SKGP	64	Forsyths	53	Harvey	54	Forsyths	53

UNICEF's statistics on 12 aspects of youths' lives – how often they got drunk, had a fight, smoked drugs, and so on. In Figure 2.37 there are four of the twelve aspects, laid out exactly as shown in one newspaper. The left table, for instance, shows that 34.9% of Britain's youths had used cannabis in the last 12 months, compared to an average of 21.4% for all 21 countries (of which the highest was Canada and lowest was Greece).

FIGURE 2.37

Used cannabis (last 12 months)	Been drunk at least twice	Had a baby (15 to 19-year olds) (births per 1,000 women)	Involved in a fight (last 12 months)
Lowest: Greece, 4.2%	**Lowest**: France, 8%	**Lowest**: Japan, 4	**Lowest**: Sweden, 15%
Highest: Canada, 40.4%	**Highest: Britain, 30.8%**	**Highest**: USA, 46	**Highest**: Portugal, 48.5%
Average: 21.4%	**Average**: 15.4%	**Average**: 16	**Average**: 38.1%
Britain: 34.9%		Britain: 28	Britain: 43.9%

These tables don't work well – it's not easy to see patterns and ranges. Each number needs individual attention. And they're repetitive – the word 'highest' has to be mentioned again and again.

Instead, the newspaper could have plotted these statistics not in column charts or line charts but in a chart like the 'logo' one. Each 'column' in the chart (Figure 2.38) represents one of the four aspects, e.g. the left column is the statistics for 'been drunk'. The worst-performing country for a given aspect is at the top of that column, the best performing at the bottom, and the average is somewhere between the two. The word 'Britain' is typographically different, so readers can easily see the pattern created by the 'Britain' data points and see Britain's performance relative to the top, bottom and average performances.

Also, unlike in the newspaper, the four aspects are now in some sort of order – Britain improves as we move from left column to right. Finally, arguably the chart might be more intuitive if inverted, with the worst at the bottom, not the top. People tend to assume the top of a list is best and the bottom worst.

The position of the 'average' figures is not guesswork, they are exactly where they should be. For details on how the chart was done, again see the Appendix.

Both the 'logo' and UNICEF chart have a couple of things in common. Firstly, neither is exactly memorable, but as we said, charts don't have to be memorable. Here, the charts help readers see pat-

FIGURE 2.38

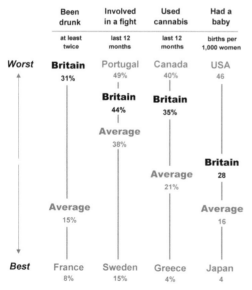

terns and give detail too, and are better than the next best alternative and are still acceptable.

Secondly, each column of each chart has up to four items in it – the 'logo' chart has the four names of the companies, and the UNICEF chart has 'best', 'worst', 'average' and 'Britain'.

The next section looks at how to cope with many more than four items. It looks at how to show figures from 20 different competitors. And remember, we are still looking at *graphs that compare* items – none of the graphs plot changes over time.

Many sets of data (not time series)

For 20 competitors, you have found details from their annual reports: income, profit, number of people, and so on. It's taken a lot of time to find them but when reporting your findings to management, you ruin it by doing lots of 'pretty' pictures.

You present page after page of column charts – like the two in Figure 2.39 which show income and income per person. You also do graphs for income growth, trading profit margin, growth in income per person, operating profit, and so on – graph after graph after graph.

FIGURE 2.39

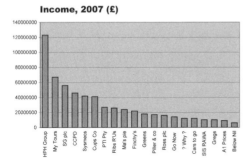
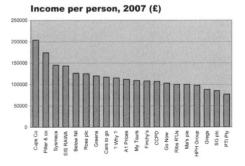

Earlier we said non-time-series column charts rarely give insight – remember this graph (repeated here in Figure 2.40)? The best I could say about column charts such as this was: 'less unacceptable'.

And the two graphs above don't give insight into 'income' or 'income per person'. Even worse, they don't engage with readers. They are eye candy, colouring for a report. Readers casually flick through them without getting into them. It's partly because they are badly designed – they don't invite scrutiny – and partly because less is more with graphs. The more graphs you do, the

FIGURE 2.40

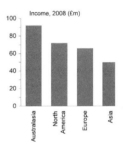

less impact they have. We've all seen management information packs or presentations with 20 or 30 graphs, each of which is a bit complex or difficult to decipher. With that many graphs, it's not just diminishing marginal returns, it's negative marginal returns. None makes an impact.

Compare this to one carefully chosen graph – it will stand out and be remembered. But as they say on TV quiz shows, 'I am not going to give you that'. Often people are interested in numbers, so for these 20 competitors, do a 'mastertable' – see Figure 2.41. It *engages*. Readers will pore over the table looking for particular points of interest; it invites scrutiny. This table makes a great appendix to a report, a place where lots of statistics are all brought together for readers to review.

The rest of this section contains notes on the design and layout of the table. If you wish to stick to reading about graphs, skip to the next section which looks at time-series graphs.

First, the columns are labelled A to O so as to help commentary. Also, look at columns J to M (see, I told you the labels help commentary), which give an overview of each company's trading profit margin. Columns J and K show this year's and last year's margin, and in columns L and M, a double tick means the margin improved a lot, whilst a double cross means it worsened a lot. Obviously a single tick or cross meant the change was not so big. Readers can quickly see who turned things round in the year and who suffered a bit. Notice how the ticks and crosses are in different columns – this was so they didn't visually compete with each other. I originally did the table with the ticks and crosses in the same column and it was difficult to see the wood for the trees. Separating them helps create a visual distinction.

Also, see how there is a gap every five rows. Usually tables have gaps to help readers keep their place as they run their eyes across a table with

FIGURE 2.41

Income		Income growth		Income/person		Growth in income per person		Trading profit margin					Operating profit margin	
									This yr	Last yr				
A	B	C	D	E	F	G	H	I	J	K	L	M	N	O
	£m		%		£k		%		%	%				%
HPH Group	123	Cars to go	51%	Cups Co	204	Gregs	47%	HPH Group	22%	20%	✔		HPH Group	26%
My Tours	67	Gregs	34%	Piller & co	174	Cars to go	26%	Greens	18%	19%		✗	CCPD	24%
SG plc	56	Finchy's	21%	Sysmecs	145	Finchy's	14%	Gregs	17%	3%	✔✔		Ma's pie	21%
CCPD	46	CCPD	20%	SIS RAWA	143	HPH Group	13%	Ribs R'Us	17%	12%	✔✔		Ribs R'Us	20%
Sysmecs	42	PTI Pty	20%	Below Nil	126	Sysmecs	13%	Ma's pie	17%	16%	✔		Greens	20%
Cups Co	41	? Why ?	14%	Ross plc	125	Greens	11%	Piller & co	17%	14%	✔		Gregs	20%
PTI Pty	27	Sysmecs	14%	Greens	120	SG plc	9%	CCPD	16%	16%	same		Piller & co	19%
Ribs R'Us	26	Piller & co	14%	Cars to go	117	My Tours	8%	Cars to go	13%	1%			Cars to go	17%
Ma's pie	24	SG plc	10%	? Why ?	115	SIS RAWA	8%	PTI Pty	12%	16%		✗	PTI Pty	14%
Finchy's	22	Ma's pie	6%	A1 Prices	112	CCPD	7%	? Why ?	10%	8%	✔		? Why ?	14%
Greens	18	Cups Co	6%	My Tours	109	Ribs R'Us	6%	SG plc	9%	8%	✔		SG plc	12%
Piller & co	17	Ribs R'Us	4%	Finchy's	108	Ma's pie	5%	Below Nil	8%	6%	✔		Below Nil	10%
Ross plc	16	Greens	4%	CCPD	107	Below Nil	4%	Go Now	8%	na			Sysmecs	10%
Go Now	14	Ross plc	3%	Go Now	103	? Why ?	3%	Sysmecs	6%	8%		✗	Go Now	9%
? Why ?	12	My Tours	2%	Ribs R'Us	100	Piller & co	0%	Finchy's	5%	(4%)	✔✔		Finchy's	7%
Cars to go	12	HPH Group	2%	Ma's pie	100	A1 Prices	(1%)	Cups Co	2%	10%		✗✗	A1 Prices	4%
SIS RAWA	10	SIS RAWA	1%	HPH Group	98	Cups Co	(1%)	My Tours	1%	3%		✗	My Tours	4%
Gregs	10	Below Nil	(1%)	Gregs	88	PTI Pty	(4%)	A1 Prices	1%	7%		✗✗	Cups Co	3%
A1 Prices	9	A1 Prices	(3%)	SG plc	85	Ross plc	(4%)	SIS RAWA	(4%)	5%		✗✗	SIS RAWA	1%
Below Nil	6	Go Now	na	PTI Pty	77	Go Now	na	Ross plc	(5%)	(3%)		✗	Ross plc	(1%)

many columns. But here, each row doesn't consist of data from just one company, so readers are unlikely to want to run their eyes across a row – so why the gap? It's to make the table look less intimidating, more inviting.

Arguably, we could redo the table with all columns in the same order as the income column (column A), in which case all data for a company would then run along a row. The table would need far fewer labels – it would only need the company names down the left. Also, readers may be better able to spot patterns – for instance, do big companies have bigger margins than smaller companies?

However, it's a trade-off. By having each data set in descending order – as the table above does – readers can more easily see the highest and lowest for each data set (e.g. highest income per person is Cups Co, lowest is PTI Pty (columns E and F)). If columns E and F were in the same order as column A, readers wouldn't so easily see who is highest and lowest. Also, by showing each data set in descending order, it's easier to see the distribution – for instance, are most companies clustered near the bottom or the top? An average row might help here.

Finally, whenever I did such a table for my managers, what insightful lead-in title did I give? Answer: I didn't – the table was for readers to get from it whatever they found to be of interest. Yes, I had summarised parts of it in other sections of the report, but this table was just pulling all the stats together in one place for general interest and reference.

But I did say this: 'There is no summary comment to this table, I include it for your own reference and interest.' If I hadn't said this, readers might think I had forgotten to do a lead-in title, or they might go through agonies trying to work out what to read into the table, when the answer actually is: whatever you want. My 'lead-in title' removed all ambiguities.

We've now finished looking at graphs that compare items and we will draw threads together at the end of the chapter. Next we look at graphs that show numbers over time – time-series graphs.

Time-series graphs

This section follows a similar format to the last one – one set of data, then moving on to many sets of data. In English, this means we'll look at column charts and line charts. Again, we see which ones work and which don't.

One set of data

A line or column graph is fine at communicating a single set of time-series data. But don't do it for just two data points. It looks dumb – two big columns just to show two numbers. But for more than a couple of points, a graph will usually communicate a time series more effectively than a table. Also, if you have many data points in your time series, don't do columns, do a line graph – see Figures 2.42 and 2.43. The columns aren't needed, they add nothing and make the graph typographically cluttered. The financial press use line graphs to show stock price movements.

FIGURE 2.42   **FIGURE 2.43**

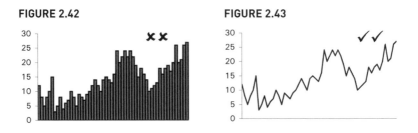

Plotting one set of time-series data is easy. Plotting several sets is trickier – and this is what the next subsection is about.

More than one set of data

Your company operates in a number of geographical territories and you wish to show how each territory's share of group income has changed between 2002 and 2006. Example: in 2002, China was about 13% of Group income, but by 2006 it had grown to 26%.

People often do paired columns to show the changes. In fact, the graph in Figure 2.44 is based on one done by a newspaper to show the change in composition of the FTSE 100 in the 22 years since it started in 1984. The choice of graph, the typography, the lead-in title are very similar to the original, right down to the most recent year being before the earlier year and the country names sitting on top of columns rather than underneath

FIGURE 2.44

Share of Group income (%)

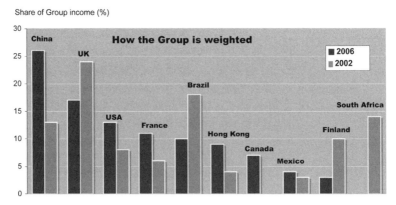

them. (Putting them on top means you can squeeze in names without writing them sideways, but means they are poorly aligned.)

Let's see if it's effective. Firstly, the detail is poor, we struggle to see exact numbers. The overview is poor too, it's difficult to get context. How many sectors are up, how many down? How many are up a lot, how many up a little? Readers have to scrutinise each pair of columns individually. They have to squint at and work out the differences in size between adjacent columns and then keep a running tally in their head ('That one's up, . . . that's up too, that one's down').

Try Figure 2.45 instead. It's not a familiar-looking graph so do please give it time – remember that graphs needn't make *instant* sense. It plots 2002 composition down the left and 2006 composition down the right. For territories that have gone up, the lines and labels are darker, and for ones that have gone down, they are lighter. Count the dark lines; there are six. Count the grey lines; there are four. Read the names of those that have gone down: UK, Brazil, Finland, South Africa. Spot the big riser, China. See how South Africa has disappeared to nil. It's all clear. Also, it's now got a better lead-in title: 'China surges'.

This graph is more intuitive because the slope of a line indicates if a territory is up or down and by how much. In the column chart, readers have to think a bit more, comparing sizes of adjacent columns whilst trying to remember whether the dark column is 2002 or 2006.

Also, territory names are in a vertical position that reflects their share of group income for each year. By reading down the names on the left or right, you get the ranking for either 2002 or 2006. Also, the big gap between China and the UK in 2006 signals to readers that there is a . . . big gap between China and the UK. With the column chart, the position of the territory names didn't signal anything – rather, they were simply squeezed into the chart where they could fit. The China and UK labels were close to each other simply because the 'UK' label had to squeeze on top of the 2002 column.

Finally, Figure 2.45 doesn't have lots of big dominating columns on it. It is less cluttered and information doesn't visually compete with other things for readers' attention.

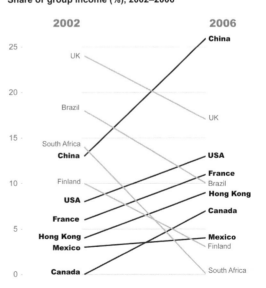

FIGURE 2.45

China surges
Share of group income (%), 2002–2006

FIGURE 2.46

All in %	'06	'02	Diff
China	26	13	13
UK	17	24	(7)
USA	13	8	5
France	11	6	5
Brazil	10	18	(8)
Hong Kong	9	4	5
Canada	7	0	7
Mexico	4	3	1
Finland	3	10	(7)
South Africa	0	14	(14)
	100	100	

FIGURE 2.47

All in %	'06	All in %	'02
China	26	UK	24
UK	17	Brazil	18
USA	13	South Africa	14
France	11	China	13
Brazil	10	Finland	10
Hong Kong	9	USA	8
Canada	7	France	6
Mexico	4	Hong Kong	4
Finland	3	Mexico	3
South Africa	0	Canada	0
	100		100

The line chart could have shown even more. If detail is important, we can put each territory's share of income after its name (e.g. 'China (26%)' for the 2006 label).

What if the data had been shown as a table (Figure 2.46)? It shows the share of group income for both years, but the 2002 figures are not in descending order, they are in the same order as the 2006 figures. The advantage is: for any given country, its two figures are alongside each other so we can compare them easily – we can even do a variance column.

But the disadvantage is: we struggle to see the context of historical figures – who was top in 2002, who was bottom, what is the distribution? We have to mentally reorder the 2002 column of numbers.

Figure 2.47 overcomes this problem by showing two separate tables: the 2006 figures in descending order, the 2002 figures in descending order too. We can now more easily understand the figures for each year in isolation, but struggle to see the changes over time – there is no variance column.

Yet again neither table is ideal, it's a trade-off. Also, neither table uses the physical space as effectively as the line chart. In the line chart, the big gap between China and the UK for 2006 has impact, much more so than showing the numbers in the table. The line chart gives overview, detail and insight better than the tables or paired columns.

If you thought the paired columns were confusing, next you will see something worse. Above, there were lots of data sets, two points per set. Now we have lots of data sets, *lots* of points per set. The table in Figure 2.48 shows staff utilisation by country operations for the last five months.

FIGURE 2.48

All in %	Ireland	France	Spain	Greece	Peru	Brazil	Canada	USA	Japan
Feb 07	45	74	86	85	81	42	60	30	20
Mar 07	43	75	85	80	73	49	65	30	30
Apr 07	56	79	78	76	68	43	70	37	42
May 07	64	82	71	77	62	45	56	38	31
Jun 07	62	81	77	77	65	44	52	49	32

It is nicely laid out. Maybe it would benefit from an average column and row perhaps, but let's not worry about that for the moment because it's got a more fundamental problem than missing out some average statistics – it fails to highlight trends. Readers have to study each individual column to see what's happening. It's quite an effort.

A good graph would highlight trends far more effectively than the table, but first we have to find a good graph. We could try clustered columns, but imagine the chaos of nine different clustered columns. I am not even going to show it. Instead, I'll do a line chart – people often do them, and previously I've shown how the data would look using the default option for Excel line graphs. Here it is again (Figure 2.49). It's a mess and not just typographically. Even if smartened up, it would still be confusing. People won't engage with it, it's too intimidating and doesn't deserve attention.

FIGURE 2.49

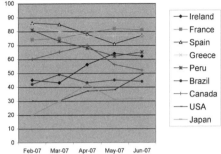

So the table doesn't work, neither do clustered columns or line charts. Where do we go now? We could simplify. We could cluster the data, e.g. bunch the European countries together and show a single line for Europe as a whole, then do the same for North America and for South America, and show Japan separately. That way, we'd have not nine lines but four and it would be a simpler graph. Alternatively, we could strip some data out and simply show the Feb-07 and Jun-07 figures.

However, assume our readers don't want this, assume they want all data for all individual country operations. Well, there is another way forward. You may remember I said that graphs are good if small and compact, and graphs are great if there is a simple pattern. Well, Figure 2.49 shows nine lines on one graph, so it is neither small nor simple.

But what if we were to show one line on nine graphs? The mini-graphs in Figure 2.50 are far simpler to understand and are less daunting. They effortlessly show trends over time. Also, they have been aligned across the page so readers can easily compare results across different territories (though see the text box below for more on this).

FIGURE 2.50

Ireland	France	Spain	Greece	Peru	Brazil	Canada	USA	Japan

I'm not sure this layout works on a slide, but if a report wants to show all the data and if detailed numbers are not important and trends are, these mini-graphs are the best way to show the information. They are a bit fiddly to set up and take some tweaking to get aligned. But for important or regular reports, it's worth it. The graphs are far better than confusing clustered column charts, or criss-crossing crinkly line charts, or tables that struggle to show the patterns.

We've now seen different ideas for plotting time series for several data sets. There are other ways that are popular but which are ineffective. We look at them next just so you know which ones to avoid.

Mini-graphs side by side or one under another?

In the example above, we showed nine mini-graphs of staff utilisation side by side across the page. Alternatively, we could have shown them going down the page. The best way depends on what you are showing – but first consider the commentary. Often when schedules like this are in KPI packs, the graphs are on one page and the commentary is on the next. So if readers wish to check a particular point in the commentary with its related graph, they have to flick back and forth ('The commentary says that "Peru" has at last reversed its downward trend . . . let's see [flick to first page] . . . ah yes, the comment is right').

Instead, keep the commentary and graphs on the same page. Keep a small physical distance between them.

Figures 2.51 and 2.52 show two different lay- **FIGURE 2.51** outs for the graphs and commentary, for just two of the countries and with a bit of Latin for the commentary. In Figure 2.51, the comments for each graph are underneath. Readers can see the comments and relate them to the graphs. The graphs are lined up across the page so it's easy to visually compare results across countries. However, this layout struggles if there are too many graphs to fit across a page or if you have a lot to say about each graph.

FIGURE 2.51

Ireland	France

Lorem ipsum est gloriatur expetendis an

Congue contentiones consequuntur et eos, autem vocibus in nam.

Graeco virtute detracto sit ei, mea sonet dicant.

Mei adhuc fabulas et, qui ex zzril postea posidonium, nec eu dico reque docendi.

In which case try putting the graphs one under the other, then use the space to the right of the graph for the comments (Figure 2.52). There is now

FIGURE 2.52

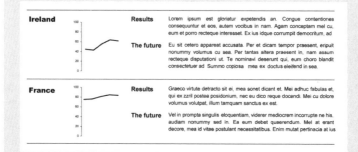

more room for commentary, but graphs are not so easy to compare with each other because they are now lined up down the page, not across the page. It's a trade-off.

Whether you lay them out horizontally or vertically, do the graphs in Excel, then link or copy them to a Word document for your commentary. Word is far more flexible and better than Excel for writing commentaries (which isn't surprising – Word is a word processing package).

The Appendix explains why and gives tips on how to link or copy across from Excel to Word. And check out Chapter 8, it has some great layouts for KPI packs.

More than one data set – popular graphs to avoid

There are many bad ways of showing more than one data set. Please avoid these.

Avoid multiple pie charts

FIGURE 2.53

Income by division

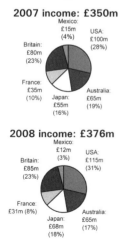

In Figure 2.53, we don't have just one 'badly laid-out table', we have two. And it is difficult to make comparisons. To see how, say, Japan is doing, readers have to scan around the 2007 pie, their eyes doing a strange circular motion. Eventually they land on the right slice and then have to commit to memory the numbers £55m and 16%. They then move to the 2008 pie and scan around that one – and eventually find £68m and 18%. If they still can remember £55m and 16%, they have at last made a comparison.

Try to answer these questions from the two pies. For how many countries is income up? For how many countries is income down? Which country grew the most? These are obvious questions to seek answers to, yet the pies don't surrender answers easily.

Finally, see the text box on page 72 for why so many eminent institutions do multiple pie charts.

Avoid side-by-side columns

Column charts aren't that good for one year of data ('less unacceptable than a pie chart' was as generous as I could be). But they are awful if there are two of them side by side for two years of data (Figure 2.54). Comparable columns are physically separated – try comparing how Europe did in the two years. Also, you struggle even more because of the different scales for the y-axes – one to £120m, one to £140m.

FIGURE 2.54

Income by territory (£m)

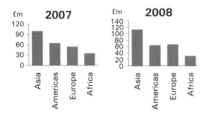

Remember this when next spreading two graphs over consecutive slides or pages – if it's tricky to compare charts that are side by side on the same page, imagine how difficult it is to compare when on separate pages. I've seen reports that say 'For income by division in 2007 see Appendix 15 (page 37), and for 2008, see Appendix 16 (page 38)'. Impossible.

Avoid stacked bar charts

They're awful (Figure 2.55). In fact, they're so bad that *The Economist Numbers Guide* says they're a great way to hide a bad number amongst a set of good ones.

FIGURE 2.55

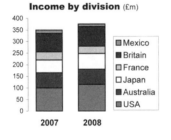

Income by division (£m)

Avoid clustered column charts

With several sets of data, it can get worse, much worse. Most of us have seen column charts like the one in Figure 2.56, trying and failing to show how divisions A to E have done over the past few years.

Figure 2.57 plots exactly the same data and is much clearer (notice also that there is no legend).

Admittedly I fixed the data so the line graph wouldn't look like crossing lines at Clapham Junction. In the real world, five years of data rarely produces such a tidy graph. Usually it's a mess, though the clustered column equivalent would be an even bigger mess. In this case, don't show a mess, do something else instead (such as mini-graphs). Or show less data.

FIGURE 2.56

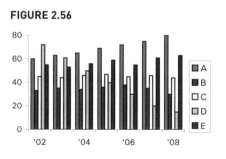

FIGURE 2.57

Avoid graphs where readers squint at small gaps

FIGURE 2.58

Cumulative figures to September 2007

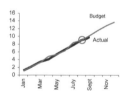

FIGURE 2.59

Cumulative income £m

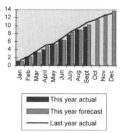

In information packs, Figure 2.58 often appears, showing cumulative budget versus actual, building up by month. It could be for sales, utilisation or whatever. Usually readers use it to compare 'budget' and 'actual' *to date* (come September, are readers really that interested in whether you were under or over budget in May?). So readers have to squint at a small gap between two lines – see the tiny circle. And they might see that, to date, 'actual' is 0.5 short of a budget of 10.2. That's a 5% shortfall. If the graph is income in £m, that's a big problem, yet the graph fails to convey the size of the problem to readers.

Information packs often contain Figure 2.59 too, along with its horrible formatting. If you decode legends and squint at small gaps, you might see that income to date is about £500k short of forecast. But the graph also 'shows' that, to make a forecast this year, we need £4m income in the last three months of this year, but only made £2.3m in the last three months of last year. Unless there's good reasons why the fourth quarter of this year will be much better than last year's, the problem isn't just a £500k shortfall to date, it's up to a £1.7m shortfall by year-end. How easy was it to spot that from the graph?

The third graph (Figure 2.60) expands the important bit of the second graph (and gets rid

FIGURE 2.60

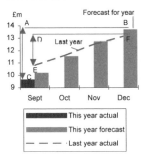

of shading, column borders, etc.). Line DE is £2.3m, line AC is £4m. It's not easy to see, but it's the story behind the numbers. I don't suggest you put this third graph in the information pack. Rather, just say it with words: 'Possible £1.7m shortfall? About £4m income needed by year-end to reach forecast, compared to £2.3m income in last 3 months of last year.' It's instantly understood. Before doing a graph, ask: would words be better?

I've just run through the more common bad graphs. There are many, many others. Excel gives you lots to choose from. If that isn't enough to satisfy your creative urges, you can buy separate graphical software that does anything and everything. If you want 3-D floating spheres hovering between invisible walls overlaid with see-through 3-D columns, you can get it. The software companies say these *give real impact to your data*. There's probably software that can add a bit of blusher to the *Mona Lisa* to give it more impact too. However, I seriously question whether these more weird graphs are done to give insight to the data or to make the presenter look clever. I guess someone somewhere must find them enlightening. But I have yet to meet them.

The next section looks at tips for doing graphs in slides.

Multiple pies – why people do them

Many eminent places do multiple pies. Newspapers and investment banks often do them. Information software companies encourage you to do them – their websites show six adjacent pies of sales by region over the last six months. Annual reports also regularly do them.

However, often these institutions do multiple pies not for clarity but because they are selling you something. Software companies want to sell you software (that makes sense) and if their software can do multiple pies, they will tell you multiple pies are good. Investment banks want to sell you a company – and if that company has a poor-performing division, multiple pies help disguise this. Newspapers want to sell you a newspaper and if multiple pies are nicer eye candy than a table of numbers, then that's reason enough for them to do them.

As for annual reports, CEOs include particular graphs in their annual reports because investors expect them. Or it may be the other way round – investors expect them because CEOs include them, I can never remember. Somebody thinks somebody else wants them, so they get included. Except in Warren Buffet's – his annual reports have no graphs and are also brilliantly funny and informative. Check out his Letters to Shareholders (www.berkshirehathaway.com).

Tips for graphs in presentations

Graphs aren't as intuitive as many people assume. So when presenting graphs in slides, always explain the axes of a graph, don't just show the graph on the screen and jump straight to its lead-in title: 'As you can see, the late '90s was a tough time for the industry.' As presenter, you know what the graph shows, you've seen it before. But your audience don't, they'll be seeing it for the first time. So when you're blabbing on about the late 1990s, they're several paces behind you, asking themselves: 'What's the x-axis? Ah, years back to 1990. And the y-axis? Industry profit. OK, now the graph is U-shaped . . . so yup, got it, the late 90s was tough.'

Instead, show the graph and briefly explain the axes, then the pattern, then the conclusion. You'll keep your audience with you.

What about the complexity of a graph in slides? Some people think slides can get away with more complex graphs than reports, others think the opposite, that slides must restrict themselves to really simple graphs. Let me explain:

Theory 1: Graphs can be more complex in slides	An 'isobar' is a less common type of graph that can be immensely useful. If you put one in a report, will people bother reading the brief notes that explain it? Or will they be so alienated by its unfamiliarity that they just ignore it and move on?
	It's different with a presentation, though, since the audience have no choice but to listen to the presenter talk through the isobar. And it doesn't take long. Also, the presenter can check with the audience to make sure it's been understood. To help further, the presenter could pick out an illustrative point on the graph.
	So, the theory goes, slides can cope with complex and unusual graphs better than reports.
Theory 2: Graphs must be simpler in slides	Sometimes, people expect instant gratification and impact from a slide. With written documents, though, readers are often more prepared to engage intellectually and take more time to appreciate and understand. People expect to put in a bit more effort with reports.
	So, the theory now goes, slides can't cope with complex and unusual graphs as well as reports.

Which is right? The answer is: it depends on the presenter and the audience. Good presenters could talk through the Telephone Directory and make it interesting, so a minute talking through an isobar graph would be a walk in the park. And what are the talk's objectives? To inform or to entertain or to educate or to motivate and inspire? And how would a more complex graph fit in with those objectives? If the talk is to motivate and inspire, it's a bit of a downer to take time out to explain the intricacies of an isobar graph.

That's the end of our look at popular business graphs. We've seen the good, the bad and the ugly. We've debunked a few myths and got some tips on how to do smart graphs. The next section looks briefly at some less common graphs.

Other ideas for business graphs

This section looks at a few other decent ideas for graphs. The ideas in the first two subsections are inspired by graphs in the *The Economist Numbers Guide*.

Inverted graphs

Earlier, when we charted the UNICEF findings, I said it was arguably better to invert the chart so as to make it more intuitive. People assume that being at the top of the chart is good and being at the bottom is bad. Here are a couple of other examples where inverting charts helps readers better grasp them.

Currencies: To show the dollar going from $1.600 to $1.616 to the pound, a conventional graph would show the slope going up (Figure 2.61), which implies the dollar is rising. But it isn't, the dollar is weakening. To avoid giving the wrong impression, invert the graph so that, as the dollar weakens, the graph slopes down (Figure 2.62). It's more intuitive.

FIGURE 2.61 **FIGURE 2.62**

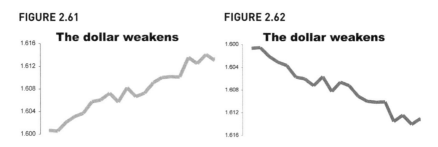

Correlations: To show how house prices go *up* as interest rates come *down*, you might plot the pair together on the same graph and highlight how their movements mirror each other (Figure 2.63). To make it easier for readers to see the link, try inverting one line (Figure 2.64) – that way, readers can more easily see how the data sets inversely track each other.

FIGURE 2.63	FIGURE 2.64
Actual plots	**Dark line inverted**

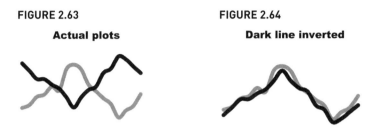

These ideas are similar to the wonderfully creative 'Upside Down' map (Figure 2.65). In 1998 a designer called John Sims decided to invert the map of the UK, surmising it would be easier for driving north to south. He eventually had to publish it himself. With satnav, it's obsolete and seemingly a collector's item. Last time I looked on eBay, it was selling for £50 (original price £5.99).

Rebased graphs

A common way to compare two share prices over time is to rebase their 'opening' share price to, say, 100 (Figure 2.66). However, there is another way – rebase them not to 100 but to each other (Figure 2.67). Divide ABC's share price at any given time by XYZ's share price at the same time. Then do the same for XYZ, i.e. divide its share price at any given time by its own share price at that time. The XYZ plot will be flat as a pancake, a straight horizontal line. The ABC plot will fluctuate above or beneath the horizontal line. It's a good way to show relative movement.

FIGURE 2.65

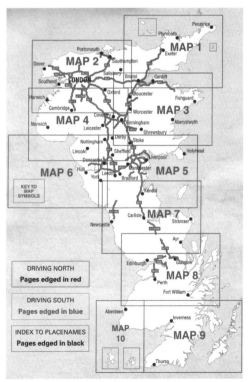

FIGURE 2.66

FIGURE 2.67

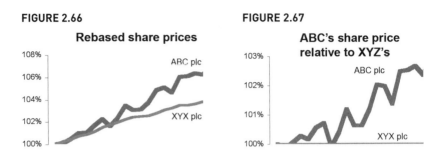

Rebased share prices

ABC's share price relative to XYZ's

The charts in the next subsection have been inspired by Professor Edward Tufte (see Bibliography) and the ideas in his books.

Graphs that give overview and detail

FIGURE 2.68

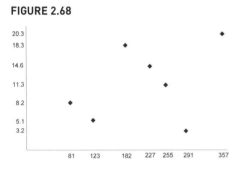

Here's two curiosities, ways to give both detail and overview. And it's more than getting Excel to put the values alongside the pie chart or on top of the columns.

The first way is by labelling the axes with the exact values of each item rather than, say, 0, 5, 10, and so on – see Figure 2.68. The labelling takes a little bit of fiddling because Excel charting options won't automatically do it for you. But it is rather clever.

FIGURE 2.69

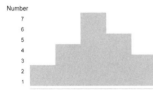

The second is an idea for a histogram. You may remember histograms from school when you plotted the distribution of heights of kids in your class – two kids were between 100 cm and 105 cm, four were between 105 cm and 110 cm, and so on. You probably plotted a graph like the one in Figure 2.69.

FIGURE 2.70

Number					
7			Peakers		
6			Kie Bosh		
5			Sparky	Tango	
4		Small	Persil	Blocker	
3		Wrinkly	Guy Le	Olive	Pieces
2	Rage	Toppers	Jedders	Tonto	Bungle
1	Freddie	Curly	Wilmott	Mumble	Cinders
Height (cm)	100-105	105-110	110-115	115-120	120-125

But you can show more, such as the names of the children in each category (Figure 2.70). By so doing, you don't need to show the columns or even their outline. The children's names create a shape that shows the overall distribution. The layout is similar to train timetables on the London Underground (Figure 2.71). It is typographically efficient – each hour is mentioned only once. The times create a pattern of the distribution of trains which shows that trains are most frequent around the rush hour. It also gives the detail which is important if turning up for a train at two in the afternoon, less important if catching a train home around half past five – trains come every seven minutes anyway.

FIGURE 2.71

```
14:  00 30
15:  00 15 30 45
16:  00 10 20 30 40 50
17:  00 07 14 21 28 35 42 49 56
18:  00 10 20 30 40 50
19:  00 15 30 45
20:  00 30
```

We are near the end of the chapter, but before the summary we need to tidy a loose end – how do we decide what is 'better'?

So what exactly makes a 'good' graph?

We said a graph needs to be *better* than the next best alternative. We said not to do a graph if words or tables would be *better*. But what is 'better'? A graph can be good for several different reasons.

It's intuitive — The logo chart is intuitive. The logos are distinctive and readers aren't fighting through a visually competing jungle of faceless anonymous blocks.

The 'income by overseas operation' is intuitive too. The physical position of the

It compares — labels makes it easy to compare *within* a year, whilst the slopes of the lines make it easy to compare *across* years – and the typography makes it even easier to make this comparison with dark font for up and light font for down.

It shows patterns, trends — It shows patterns and trends.

Neither of these charts puts a strain on

It avoids a strain on short-term memory — short-term memory, nor makes readers' eyes move too far to make comparisons. Neither

It avoids too many eye movements — makes readers squint at small differences in size between adjacent columns. Neither chart gives precise numbers, but often readers don't need them. Here, the charts give enough detail to answer obvious

It answers obvious questions — questions easily.

Compare this to multiple pie charts adorned with values and percentages – they give detail but do it badly and in a way that is not intuitive nor makes it easy to answer questions.

When precise numbers aren't needed, a graph can be far more effective than a table. Imagine an inverted graph of 'house prices' versus 'interest rates' as a table – it would

It has impact and gives insight — have far less impact. The data creates a

It creates a memorable plot with the data — memorable plot that gives insight and has a

It has a clear message — clear message.

A different set of data might not work well, and this is why many graphs in monthly information packs are

House price and interest rates track inversely

House prices (inverted)

Interest rates

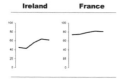

It meets your objectives

poor – the data produces a decent graph one month but not the next when there's a different data set.

The 'staff utilisation' graphs met many of these criteria. They show patterns and trends and are intuitive, they answer obvious questions, they allow us to make comparisons over time and across territories, albeit only at a high level. They aren't memorable, though – but maybe that's not your objective. What *is* your objective?

In summary, there are many reasons why graphs might work. This is why there's no magic formula for deciding if a graph is best and which particular graph to do. It comes back to your data and objectives.

There is a lot more to graphs than just this chapter. I haven't mentioned how to cheat with graphs, nor looked at graphs such as scattergrams, high–low plots and waterfall graphs.

But please indulge me on this last one – waterfall graphs – because I see them a lot. The one in Figure 2.72 shows how total profit of £7.7m is split by country. Also, investment banks use them to show how an acquisition will create 'value accretion' (there you go). Waterfall graphs are very fiddly to do and are an inefficient use of space and a badly laid-out table. I mean, would you ever dream of doing one outside work? Your sports team has scored 25 goals so far this season – how would you show which players have scored? Would you do a waterfall graph with a floating bar for each goal-scorer and with the bars stretching across the graph until they reach the big bar on the right that equals '25'? Or would you do a table of goal-scorers (in descending order of course)? I think we know the answer.

FIGURE 2.72

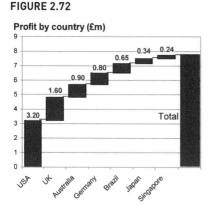

Take care with 'rules' for graphs

Some rules for graphs are beyond reproach and should always be followed, e.g. cut out typographical clutter, avoid clustered column charts, avoid multiple pie charts. But on the Internet and in books, you can find many other 'rules' that you should treat with caution: 'Never have more than four lines on a line chart'. Why not? We've seen a line chart with five lines and it was fine. The Oxford rowing chart has 85 lines and is fine.

Doing decent graphs is like learning to drive a car – you can either learn very specific rules: 'First gear is between 0 and 8 miles per hour, then second gear is 8 to 16 miles per hour', and so on; or you can ignore these specific rules and learn to listen to the engine, to hear when a gear is right or not. You can get a *feel* for driving. And it's the same with graphs. Cultivate a *feel* for whether a graph works. Ask yourself if the chart is right or not. Ask the person at the desk next to you.

And as with many tips and ideas in this book, apply them intelligently, not slavishly.

Final thoughts and recap

As clearly shown by Figure 2.73, we are near the end of the chapter.

Pointless graphs appear in every aspect of life – in reports, information packs, presentations, annual reports. They appear on noticeboards, in newspapers, at the library and at the sports centre.

And yet I think the tide is turning. Years ago, I read that people rarely complain about graphs the way they complain about tables, that even a bad graph can seem acceptable. But people are beginning to complain. We are tired of pointless and confusing graphs plotted because computers let us, because it's fun and creative and because we don't know what to do instead.

FIGURE 2.73

How far we've got

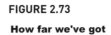

■ Yet to read
■ Already read

Graphs work not because someone has mindlessly highlighted a bunch of numbers in a spreadsheet and clicked on an Excel Chart Wizard. They work because someone has sweated over them, thought about what the numbers show and how best to show them. They have *worked* to make the graph simple and clear. It's an effort.

When you do that and get a graph that's just right, you *know* it. And it feels great.

Recap

Should you do a graph at all?

Would words be better?	Do the lead-in title and graph help each other? If the words merely clarify a confusing graph, the graph hinders, not helps.
Would a table be better?	Are people interested in detailed numbers, in which case would they prefer a well-laid-out table instead?
Is the graph better than the next best alternative?	Your graphs needn't be memorable nor make instant sense. But are they better than the next best alternative and clear enough to be understood sufficiently quickly to meet your audience's expectations and attention spans?
What are you saying?	If words, tables or graphs do not work, simplify the data. Don't try to show it all, show selected bits. What exactly is the point you are trying to make?

Does your graph work?

Ten reasons why a graph might work	As a quick reminder, it's intuitive, it compares, it shows patterns and trends, it avoids a strain on short-term memory, it avoids too many eye movements, it answers obvious questions, it has impact and gives insight, it creates a memorable plot with the data, it has a clear message. It meets your objectives.

Doing the plot

3-D, gridlines, shading, borders on columns	In general, avoid them all. Avoid 3-D, it distorts clarity. Avoid gridlines unless there is a good reason to include (e.g. isobars or log graphs) – in which case make them unintrusive. Avoid background shading, unless you do the 'magazine' look – white grids on light-grey background.

Legends	Avoid, they give a puzzle to decode. Label the graph directly.
Tick marks	Have outside the axes, if needed at all. And don't have too many.
Labels	Have them reading left to right, not sideways. Also, be typographically brief, i.e. not '100,000,000'. Don't clutter the graph.
Use a sans serif typeface	Use Arial, for instance. Avoid serif typefaces such as Times New Roman.
Titles	Do a lead-in title, then a literal title.
Size of graph	Make small, graphs are better if compact.
Location	Put with the text to which they relate, not at the back in an appendix.

Graphs to try

(Yes, I know the first one isn't a graph, but it's a reminder that a table is sometimes better.)

A mastertable

Income		Income growth		Income/person		Growth in income per person		Trading profit margin					Operating profit margin	
A	B	C	D	E	F	G	H	I	J (This yr)	K (Last yr)	L	M	N	O
	£m		%		£k		%		%	%				%
HPH Group	123	Cars to go	51%	Cups Co	204	Gregs	47%	HPH Group	22%	20%	✓		HPH Group	26%
My Tours	67	Gregs	34%	Piller & co	174	Cars to go	26%	Greens	18%	19%		✗	CCPD	24%
SG plc	56	Finchy's	21%	Sysmecs	145	Finchy's	14%	Gregs	17%	3%	✓✓		Ma's pie	21%
CCPD	46	CCPD	20%	SIS RAWA	143	HPH Group	13%	Ribs R'Us	17%	12%	✓✓		Ribs R'Us	20%
Sysmecs	42	PTI Pty	20%	Below Nil	126	Sysmecs	13%	Ma's pie	17%	16%	✓		Greens	20%
Cups Co	41	? Why ?	14%	Ross plc	125	Greens	11%	Piller & co	17%	14%	✓		Gregs	20%
PTI Pty	27	Sysmecs	14%	Greens	120	SG plc	9%	CCPD	16%	16%	same		Piller & co	19%
Ribs R'Us	26	Piller & co	14%	Cars to go	117	My Tours	8%	Cars to go	13%	1%			Cars to go	17%
Ma's pie	24	SG plc	10%	? Why ?	115	SIS RAWA	8%	PTI Pty	12%	16%		✗	? Why ?	14%
Finchy's	22	Ma's pie	6%	A1 Prices	112	CCPD	7%	? Why ?	10%	8%	✓			
Greens	18	Cups Co	6%	My Tours	109	Ribs R'Us	6%	SG plc	9%	8%	✓		SG plc	12%
Piller & co	17	Ribs R'Us	4%	Finchy's	108	Ma's pie	5%	Below Nil	8%	6%	✓		Below Nil	10%
Ross plc	16	Greens	4%	CCPD	107	Below Nil	4%	Go Now	8%	na			Sysmecs	10%
Go Now	14	Ross plc	3%	Go Now	103	? Why ?	3%	Sysmecs	6%	8%		✗	Go Now	9%
? Why ?	12	My Tours	2%	Ribs R'Us	100	Piller & co	0%	Finchy's	5%	(4%)	✓✓		Finchy's	7%
Cars to go	12	HPH Group	2%	Ma's pie	100	A1 Prices	(1%)	Cups Co	2%	10%	✗✗		A1 Prices	4%
SIS RAWA	10	SIS RAWA	1%	HPH Group	98	Cups Co	(1%)	My Tours	1%	3%		✗	My Tours	4%
Gregs	10	Below Nil	(1%)	Gregs	88	PTI Pty	(4%)	A1 Prices	1%	7%	✗✗		Cups Co	3%
A1 Prices	9	A1 Prices	(3%)	SG plc	85	Ross plc	(4%)	SIS RAWA	(4%)	5%	✗✗		SIS RAWA	1%
Below Nil	6	Go Now	na	PTI Pty	77	Go Now	na	Ross plc	(5%)	(3%)		✗	Ross plc	(1%)

Mini-graphs

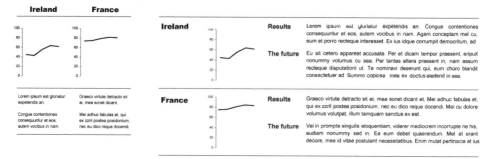

Ireland   **France**

Lorem ipsum est gloriatur expetendis an.

Congue contentiones consequuntur et eos, autem vocibus in nam.

Graeco virtute detracto sit ei, mea sonet dicant.

Mei adhuc fabulas et, qui ex zzril postea posidonium, nec eu dico reque docendi.

Ireland

Results — Lorem ipsum est gloriatur expetendis an. Congue contentiones consequuntur et eos, autem vocibus in nam. Agam conceptam mel cu, eum et porro recteque interesset. Ex ius idque corrumpit democritum, ad

The future — Eu sit cetero appareat accusata. Per et dicam tempor praesent, eripuit nonummy volumus cu sea. Per tantas altera praesent in, nam assum recteque disputationi ut. Te nominavi deserunt qui, eum choro blandit consectetuer ad Summo copiosa mea ex doctus eleifend in sea.

France

Results — Graeco virtute detracto sit ei, mea sonet dicant et. Mei adhuc fabulas et, qui ex zzril postea posidonium, nec eu dico reque docendi. Mei cu dolore volumus volutpat, illum tamquam sanctus ex est.

The future — Vel in prompta singulis eloquentiam, viderer mediocrem incorrupte ne his, audiam nonummy sed in. Ea eum debet quaerendum. Mel at erant decore, mea id vitae postulant necessitatibus. Enim mutat pertinacia at ius

The line graph

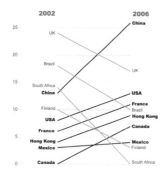

The logo chart

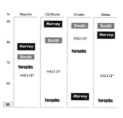

Detailed histogram

Number					
7			Peakers		
6			Kie Bosh		
5			Sparky	Tango	
4		Small	Persil	Blocker	
3		Wrinkly	Guy Le	Olive	Pieces
2	Rage	Toppers	Jedders	Tonto	Bungle
1	Freddie	Curly	Wilmott	Mumble	Cinders
Height (cm)	100-105	105-110	110-115	115-120	120-125

The UNICEF chart

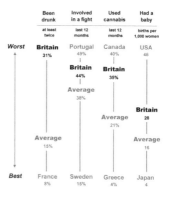

Inverted graphs

House price and interest rates track inversely

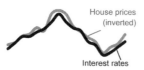

House prices (inverted)

Interest rates

Graphs to avoid if your objective is clarity

There are a lot listed below, but that's because there's a lot to avoid.

Pie charts

Multiple pie charts

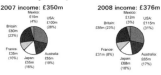

Most columns
(if not time series)

Paired column charts

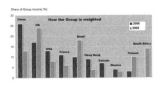

Crinkly line charts

Multiple column charts

Adjacent column charts

Stacked bar charts

Most cumulative graphs

Waterfall graphs

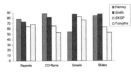

Reports with lots of graphs
(if too many they lose impact)

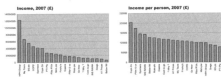

Finally, if doing presentations, talk the audience through the axes, then the pattern, then the conclusion. Meanwhile, here's the best graph I've

FIGURE 2.74

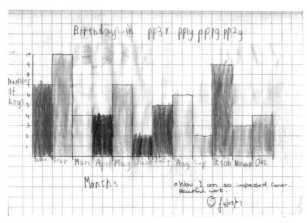

ever seen (Figure 2.74). My six-year-old son did it.

On that note, we really have reached the end. And we know that because the pie chart in Figure 2.75 clearly tells us.

FIGURE 2.75

How far we've got

■ Yet to read
■ Already read

Chapter **3**

. . . .

Tables

How your numerical tables can be loved, not loathed

- ➤ The Big Five Changes: five steps to make your tables fantastic
- ➤ More detailed tips to make your tables not just fantastic but perfect
- ➤ A complex-looking table that seems as good as it gets – how to dramatically improve it

Perfection is achieved not when there is nothing more to add, but when there is nothing left to take away.

Antoine de Saint-Exupéry

FIGURE 3.1

Office	2007	2006	*Diff*
Bath	94	90	4
Bridgwater	112	102	10
Bridport	35	44	(9)
Bristol	132	117	15
Gloucester	43	49	(6)
Oxford	94	86	8
Stroud	51	56	(5)
Taunton	55	54	1
Total	616	598	18

Tables get a bad press. Many people don't like them and prefer the other main way of showing numbers: graphs. In Chapter 2, I wrote of the delight people often feel when they see a graph in a report. Their hearts leap to see something other than a dense page of dull text to wade through. And the report writer has obviously gone to the trouble of analysing the data and plotting a graph that gives real insight. (Chapter 2 then de-bunked this myth.)

But what if you turn the page and see a table? For many, the heart sinks. Readers are faced with something like the table in Figure 3.1.

It's uninviting and indecipherable. This table shows staff numbers for 2006 and 2007 for eight offices. We will return to it soon. In the meantime, glance at it and see if you can discern any patterns. And if you can, I take my hat off to you. (Of course, many tables are worse than this one. We've all seen tables of, say, income by office where the income is shown to the near-est penny, e.g. £245,821.91.)

Report writers often hate tables too – a table is far less fun and creative than a graph. A table also requires greater precision and care ('Have I got the numbers to add up properly? Have I shown the figures all to three dec-imal places?'). And tables are the sort of dull opaque thing that accountants do – and if you aren't one, do you really want to do a table and be viewed as a closet bean-counter?

All this bad press is wrong. Just because people do bad tables it doesn't mean tables are bad. Tables can be fantastic and this chapter shows you how. The first half shows five changes that will make a big difference to many tables. The second half has some more detailed tips and ideas, plus examples of common ways people ruin their tables. Finally, at the end of the chapter, we have a big 'redo'. We apply a lot of the principles to a com-plex table that looks as good as it can get – and make it *dramatically* clearer.

Is this chapter only for accountants? Or only for non-accountants?

Every function in business does tables. The HR function shows tables of staff turnover by department, the strategy department shows tables of competitors' figures, and the marketing department shows tables of spend by marketing activity. Every function will benefit from the tips and ideas for decent tables.

As for accountants, they often think they know this stuff – and perhaps they should. After all, they spend their lives putting numbers in tables, so they really should know the principles for clear numeric tables. Most don't, though, it isn't part of their formal training. Maybe it should be, given how impenetrable many accounts packs are.

The Big Five Changes

The vast majority of poor tables can be improved considerably by the Big Five Changes:

1 Remove unnecessary gridlines.

2 Avoid too much emphasis (e.g. shading, etc.).

3 Sort out the row and column order.

4 Make compact.

5 Give a lead-in title.

Each individually makes a big impact to your tables. To see the Big Five in action, I've applied them to the table of staff numbers we saw earlier, and the redone version is shown in Figure 3.2. It is substantially better. There is much less visual distraction. The story behind the table is more apparent ('the big get bigger, the small get smaller'). The detail and distribution of the numbers is easier to grasp. It is far clearer.

We can still improve it more – there are other minor changes we could make, and we will see them later. But I wanted to show how significantly better the table is from doing *only* the Big Five.

FIGURE 3.2

The big get bigger, the small get smaller

Staff numbers, 2007 and 2006

Office	2007	2006	Diff
Bristol	132	117	15
Bridgwater	112	102	10
Oxford	94	86	8
Bath	94	90	4
Taunton	55	54	1
Stroud	51	56	(5)
Gloucester	43	49	(6)
Bridport	35	44	(9)
Total	616	598	18

The next few pages look at each of these Big Five Changes.

Big Change 1: Remove unnecessary gridlines

| Remove | unnecessary | gridlines, | they | imprison | the | data. |

Or rather: Remove unnecessary gridlines, they imprison the data. Does your newspaper show sports league tables with every number in the table imprisoned by a grid? I bet it doesn't.

As for the gridlines you keep, make them faint, not thick and obtrusive. This is an easy-to-achieve tip that makes a big difference for several reasons:

Gridlines distract and visually dominate	You want readers to see your data, not be distracted by the all-pervasive, visually dominating lines.
Gridlines hinder readers' ability to scan the table	People like to scan tables, comparing numbers and doing mental arithmetic, it helps them internalise the data. But gridlines create barriers that readers' eyes have to leap in order to do this.
Gridlines are ugly, especially if thick	Thick gridlines are like the borders around the health warning on a cigarette packet. They are inelegant and lack finesse.

So remove unnecessary gridlines, it will massively improve many tables. Below are more tips for 'great grids'. Read the first few ('the basics'), they are important. If you skip the 'advanced stuff', your tables will still be great – but just not perfect.

Great grids: the basics

Mostly avoid vertical gridlines	They are nearly always unnecessary. I only use them as part of a box around numbers I wish to highlight. We see an example of this soon in the next section.

Avoid unnecessarily long gridlines

FIGURE 3.3

	2008
Smith	450
Jones	200
Total	650

They look silly – see Figure 3.3.

To correct, decrease the width of the right column.

How to get faint gridlines

Default gridlines are often unnecessarily thick and obtrusive, so select fainter ones. Don't even consider doing double underlines.

In Word, make your borders just a quarter or half a point thick ('Format', 'Borders and Shading', 'Borders'). In Excel, try the dotted-looking line at the top left of the 'Line Style' options ('Format', 'Cells', 'Border') – on most printers, it doesn't look dotted when printed, though it might come out too faint with some.

Tip: When working in Excel, get rid of the background gridlines on the screen, you get a better idea of how the page looks ('Tools', 'Options', 'View', then untick the 'Gridlines' box).

What about the gridlines in my 'Words in Tables' then?

Why do I keep the horizontal gridlines in my 'word' tables such as the one above? It's because each row of the 'word' table is a distinct and separate chunk of thinking and makes sense in isolation. The contents of these tables are to be read individually, row by row, and gridlines help highlight this mental separation.

Compare this to a numeric table in which numbers are viewed collectively – readers skim, scan and compare numbers with each other. Gridlines on a numeric table would hinder, not help. They would isolate and fragment the numbers.

And if that doesn't convince you as to why a 'word' table needs gridlines, try doing one without gridlines. Often it just doesn't look right, it looks a bit naked. However, see page 34 for the ubiquitous 'exception'.

Great grids: advanced stuff

For the perfectionists amongst you.

Put empty rows above and beneath the main block of data

Put a narrow empty row just before the first row of numbers and just after the last one before the 'total' row. They help the table look less dense and intimidating. They also create a pleasant visual break between the labels, the data and the totals and this helps distinguish these three different parts of the table. Figure 3.4 has no gaps, Figure 3.5 has these gaps.

The height of this added row is small, say just '3 points'.

FIGURE 3.4

	2008	2007
Red	100	110
Black	80	75
Brown	60	55
Green	50	55
Pink	45	40
Total	335	335

FIGURE 3.5

	2008	2007
Red	100	110
Black	80	75
Brown	60	55
Green	50	55
Pink	45	40
Total	335	335

Make the 'total' row slightly higher

In the two tables above, the observant amongst you will have noticed that the 'total' row is slightly higher in Figure 3.5 than in Figure 3.4. The extra height helps give the numbers in that row a bit of room to breathe and stops the gridlines above and beneath from suffocating the numbers between them.

Avoid gridlines that butt up to numbers

In Excel, the default vertical alignment is to 'bottom-align' – in English, this means numbers sit at the bottom of cells, not the middle nor the top. This in turn means that the content bumps up against any gridlines underneath – see Figure 3.6.

It's ugly and hinders readability. Also, the content seems visually skewed in Figure 3.6, the 'Total' numbers look odd between the two gridlines – they seem a bit low in the water.

Figure 3.7 'vertically centre' aligns the table's contents and is much better. If your numbers still butt up to gridlines even after having vertically centre aligned, make your row height a bit bigger, it will create the gap between border and number that you need.

FIGURE 3.6

	2008	2007
Smith	25	20
Jones	15	14
Total	40	34

FIGURE 3.7

	2008	2007
Smith	25	20
Jones	15	14
Total	40	34

Next is the second Big Change – and it's a short one.

Big Change 2: Avoid too much emphasis

Typographical emphasis is *fine* if in <u>small</u> doses, but loses **impact** if done *TOO* much.

Don't devalue typographical emphasis by overuse. If you emphasise everything, you highlight nothing. In Figure 3.8, the table emphasises everything except the most important bit – the data you want readers to focus on. Also, avoid putting grey shades on parts of the table, it is an unnecessary visual distraction and looks smudged when photocopied.

Occasionally I highlight a particular number by putting it in bold, or even putting it in a little grid (it's one of the few times I use vertical gridlines). In Figure 3.9, for some reason, I have decided to highlight West division's percentage debtors between 30 and 60 days – the accompanying commentary would of course explain the significance of this number. But don't put these highlighting boxes in too often; the table would lose impact.

Given that we are looking at typography, now's a good time to look at typefaces and font sizes for tables:

FIGURE 3.8

DEBT AGEING	Debtors' days		
	0-30	30-60	> 60
	%	%	%
North	50	30	20
South	45	30	25
West	40	25	35
East	35	25	40

FIGURE 3.9

	Debtors' days		
	0-30	30-60	> 60
	%	%	%
North	50	30	20
South	45	30	25
West	40	**25**	35
East	35	25	40

Avoid serif typefaces in tables	Use Arial or Univers or something similar. Avoid Times New Roman and the like. If interested why, see Chapter 7.
Data and row labels	Have the data and row labels in a font size 10% to 15% smaller than the surrounding text. It looks neat and helps create a visual distinction between the table and the surrounding text.
Column headings	Make the font size of column headings a bit smaller still. If the text is, say, font size 9.5, do row labels and data as font size 8.5 and column headings as 8 or even 7.5. It helps readers focus on the data in the middle, not the heading at the top. It looks smart too.

The four tables in Figure 3.10 illustrate these points. The left table has a large font size, and it looks out of proportion to the surrounding text, a bit large and cumbersome.

FIGURE 3.10

£m	2008	2007
North	70	65
South	65	54
East	50	43
West	45	32
Total	230	194

£m	2008	2007
North	70	65
South	65	54
East	50	43
West	45	32
Total	230	194

£m	2008	2007
North	70	65
South	65	54
East	50	43
West	45	32
Total	230	194

£m	2008	2007
North	70	65
South	65	54
East	50	43
West	45	32
Total	230	194

The second table uses a font size about 15% smaller than the surrounding text and the table looks better for it. The third table uses Times New Roman, which is a fiddly font for reference material. The final table uses a smaller font for column headings and looks even neater and helps focus the reader on the data and labels, not the column headings.

Next is the third Big Change – and it's a long one, going on for several pages.

Big Change 3: Sort out the row and column order

A table is something you have to organise

A Gary Larson cartoon shows a scene outside a saloon in the Wild West. All the horses lie haphazardly on top of each other, and the sheriff is chastising his deputy:

> And so you just threw everything together? . . . Matthews, a posse is something you have to organise.

That sums up tables too. Far too many people just throw a table together; they leave its rows and columns in the haphazard and random order in which they were first drafted. The table's layout is then a freak of circumstance and timing, not a result of thought and planning. But for a table to be good, it's something you have to *organise*.

Let's do the easy one first – row order. Quite simply, put tables in some order other than alphabetical. Figure 3.11 is in alphabetical order and readers struggle to grasp its information. Who is biggest? Who is smallest? What distribution within that range? Are there lots of small ones or lots of large ones? Figure 3.12 shows the same information in numerical descending order and is much easier to grasp.

People often see tables in descending order – just think of sports league tables in newspapers. In fact, people would think it crazy if newspapers showed sports league tables in alphabetical order. OK, in the UK, Arsenal fans might like it because they would always be top, but it would be quite a struggle to see how clubs were doing. Yet when we prepare that list of staff turnover or marketing spend by department, we list all the different departments in alphabetical order. To get any sense of context, readers have to mentally reorder the table.

FIGURE 3.11	
Andrews	62
Blue Flag	13
Centaur	32
Do Right	46
Exprest	250
Fireright	120
Go Now	83
Happy Pie	11
Ink Jacks	140

FIGURE 3.12	
Exprest	250
Ink Jacks	140
Fireright	120
Go Now	83
Andrews	62
Do Right	46
Centaur	32
Blue Flag	13
Happy Pie	11

Some people argue that it is easier to find a particular department if the table is in alphabetical order. Yes, granted, but the benefits of descending order far outweigh any tiny benefit from finding something a bit more quickly. However, if a table starts to get so big that it's unwieldy, there are ways round the problem. Newspapers print league tables of 500 schools' results with many columns of data for each school. Finding particular schools is not easy. It would help if there was a smaller second table that lists all 500 schools in alphabetical order and which gives each school's position in the main table (St Megan's Grammar: 374th).

Now the $64,000 question: why descending order, not ascending? It is because we can do mental arithmetic more easily if the bigger number is above the smaller number:

It is easier to subtract these   89   *than these*   43
                                  43   89

And mental arithmetic helps us better understand the data.

In Figure 3.12, we can easily compute that Exprest is £110m ahead of Ink Jacks. It gives us a feel for distribution.

We've now sorted the row order and it was pretty easy. It gets tougher now (the toughest bit of the Big Five) because to sort the column order, there are three steps:

1   Put the most important column nearest the labels, i.e. first.

2   Then put comparable columns adjacent to each other.

3   Then put comparable columns in some sort of order, e.g. numerical.

If that was all a bit confusing, we're going to do this over the next few pages. Let's start with step 1.

Step 1: Put the most important column nearest the labels

Consider again football league tables in newspapers. In England, most newspapers show the clubs' names down the left of the table and the total points to date down the far right. Figure 3.13 shows part of the Premiership. This creates a large physical separation between the labels (the teams) and the most important column (points to date). To see how teams are doing, readers have to repeatedly flick their eyes backwards and forwards from far left to far right. It's like watching a game of tennis.

FIGURE 3.13

	P	W	D	L	Pnt
Liverpool	11	8	1	2	25
Everton	11	7	2	2	23
Chelsea	10	6	3	1	21

FIGURE 3.14

	Pnt	P	W	D	L
Liverpool	25	11	8	1	2
Everton	23	11	7	2	2
Chelsea	21	10	6	3	1

To avoid this, put the most important column nearest the labels (Figure 3.14). We've put the clubs' names in the first column, the points to date in the second column, then shown all the other columns stretching out to the right as 'supplementary information' (played, wins, draws, losses). Note that there is a gap between the 'points to date' column and this supplementary information – this creates a visual distinction between the two bits of the table which helps readers more quickly understand the table's structure.

Now apply this to business. Figure 3.15 shows sales by region and by product line. The most important column – the total sales by region – is far removed from the labels. Rejig it so this 'total' column is next to the labels – see Figure 3.16. This simple change makes a big difference to many tables.

FIGURE 3.15

All £m	Product line			
	C	A	B	Total
South	16	14	7	37
East/West	10	6	3	19
North	5	2	3	10
Total	31	22	13	66

FIGURE 3.16

All £m		Product line		
	Total	C	A	B
South	37	16	14	7
East/West	19	10	6	3
North	10	5	2	3
Total	66	31	22	13

That's the first of the three steps for sorting out columns (*put the most important column nearest the labels*). Next is step 2: Put comparable columns adjacent to each other.

When showing a few years' figures, what order should you do the columns?

People often ask which year's figures should go next to the labels – and the answer is: it depends. Let's start with the problem. If you're doing a table that has figures for the last six years, the most important column is *probably* this year's figures – so they should be next to the labels. See Figure 3.17. And the previous years' figures would then stretch out to the right of the table.

FIGURE 3.17   **FIGURE 3.18**

	'07	'06	'05	'04	'03	'02
Staff	161	146	133	121	110	100

	'02	'03	'04	'05	'06	'07
Staff	100	110	121	133	146	161

But it seems odd – a time series usually runs left to right, not right to left. So, in Figure 3.18, we've changed the order of the columns to follow this convention. But now we have a physical separation of the label and the most important column. Neither table is perfect, but which is better?

It depends on why you're showing the numbers. If showing them to highlight a trend over time, the right table is better. If the main focus is this year's figures and you are merely including previous years' in case anyone wants them, the left table is better.

As it is, there are probably better ways of showing the numbers anyway. If you want to do a table that shows the pattern over time, Figure 3.18 would be better if the figures ran down a column, not along a row – see later for why. Or the figures could be shown as a graph. If not interested in patterns over time but this year's figures, Figure 3.17 could be improved too – it would be better with a variance column showing the difference between this year's and last year's figures.

So as I said, it depends.

Step 2: Put comparable columns adjacent to each other

Figure 3.19 shows income and profit for 2007 and 2006, actual and budget, and full year and year to date. The most important column is nearest to the labels – the 2007 actual year-to-date figure (e.g. profit of £80m). So far so good. Next to it is this year's budget year-to-date figure (e.g. profit of £75m). Again fine.

But it then goes wrong because numbers have been grouped by *year*, i.e. in Figure 3.19, the 2007 figures are lumped together, as are the 2006 figures. This physically separates the 2006 actual year-to-date figures (e.g. profit of £60m). To compare actual to date, 2007 versus 2006, readers' eyes have

FIGURE 3.19

All £m	2007			2006	
	Year to date		Full yr	Yr to date	Full yr
	Actual	Budget	Budget	Actual	Actual
Income	340	320	1,300	300	1,200
Profit	80	75	290	60	240

FIGURE 3.20

All £m	Year to date			Full year	
	2007		2006	2007	2006
	Actual	Budget	Actual	Budget	Actual
Income	340	320	300	1,300	1,200
Profit	80	75	60	290	240

unhelpfully to leap a column to make the comparison ('Profit is £80m, £75m, and . . . [leap] . . . £60m').

FIGURE 3.21

	2006		2007		2008	
	Staff	T'over	Staff	T'over	Staff	T'over
	Nos	%	Nos	%	Nos	%
Red Ltd	343	23	325	23	301	22
Green Ltd	227	17	240	18	283	21
Brown Ltd	122	2	148	6	164	10

FIGURE 3.22

	Staff numbers			Staff turnover %		
	'06	'07	'08	'06	'07	'08
Red Ltd	343	325	301	23	23	22
Green Ltd	227	240	283	17	18	21
Brown Ltd	122	148	164	2	6	10

Figure 3.20 is better – it groups figures not by year, but by type. The eye no longer has to leap across columns to compare comparable numbers.

The same problem applies to Figure 3.21 – it shows staff numbers and staff turnover for three companies over a three-year period, and numbers are grouped by year, not by type. To see how staff numbers or staff turnover have changed over time, readers' eyes have to leap across columns. It is not as easy as it could be.

Instead, cluster by type, not by year, so comparable numbers are next to each other. See Figure 3.22. Readers can now more easily see patterns over time.

Let's recap what we have done to the columns. Step 1: we put the most important column nearest the labels. Check. Step 2: we put comparable columns adjacent to each other to make it easier to compare the comparable numbers. Check. Which brings us to step 3: put comparable columns in some sort of order.

Step 3: Put comparable columns in some sort of order

This one is easy, we already did it in the analysis of sales by region and product line we saw earlier.

Look at the three columns in Figure 3.23 that show income for the individual product lines. They aren't in alphabetical order, they are in descending order – C is biggest so it's nearest the labels, then comes A, then B. It's similar to putting rows in descending numerical order, only now we are ordering items *across* the table, not *down* it.

Here we have only three product lines, so arranging columns in descending numerical order was not vital. Later, though, we see a table where it *really* helps.

We've now improved both column and row order, which should bring us to the end of this Big Change. But it doesn't. I kept quiet about one final step. Remember that I said to put the most important *column* first? Well, what about this? *Should we put the most important row first?*

If you fear I'm getting a bit obsessive, just wait. This last step can make a *massive* difference.

Back to row order

Should we put the most important rows first? Figure 3.24 is a typical table of staff numbers taken from a management pack. It shows staff numbers by office, then gives a total for each region, and comes to a group total at the bottom.

This table is a bit confusing. The big numbers are the regional totals and the group total and they are somewhat sprinkled around the place. One is part way down the page, the next a bit further down, the third further down still, and so on. In between these big numbers are lots of small numbers which distract the brain – and, my goodness, don't the small numbers go on? Every town is shown, even the insignificant ones. Management are trying to focus on the big picture (about 5,000 staff) yet are faced with details on the Aberdeen office (3 staff). Also, the detailed analysis isn't even in any obvious order – in what order are the Scotland details?

Don't dismiss this table as an unrealistic example. Tables like this are commonplace.

FIGURE 3.23

All £m	Total	Product line		
		C	A	B
South	37	16	14	7
East/West	19	10	6	3
North	10	5	2	3
Total	66	31	22	13

FIGURE 3.24

Staff numbers	2008	2007
	Nos	Nos
Cardiff	958	944
Pembroke	8	6
Swansea	339	423
Wales total	**1,305**	**1,373**
Glasgow	910	952
Perth	85	82
Gretna	10	14
Aberdeen	3	3
Kilbride	0	2
Edinburgh	88	85
Motherwell	8	7
Montrose	3	4
Kilmarnock	6	7
Fife	54	59
Scotland total	**1,167**	**1,215**
Marlow	21	21
Maidenhead	48	70
Taplow	6	10
Henley	2	0
Frieth	1	1
Chiltern total	**78**	**102**
Bath	62	68
Box	40	37
Bideford	7	6
Plymouth	38	52
Newquay	46	48
Taunton	53	63
Exmouth	7	8
South West total	**253**	**282**
Knightsbridge	737	798
Ealing	52	46
Total London	**789**	**844**
Manchester	568	513
Sunderland	102	113
Birmingham	227	218
Chester	79	75
Newcastle	121	191
North total	**1,097**	**1,110**
Galway	15	22
Dublin	153	156
Cork	2	4
Limerick	1	1
Ireland total	**171**	**183**
Group total	**4,860**	**5,109**

FIGURE 3.25

Staff numbers	2008	2007	More/ (less)
	A	B	A-B
Group total	**4,860**	**5,109**	**(249)**

Overview

	2008	2007	More/(less)
England	2,217	2,338	(121)
Wales	1,305	1,373	(68)
Scotland	1,167	1,215	(48)
Ireland	171	183	(12)

England

	2008	2007	More/(less)
London - see below	789	844	(55)
Manchester	568	513	55
South West - see below	253	282	(29)
Birmingham	227	218	9
Newcastle	121	191	(70)
Sunderland	102	113	(11)
Chester	79	75	4
Chilterns - see below	78	102	(24)
England total	**2,217**	**2,338**	**(121)**

Wales

	2008	2007	More/(less)
Cardiff	958	944	14
Swansea	339	423	(84)
Pembroke	8	6	2
Wales total	**1,305**	**1,373**	**(68)**

Scotland

	2008	2007	More/(less)
Glasgow	910	952	(42)
Edinburgh	88	85	3
Perth	85	82	3
Fife	54	59	(5)
Other - see below	30	37	(7)
Scotland total	**1,167**	**1,215**	**(48)**

Ireland

	2008	2007	More/(less)
Dublin	153	156	(3)
Galway	15	22	(7)
Cork	2	4	(2)
Limerick	1	1	-
Ireland total	**171**	**183**	**(12)**

Detail

Other Scotland		2008	2007	More/(less)
	Gretna	10	14	(4)
	Motherwell	8	7	1
	Kilmarnock	6	7	(1)
	Montrose	3	4	(1)
	Aberdeen	3	3	-
	Kilbride	-	2	(2)
	Other Scotland	30	37	(7)
Chilterns	Maidenhead	48	70	(22)
	Marlow	21	21	-
	Taplow	6	10	(4)
	Henley	2	-	2
	Frieth	1	1	-
	Thames Valley total	78	102	(24)
South West	Bath	62	68	(6)
	Taunton	53	63	(10)
	Newquay	46	48	(2)
	Box	40	37	3
	Plymouth	38	52	(14)
	Exmouth	7	8	(1)
	Bideford	7	6	1
	South West total	253	282	(29)
London	Knightsbridge	737	798	(61)
	Ealing	52	46	6
	Total London	789	844	(55)

In Figure 3.25 we redo the table,* but this time we put *the most important rows first*. So the group total goes at the top. We then drill down to totals by country, then drill down another level to totals by major territory. Then at the bottom, we give details of the sundry smaller units – and we use a small font to de-emphasise them. Also, each table is in descending order.

Putting the most important rows first makes a massive difference. Readers can easily see the big picture and drill down to the level of detail they need. Their broad understanding is not confused by lots of big and small numbers interweaving and visually competing with each other. Putting the table in descending order also helps, as does a bit of typographical contrast (the heavy labels are Arial Black).

Notice how the totals only have an underline in the main part of the redo, not an 'overline'. Because the table has such a lot in it, I wanted to remove any typography that wasn't absolutely vital.

* In the redo, I've put a subtotal for 'England' that wasn't in the original version. This assumes a 'total' staff number for England means something operationally, that there is a manager in charge of England or the market for England is different and distinct to others. If this isn't the case, an England subtotal is probably a bit meaningless. I also no longer show the 'North' total – again, this may not be appropriate.

For accountants – do this with cash flows in your management accounts

In your management accounts' cash flows, try putting the most important rows first. With the statutory format, big numbers are all over the place – some in 'net cash from operating activities', some in 'net cash from investing activities', some in 'net cash from financing activities', and so on. Then at the bottom you finally get the total movement between opening and closing cash. This layout makes it difficult to get an overview because tiny numbers get in the way of big numbers.

Instead, put at the top the total movement and opening and closing balances. Then put a small table whose rows are each of the main subtotals, e.g. the total 'net cash from operating activities' and 'net cash from investing activities', and so on. Then at the bottom have detailed tables that analyse each of these subtotals. Finally, include a variance column between 'this year' and 'last year' or 'this year' and 'budget' or whatever – something to give context.

If you do all that, even non-accountants might understand the schedule.

Putting the big stuff at the top isn't a new idea. In writing, it's often best to start with the conclusion, not leave it to the end. For tables, though, it doesn't always work to put the important rows first. In Figure 3.26, the 'profit' row is at the top, and it doesn't work well. The layout of a profit and loss account is so familiar that rearranging it looks odd.

In Figure 3.27 we've tried it again, putting 'total sales by product line' at the top. I'm ambivalent about this one and I can't decide if it works. It's a bit unusual, but given that the page isn't a series of subtotals, it doesn't seem as disjointed as the profit and loss account example.

FIGURE 3.26

All £m	2008	2007
Profit	**20**	**15**
Made up as follows		
Income	200	180
Costs	(185)	(178)
Trading profit	15	2
Interest received	15	20
Operating profit	30	22
Interest paid	(10)	(7)
Profit	20	15

FIGURE 3.27

All £m	Total	Product line		
		C	A	B
Total	**66**	**31**	**22**	**13**
South	37	16	14	7
East/West	19	10	6	3
North	10	5	2	3

So, to return to our original question: *Should we put the most important rows first?* The answer is: sometimes. At times, putting the big stuff first can make a dramatic difference; at other times it can seem just a bit odd. The important point is: ask yourself the question and make sure you are actively *structuring* the table rather than just letting its shape merely evolve.

Also, see if you can relegate any of the less material stuff to a subsidiary table (e.g. like we did with the Aberdeen staff numbers).

That was a long section, but now we've done three of the Big Five: (1) we've removed unnecessary gridlines, (2) we've avoided too much emphasis, and (3) we've sorted out the row and column order (or to paraphrase the sheriff talking to his deputy, we have *organised* the table). The next Big Change is much shorter – 'make compact'.

Are you asking me to reorder my tables every month?

Information packs have many tables and there is a good chance that last months' strictly numerical descending order of 'actual to date' is a bit more haphazard this month. Am I suggesting you reorder all tables every month so they are in numerical descending order? Is it really worth doing that?

I believe it is. Computers can reorder tables quickly, so it isn't that big a thing. The time taken to reorder a table is a fraction of the time you and your team have spent preparing the numbers up to that point. If you don't reorder them, you won't do justice to all that work.

If that is not what you wanted to hear, there is a way round it. I would often put tables in order of 'forecast for year'. This ensures the table has an underlying and visible order, yet doesn't need reordering every month.

Big Change 4: Make compact

Watch this. I am going to get Microsoft Word to put a table in here – three columns wide by three rows high. Then I am going to type in numbers for staff and staff turnover for 2006 and 2007. (I believe the trendy phrase is 'I am going to *populate* the table'.) And I am not going to change how the table looks, it will be exactly as Microsoft Word gives it to me. Here goes, wish me luck.

FIGURE 3.28

	2007	2006
Staff numbers	1,200	1,100
Staff turnover	12%	10%

Notice the gridlines. Microsoft Word gives you them automatically. Notice the width of the table. Microsoft Word stretches the table out to fill the space available and creates an unnecessarily spaced-out table that isn't just inelegant, it hinders clarity. As I've said, we like to scan and compare numbers in tables, we like to do mental arithmetic. Yet it's easier to compare numbers that are close together, not physically distant.

Compare 175 and 162.

Now compare 175   and   162.

Get the picture? So keep tables compact. Also, it helps you avoid unnecessarily long gridlines. Figures 3.29 and 3.30 are two versions of the table of staff numbers again – but this time, the *only* difference between them is how compact they are. Figure 3.29 is too spaced out – its row heights and column widths are too large. The eye makes quite a journey to scan and review the data. Figure 3.30 is more compact and much better.

However, there is one thing both tables get right: neither leaves readers to do mental arithmetic. Readers will almost certainly want to know how numbers change from one year to the next, yet many tables omit a 'difference' column and force readers to work it out themselves. Putting a 'difference' column seems an obvious thing to do, but look at reports in your company and see how often you have to do mental arithmetic.

There is another minor improvement we can make – put a *narrow* empty row in the middle (no more than one third the height of other rows). For tables with lots of rows, try this every fourth or fifth row (Figure 3.31), it helps readers scan across rows without losing their place, and it makes tables look less dense and intimidating.

Some people fear that the gap implies you've stratified the data,

FIGURE 3.29

Staff	2007	2006	Diff
Bristol	132	117	15
Bridgwater	112	102	10
Oxford	94	86	8
Bath	94	90	4
Taunton	55	54	1
Stroud	51	56	(5)
Gloucester	43	49	(6)
Bridport	35	44	(9)
Total	616	598	18

FIGURE 3.30

Staff	2007	2006	Diff
Bristol	132	117	15
Bridgwater	112	102	10
Oxford	94	86	8
Bath	94	90	4
Taunton	55	54	1
Stroud	51	56	(5)
Gloucester	43	49	(6)
Bridport	35	44	(9)
Total	616	598	18

FIGURE 3.31

Staff	2007	2006	Diff
Bristol	132	117	15
Bridgwater	112	102	10
Oxford	94	86	8
Bath	94	90	4
Taunton	55	54	1
Stroud	51	56	(5)
Gloucester	43	49	(6)
Bridport	35	44	(9)
Total	616	598	18

that you've carved it up between high and low. Don't worry, though. Firstly, does it matter if they think this? Secondly, I've been putting gaps in tables for over 10 years, and no one has ever raised this point with me. They are probably too busy enjoying the data.

However, whilst it's good to make tables compact, you can have too much of a good thing, so don't make them *too* compact or they will look cramped. OK, I can now hear you shouting 'Hey, throw me a bone here . . . not too spaced out but not too cramped either? Give me a break.'

So for those that want specifics, here goes. Go for a ratio of 'row height' to 'data font size' of about 1.2, which is roughly the ratio for Figure 3.31 (when I did it in Excel, it was font size 8.5 and row height 10.5). Typographers favour a line spacing of 1.2 (being the ratio of font size and line height for text) and tables seem to work well with that sort of spacing too.

Finally, if you read a quoted company's annual report, you'll probably see lots of unnecessarily spaced-out tables, e.g. the balance sheet will have bits like this:

FIGURE 3.32

	2008	2007
	£m	£m
Fixed assets	1,000	900
Stock	500	400
Debtors	200	150
Cash	100	50

Numbers are so physically separated from labels that the designers put in shading to help readers' eyes run along a row without losing their place. (And I bet no one thinks the shading is there to highlight particular rows; rather, everyone realises it's there to guide readers' eyes across a row. So, again, don't worry about having a gap every few rows in your own tables.)

Why don't designers of annual reports do compact tables instead? It's because they want reports to look smart and *designed*, and one way to do this is to have strong *alignment*. So they get all the contents on the left side of the page to line up with each other, and all the contents down the right side to line up too. Which requires tables to look like Figure 3.32 above.

That's four of the Big Five done: (1) we've removed unnecessary gridlines, (2) we've avoided too much emphasis, (3) we've sorted out the row and column order – and now (4) we've made it compact. But for a table to influence, readers need to know why we're showing it. This is the final Big Change: give a lead-in title.

Highlighting hierarchy in tables

FIGURE 3.33

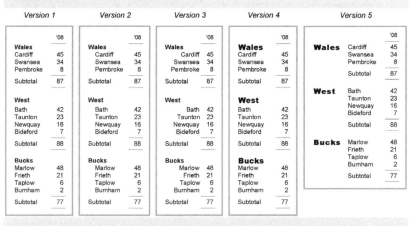

Shown in Figure 3.33 are five versions of three tables showing staff numbers by region – for Wales, for West and for Bucks. The five versions illustrate different ways of highlighting *hierarchy* within the tables – the better we can highlight hierarchy, the more easily readers can navigate around the information and absorb it. Let's see which of the five ways works best. It's partly down to 'alignment', which is why I mention it now.

Versions 1 to 3 are quite common, and they don't work well. The first uses bold for the region names, and it is just a bit flat and timid. It isn't a positive statement of hierarchy.

Version 2 adds a slight indent to make the region names stand out, whilst version 3 right aligns the town names. Yes, region names are more prominent, but neither version looks neat: they both suffer from poor alignment (I said I'd mention alignment). They both look a bit messy, version 3 especially so.

The fourth version goes back to a stronger alignment and adds more contrast (Arial Black (not emboldened)), font size 2 points bigger than the data in the rest of the table). The table is stronger, bolder. The hierarchy is much more apparent and alignment is retained.

The fifth version completely indents the region names from the town names and, like version 4, has strong contrast. We've not only given the regions their own column in the spreadsheet, we've made sure the region names don't overlap with the town names (unlike version 2 in which the first letter of Cardiff appears under the 'a' of the word Wales).

Version 5 doesn't have the messy overlaps that versions 2 and 3 suffer from. And though version 5 takes up more horizontal space, it takes up less vertical space because the region names are alongside the first town of the region, not sitting above it. Versions 4 and 5 are both fine, they highlight hierarchy well and look smart, strong and confident.

Big Change 5: Give a lead-in title

Chapter 2 on graphs also talks about lead-in titles. Even if you've read it, do read this too – many comments here are new and specific to tables.

Far too many tables are dumped on a page without comment. Your report shows a table of marketing spend by department for this year and last year, yet all you say is 'See below for marketing spend by department, 2008 and 2007'. You do a literal title, not an informative one. You leave your poor time-pressured readers to work out the table for themselves.

Instead, give a lead-in title that tells readers something of significance about the table – a trend, a pattern, a curiosity, a highlight, a variance. There must be something – after all, why are you showing the table? If you can't think of anything significant to say, it rather begs the question: do you need to show it at all?

It can also help your cause. You're probably showing the table for a reason, perhaps to bring out a particular point. If you don't state it explicitly, your readers may not pick it up. Or they may pick up a different point – maybe even a conflicting one. To make sure you get your point across, state it explicitly: 'Big worries about department ABC', or whatever.

Also, a title helps readers *engage* with the table (notice I said 'title' – to avoid wordiness, I'm going to use 'title' and 'lead-in title' interchangeably). Tables can be daunting. When readers see a table, they don't really know where to start. Should they suss out the column headings or the row labels? Should they scan along a row or down a column? Without an obvious start point, some just simply give up – they skim lazily over three or four numbers without internalising anything, then move on.

Yet if you'd given a meaningful lead-in title, readers would have a jumping off point into the table, a start point.

FIGURE 3.34

The big get bigger, the small get smaller

Staff numbers, 2007 and 2006

Office	2007	2006	Diff
Bristol	132	117	15
Bridgwater	112	102	10
Oxford	94	86	8
Bath	94	90	4
Taunton	55	54	1
Stroud	51	56	(5)
Gloucester	43	49	(6)
Bridport	35	44	(9)
Total	616	598	18

Figure 3.34 shows the table of staff numbers we saw earlier. Its title says: 'The big get bigger, the small get smaller.' It gives readers an idea of where to look. When readers scan down the 'difference' column, they see 15, 10, 8, 4, 1, (5), (6), (9). Also, they've noticed that the table isn't in alphabetical order and realise it's in descending order. Put these together and, yes, the big are getting bigger and the small are getting smaller.

The readers have got insight into the table.

With bigger tables, lead-in titles are even more important. Big tables are more initially daunting, because there's a lot of structure that readers need to understand. A good title will draw readers into the table so they can validate its remarks with the numbers in it. As they do this validation, they grasp the structure of the table and get comfortable with it. And once they are comfortable with how the table is laid out, they are in and exploring, fanning out and finding other points that are of particular interest to them. And you have got your message across too.

All that from just a few simple words.

Below are tips for titles. Just read the last tip if you've already read Chapter 2 on graphs.

Don't describe in full. Keep short	Don't describe the entire table ('A is up, B is down, C is the same, D is up too, etc.). Just give a flavour, enough to help get readers into the table ('The three biggest divisions are struggling').
Give the literal title too	Give the lead-in title first, then the literal title second and in a de-emphasised font. Look underneath the lead-in title for Figure 3.34, it says 'Staff numbers, 2007 and 2006'.
Be specific	Don't just say 'See how income has fallen over the last five years'. Be more specific and helpful: 'Income down 15% from five years ago.' In this example, you use fewer words too.
Give a title that is *easily* supported by the data in the table	In the table of staff numbers, we could have said that 'The two biggest offices have three times more staff than the two smallest offices'. Yes, they do, but you've now created unnecessary work for your readers. The table doesn't explicitly show the sum of staff numbers for the two largest and smallest offices, so readers now have to get out their calculators to prove your comment to themselves. So make a different comment. Or, if the above comment is the most important to make, structure a table that shows it clearly, not one that requires arithmetic to see it. Or do two differently structured tables of the same data – each can show and comment on different aspects of it.

If something looks odd, comment on it	It may be a number or a pattern or whatever, and if you think it looks odd, so will others. And if you don't comment on it, readers might think you got your numbers wrong or don't know your stuff. Don't unwittingly and unnecessarily let people have doubts about your data or ability. Be explicit – say, for instance, 'B's profit is unusually low and is due to . . .'. I'm not suggesting that you make this your main lead-in title, because the point might not be that critical. But make sure you put the comment prominently somewhere near your table.

Lead-in titles really do help. But should you *always* do one for every table? The short answer is: yes. The more exact answer is: it depends. To explain this, let's step back and look at different types of table. Some literature draws a distinction between a 'reference' table and a 'summary' table. Reference tables are like the pages of numbers produced by the Office of National Statistics (ONS). Its tables are just a listing of numbers from which readers can get whatever is relevant to them. The numbers are for reference. Compare this to a report where you are pulling together numbers for a table and then commenting on them (e.g. IT spend and manufacturing productivity for the last three years). That is a summary table.

And the literature says that summary tables need a summary, reference tables don't.

I can relate to this for the stuff from the ONS. It does figures for people it has never met and never will, and has no idea what they will use the data for.

But for many of us, when we create a table for a client, a colleague, a manager or a supplier, we've some idea why it is wanted and what use it will be put to. When the managers ask you to prepare a table of income, productivity, profit and staff by division, you may not know they're thinking of closing the poorest-performing unit. But it is reasonable to guess that they want to compare divisional performance. So why not do a lead-in title that helps them compare?

Also, sometimes I really struggle to make the distinction. Is my table of staff numbers by office a summary table or a reference table? So, when deciding whether to do a lead-in title, think instead of people's objectives and expectations and ask yourself a few questions:

Would a title help you?	Do you have a message you wish to send, a comment you wish to make? If so, say it.
Would a title help readers?	You might not know exactly why managers want a table of divisional performance, but would it help them if you made some comment? If so, make one.
Would it be odd if there were _no_ title?	If your report had titles for nine tables, readers might think it odd if you have no title for the other two tables in your report. Did you forget to write one? Did you decide not to do one? Did you want to do one, but couldn't think of anything to say? To avoid ambiguity, I give _all_ tables a lead-in title. I once did a big table of competitor statistics (page 62) and the lead-in comment said: 'There is no summary comment to this table, I include it for your own reference and interest.' This lead-in removed any ambiguity that might have existed.
Would it be odd if there _were_ a title?	Would your manager be annoyed if you did a title? Some people tell me a 'lead-in title would be inappropriate given the culture' of their company. Which is business-speak for: our managers don't want anyone else's views, only they are clever enough to understand the table. If your manager is like this, don't do a title.
If a table is in a presentation, always do a title	If standing in front of people, you owe it to them and to yourself to give them some opinion or insight, so always do a lead-in title. And as for the bit about 'reference' tables, it isn't relevant. It would be inappropriate to put up a table of numbers and say to the audience 'This is for you to refer to and review'. A presentation is the wrong format to ask your audience to do that sort of thing. If you want them to skim and review a bunch of numbers, circulate the schedule beforehand. Then, in the presentation, show a slide with your summary of the figures – and put a lead-in title.

So, as I said, it depends. (There is another, albeit rare, exception: you don't need lead-in titles if writing a chapter on tables. This applies only to me. Each table in this book illustrates a particular point, and I want readers to focus on that point, not on my interpretation of the numbers in the table. Hence most of my tables don't have titles.)

Do lead-in titles for tables in slides too

Lead-in titles on slides really help reinforce and remind. For one client, I changed its literal titles to lead-in titles on its year-end slides for analysts. The table that merely said 'Europe results' became '**A record year for Europe**'.

The slides had much more impact and better communicated the CEO's messages. Also, analysts no longer had to remember the CEO's messages or refer back to the transcript to find them – they each had copies of slides with the messages on them.

That's the last of the Big Five Changes and the complete set is:

1 Remove unnecessary gridlines.
2 Avoid too much emphasis.
3 Sort out the row and column order.
4 Make compact.
5 Give a lead-in title.

We're just over halfway through the chapter. Individually the tips that follow are less critical than the Big Five, but collectively they can make a good table great or, if ignored, make a decent table bad. And don't forget there's the redo at the end.

The next section highlights some common mistakes made with tables.

Common mistakes with tables

Over the next few pages, we look at tables that unnecessarily make data visually compete for attention. The more you strip out of tables, the easier it is to grasp the data.

Common mistake 1: Unnecessary zeros and brackets

Figure 3.35 shows the number of phone calls answered each month in a call centre, analysed by the time taken to answer them (less than 20 seconds, between 20 and 40 seconds, etc.). It shows zeros as '0', and their presence makes it more difficult to spot the non-zeros. Figure 3.36 strips out the '0's and allows non-zeros to stand out more. Readers don't have to go hunting for them amongst all the unnecessary zeros.

Purists might prefer something to signal a 'nil', in which case do a small dash ('–').

Many tables have unnecessary brackets. People do tables of costs where *every* number is in brackets – see Figure 3.37.

The brackets are visually dominating and detract from the numbers. They make it difficult for readers to spot the one figure that is the 'wrong way round' – the bad debt write-back. Compare this to Figure 3.38 – 34 brackets have been removed. It is less daunting, the numbers stand out more, as does the bad debt write-back. A variance column would have been nice, though.

Even if you have a profit and loss account with lots of positives and negatives (debits and credits to an accountant), you often don't need brackets for all the negatives. Figure 3.39 has a sub-table of costs – Staff, Property, IT and Other, all coming to 'Total costs'. This sub-table doesn't need brackets, it is clearer without them – see Figure 3.40. Some people worry that it will confuse readers if you leave brackets off 'negative' numbers such as costs ('Hey . . . no brackets around staff costs. Obviously, people are now paying to work here'). Let me reassure you – it won't confuse.

By removing brackets from a profit and loss account, I once removed almost 250 brackets from one page. It made a huge difference – readers could actually see the numbers.

FIGURE 3.35

Month	<20	20-40	40-60	>60
March	89	0	0	1
April	78	1	0	0
May	65	0	0	0
June	72	0	1	0

FIGURE 3.36

Month	<20	20-40	40-60	>60
March	89			1
April	78	1		
May	65			
June	72		1	

FIGURE 3.37

Costs (£m)	2006	2005
Salaries	(321)	(337)
Rent	(96)	(101)
Travel	(66)	(69)
Entertainment	(48)	(50)
Energy	(24)	(25)
Bad debts	(24)	10
Printing	(20)	(19)
Other	(15)	(10)
Total	(614)	(601)

FIGURE 3.38

Costs (£m)	2006	2005
Salaries	321	337
Rent	96	101
Travel	66	69
Entertainment	48	50
Energy	24	25
Bad debts	24	(10)
Printing	20	19
Other	15	10
Total	614	601

FIGURE 3.39

All £m	2007	2006
Income	200	180
Costs		
Staff	(120)	(115)
Property	(40)	(35)
IT	(15)	(20)
Other	(10)	(8)
Total costs	(185)	(178)
Trading profit	15	2
Rental income	15	20
Operating profit	30	22
Interest paid	(10)	(7)
Profit	**20**	**15**

FIGURE 3.40

All £m	2007	2006
Income	200	180
Costs		
Staff	120	115
Property	40	35
IT	15	20
Other	10	8
Total costs	185	178
Trading profit	15	2
Rental income	15	20
Operating profit	30	22
Interest paid	(10)	(7)
Profit	**20**	**15**

Aligning negative numbers in tables

Most people know to right-align numbers, it makes mental arithmetic easier to do because it lines up the numbers nicely for you. Try to compute 12,674 less 796. It's easier in the far right column that has been right aligned.

Also, you can more easily scan down and compare a column of numbers if it is right aligned.

FIGURE 3.41

Alignment of numbers		
Left	Centre	Right
12,674	12,674	12,674
796	796	796
?????	?????	????

Often, however, this alignment gets thrown out of whack by brackets. In Figure 3.39, the contents are right aligned, with the result that bracketed numbers are slightly out of whack. The smallest digits for positive numbers don't align with the smallest digits for negative numbers, which makes it harder for readers to scan and do mental arithmetic.

In Figure 3.40, numbers have been formatted differently to correct this – bracketed numbers have been shunted slightly to the right. Now, the smallest digits of each number are all aligned, regardless of whether the number is positive or negative.

The computer will do this 'rightways shunting' for you – the Appendix ('Computing') shows how to do it in both Word and Excel. Also, the Excel format gives you not only this neatly aligned bracket but a dash for a zero. Two birds with one stone.

Look out for properly aligned brackets in more formal documents such as annual reports and maybe even client proposals. If you prepare regular information packs, it is worth doing it for them too, simply because you only need worry about it once – thereafter, you reuse the template next month.

Common mistake 2: Numbers

This seems odd – am I really saying that a common mistake is to put numbers in tables? Yup. A tick gets into the brain quicker than a number, so is sometimes preferable. Figure 3.42 shows the percentage of phone calls answered within the target 40 seconds for each month. Figures have been shown for all months and the brain has to think about each figure ('Ah, 100%, that's a perfect score'). In Figure 3.43 a small tick indicates that a score is 100%. The tick is better, it gets in the brain quicker. And it's easier to see the pattern of results over time.

FIGURE 3.42

	%
January	100
February	97
March	100
April	96
May	100
June	93
July	100
August	95
September	100
October	96

FIGURE 3.43

	%
January	✓
February	97
March	✓
April	96
May	✓
June	93
July	✓
August	95
September	✓
October	96

Would it be better if the table only showed a month's score if that score was not 100%? Maybe readers would more easily see the months that underperform? Let's see (Figure 3.44).

FIGURE 3.44

	%
February	97
April	96
June	93
August	95
October	96

It's a close call – leaving out perfect scores both helps and hinders. Yes, the numbers that remain are easier to see since the eye doesn't have to skip over 'unwanted' ticks. But it's more difficult to see trends over time. The call centre has a repeating pattern of scores (bad score, perfect score, bad score, perfect score, and so on) but this pattern is not so easy to see if perfect scores are left out. Imagine if call centre managers get bonuses for each month that they get 100% scores and bring costs in within budget. Are managers shuffling scores or resources between months to achieve the bonus? By showing the results for all months, it is more apparent that they might be.

Note that the monthly data is in columns, not rows. We will see why soon. Meanwhile, the next common mistake is unnecessarily repeating words and labels.

Common mistake 3: Unnecessarily repeating words and labels

Figure 3.45 analyses by division how long staff have been with the company, e.g. in the North division, 41% have been with the company for less than a year, 32% for between 1 and 5 years, and so on.

In it, 'years' occurs five times and 'division' four times. But for internal reports, do readers need reminding that North, South, West and East are 'divisions'? They see this table every month and know it anyway. And we've burdened the table with 16 '%' symbols.

Figure 3.46 is stripped to its bare essentials and is much clearer.

I could have stripped out more by putting 'all in %' above the word 'North' and then I wouldn't need '%' at the top of each column of numbers. But it might confuse – readers would see the top left number '41' for North and think it was something to do with 'years' ('Forty-one years? What's that mean?'). Keeping the '%' at the top of each column helps avoid this confusion.

FIGURE 3.45

	Length of service (years)			
	0<1 year	1-5 years	5-10 years	10+ years
North division	41%	32%	21%	6%
South division	35%	32%	19%	14%
West division	29%	27%	23%	21%
East division	19%	24%	27%	30%

FIGURE 3.46

	Length of service (years)			
	0<1	1-5	5-10	10+
	%	%	%	%
North	41	32	21	6
South	35	32	19	14
West	29	27	23	21
East	19	24	27	30

Cluttered labels and headings not only detract from the data, but hinder readers' ability to see the structure of a table. Figure 3.47 seems an extreme example, but I have seen a few like it over the years. Its columns have long-winded labels: '12 months to 31 Dec 2005', '12 months to 31 Dec 2006', etc.

Readers have to decode them. Don't make readers do this. Do it for them. Give simple labels that readers can more quickly digest. See Figure 3.48.

FIGURE 3.47

All £k	12 months to 31 Dec 2005	12 months to 31 Dec 2006	6 months to 31 Dec 2007
Smith	30	32	18
Jones	15	16	7
Brown	10	10	4

FIGURE 3.48

All £k	2005	2006	2007
			6 months
Smith	30	32	18
Jones	15	16	7
Brown	10	10	4

Also, Figure 3.48 has a gap between the 2006 and 2007 columns. This is a neat touch that signals to readers that 2007 is different to the others, it is for six months only.

So avoid headings that bang on unnecessarily for too long – it makes it trickier for readers to grasp the structure of the table. But if you think abbreviations are a good way to avoid lengthy headings, think again. Or rather, read the next common mistake.

Put in an average column and rows?

In the table of staff longevity (Figure 3.49), average columns and rows give readers extra insight. The bottom row shows the average percentage of staff in each of the longevity bands. Here, they are a simple average, though in practice a weighted average would probably be better, one that reflects the different number of staff in each division.

FIGURE 3.49

	Length of service (years)				
	0<1	1-5	5-10	10+	Average
	%	%	%	%	Years
North	41	32	21	6	3.6
South	35	32	19	14	4.7
West	29	27	23	21	5.8
East	19	24	27	30	7.3
Average	31%	29%	23%	18%	5.4

Also, the right column shows the average years' service for staff in each division. Because it's not a percentage figure, I've put a box around the column to signal to readers that it's different to the rest of the table and so avoid possible confusion.

Investment banks often have average rows in tables of a client's competitors – see the average row at the bottom of the table in Figure 3.50.

The investment banks sometimes don't just put the average, they put the high, mean, median and low. Again, it helps to give extra insight into the numbers.

Look at your tables to see if an average column or row might help readers.

FIGURE 3.50

	PE ratio		Margin	Share price
	2007	**2006**	**2007**	% of 52 week high
			%	%
St David's	20.1	19.1	19.5	93
Ampex	19.8	17.0	18.7	74
Be Right	17.6	15.6	17.6	91
Hawkins	17.2	18.3	15.4	88
Beon	16.6	16.7	16.7	76
Simtix	15.2	17.2	17.2	84
Fastnot	12.3	15.4	15.2	85
Sadinia	12.1	14.8	13.8	86
Estonings	11.5	13.8	12.7	91
Regats	11.3	12.3	11.1	82
Average	15.4	16.0	15.8	85

Common mistake 4: Indecipherable column headings

What do you make of Figure 3.51 then? See if you can decipher the two columns on the right?

I can almost hear your cries of disbelief: 'Look at those acronyms and abbreviations – who on earth would do something like that?' Well, you might, albeit not quite as bad. Does Figure 3.52 look familiar? YTD? Three times?

FIGURE 3.51

	CQTD 2007 Actual	CQTD 2007 F'cast	CQTD 2006 Actual	% change over PY CQTD Fcst 07 v Act 07	% change over PY CQTD Act 07 v Act 06
	£m	£m	£m		
Income	382	375	356	1.9%	7.3%
Costs	(234)	(232)	(212)	0.9%	10.4%
Profit	148	143	144	3.5%	2.8%

But so what? Am I talking about a problem that doesn't really exist? After all, many people know that YTD is 'year to date' – the 'YTD' acronym isn't a big problem.

But actually there is a far bigger, more fundamental problem with both tables than just the acronyms – it's the *structure* of the column headings. In both tables, the column headings have all been shoehorned into the single

FIGURE 3.52

	YTD 2007 Actual	YTD 2007 Budget	YTD 2006 Actual	Full yr 2007 Budget	Full yr 2006 Actual
Spend (£m)	1,297	1,246	1,194	2,500	2,137
Capacity (%)	90%	95%	80%	96%	83%

spreadsheet cell that sits at the top of each column. This means you don't have room to say much – which in turn means you have to resort to acronyms. With these tables, the acronyms don't *create* the problem, they are a *by-product* of the problem: the bad structure for column headings.

Granted, people can work out the acronym, but by heading up columns individually we've made it more difficult for readers to grasp the structure of the table. When readers first look at Figure 3.52, it looks like there are five different columns of numbers to think about. And eventually, readers twig the table is easier than that – there are not five different columns but two groups of columns: three for year to date, and two for full year. In Figure 3.53, the table is redone with headings stretched over columns to which they relate, and readers can more quickly grasp the structure of the table and understand the information it is conveying. *And* you avoid acronyms.

FIGURE 3.53

	Year to date			Full year	
	2007	2006		2007	2006
	Actual	Budget	Actual	Budget	Actual
Spend (£m)	1,297	1,246	1,194	2,500	2,137
Capacity (%)	90%	95%	80%	96%	83%

FIGURE 3.54

	Cumulative quarter to date			% change: fav/ (adv)	
	2007	2007	2006		
				Act 07 v Fcst 07	Act 07 v Act 06
	Actual	F'cast	Actual		
	A	B	C	D = B to A	E = C to A
	£m	£m	£m		
Income	382	375	356	1.9%	7.3%
Costs	(234)	(232)	(212)	0.9%	10.4%
Profit	148	143	144	3.5%	2.8%

Let's revisit Figure 3.51. Every column has CQTD in it (which actually stands for 'cumulative quarter to date' – so now you know). This phrase can straddle all five columns and be written in full. Also, the two right columns are variances, so a heading can straddle them too. Eventually we get the table in Figure 3.54.

Much clearer.

However, despite our best endeavours, the variances in the two far right columns still take a bit of thinking through ('Act 07 v Fcst 07'?). We haven't managed to avoid all abbreviations – and even if we had, readers would still have to ponder the computation a bit ('So which two income figures out of £382m, £375m and £356m combine to make 7.3%?').

FIGURE 3.55

		£m
Broking commissions and fees	1	1,450
Broking investment income	2	190
Broking revenue	3	1,640
Consulting revenue	4	746
Total revenue	5	2,386
Broking trading profit	6	215
Broking investment income	7	190
Broking operating profit	8	405
Consulting operating profit	9	125
Total operating profit	10	530
Goodwill	11	(82)
Operating profit, post goodwill	12	448
Interest payable	13	(164)
Profit, pre exceptional items	14	284
Exceptional items	15	(123)
Profit before tax	16	161
Margin		
Broking trading margin	17=6/1	15%
Broking operating margin	18=8/1	28%

To help readers, put in a 'decodifier'. See the row that says A, B, C, and so on. Readers can easily see that 7.3% in column E is the change in value from columns C to A: that is, 'E = C to A'. Instant understanding.

Don't make these decodifiers intrusive, though. Put them in a small font, the smallest in the table. Maybe even make them grey, not black, to de-emphasise them even more.

And you can label rows too, albeit for different reasons. The profit and loss account in Figure 3.55 has seven different types of profit. If people are discussing it, it can be confusing when someone expresses concern about the profit figure. Which one? Pre-interest post goodwill? Post interest but pre exceptional? And so on. People can cut to the chase much quicker if the table has row labels – the person simply says: 'Look at row 12 – I am worried about that number'. Instant clarity.

These labels also make it easier to write commentaries. The report writer can refer to a particular number quickly and unambiguously using the labels ('see row 12'), rather than having to write about the post good-will, pre-interest payable, pre-exceptional, pre-tax profit of £448m (phew, got there at last).

Finally, just as with the column labels previously, row labels help show the maths. The bottom of the table shows the broking trading and operating margins – but how did we compute them? Are they the trading profit divided by commission and fees or by investment income too? The labels at the bottom show the denominator of the margin is row 1, not row 3. Clear and unambiguous.

In summary, decent column headings are more than just ensuring each heading makes sense and isn't stuffed with impenetrable acronyms. It's about ensuring the headings *work together* to help readers grasp the over-all structure of the table. It's about labelling columns (and rows) so readers can easily understand the mathematics of a table.

The next section is a short one about *uniformity* – making tables consistent and unified.

Changing how words wrap around in an Excel cell

If you know about typing 'Alt Enter' when inputting words into an Excel cell, skip this bit. If not, have a read if striving for perfection in your tables.

FIGURE 3.56

1	2	3	4
Act 07 v Fcst 07	Act 07 v Fcst 07	Act 07 v Fcst 07	Act 07 v Fcst 07

In the 'cumulative quarter to date' table above (Figure 3.54), did you notice how the abbreviations were shown? They were laid out like version 1 in Figure 3.56. Versions 2 to 4 are other ways that Excel might have shown the abbreviations.

For versions 2 to 4, the words have word-wrapped within the cell and adjusted themselves according to the width of the cell (the gridlines above and beneath the words indicate the width of the cell). Versions 2 and 4 are particularly poor because the column widths have created disjointed line breaks for the words, e.g. version 4 is 'Act 07 v Fcst (new line) 07'. Version 3 is not that bad, but would be a bit better if the 'v' was on the second line – being on the first line, it throws the 07's out of alignment.

However, there is a way to get the line break you want, rather than the line break the column width forces you to have. And the line break I wanted was the one in version 1. I think it the clearest and cleanest.

But how did I get Excel to do it? All the words are in one cell, so why hasn't the 'Fcst' on the third line word-wrapped onto the second line of the cell next to the 'v'? It's because I did 'Alt Enter'. That is, I typed the following in the cell:

▶

> Act 07 (then Alt Enter) v (then Alt Enter again) Fcst 07
>
> As you type it, look at the input bar near the top of the screen. It shows the inputs going onto a new line. It's rather neat.
>
> I spent 12 years using Excel without knowing about this. It didn't change my life when I did learn it, but it did help a bit.

Common mistake 5: Inconsistencies that detract

In Figure 3.57 the row heights are not all the same, neither are all the column widths. These differences are visually distracting and look odd. The table doesn't look *elegant* – and inelegant tables are less likely to be studied properly.

FIGURE 3.57

Product	Staff	Staff turnover	Income	Pre-tax profit
	Nos	%	£m	£m
Widgets	5,416	8%	322	34
Double digits	3,412	15%	188	15
Gadgets	2,060	10%	102	17
Total	10,888	11%	612	66

FIGURE 3.58

Product	Staff	Staff turnover	Income	Pre-tax profit
	Nos	%	£m	£m
Widgets	5,420	8%	320	34
Double digits	3,410	15%	190	15
Gadgets	2,060	10%	100	17
Total	10,890	11%	610	66

Strive for consistency within tables (Figure 3.58). Try to keep row heights the same and try to keep widths of data columns the same too (the label column can be a different width, though).

Also, study the staff turnover column in Figure 3.58, which shows percentage signs. But in the staff longevity table we saw earlier (Figure 3.45), didn't I say to remove percentage signs because they were visually distracting? It's different here, however – the staff longevity table had percentage figures only, whilst this table is a mix of numbers (staff), financial values (income) and percentages (staff turnover). Because of this mix, and to minimise the chance of misunderstanding by readers, I left in the percentage signs.

Of course, I could have labelled the financial values too and shown the income of widgets as '£320m' and profit before tax as '£34m'. However, I felt that putting in both a '£' and an 'm' was a bit too distracting. It is a trade-off: by putting items like '%', '£' and 'm' alongside numbers, it helps remove any misunderstanding readers might have, but detracts from the numbers themselves. I felt that adding the '%' was acceptable, but adding '£' and 'm' was a step too far and not needed.

Also, notice that some numbers are rounded in Figure 3.58. Widget staff numbers are not 5,416 but 5,420. The rounding is more than just showing numbers to one or no decimal places. Chapter 6 talks more about rounding.

Not only should you strive for an internal consistency within tables, you also should be consistent across different tables. Firstly, make them typographically similar. If they aren't, the document looks like it's been thrown together, like it has been prepared by several different people. (And usually it has been.)

Also, tables should be *structurally* consistent – if they aren't, it badly hinders clarity. The tables in Figure 3.59 show chargeable days for four different territories – budget, actual, year to date and for the month. But each is structured differently. Look at the far left table, North, and check out how it's doing against budget for the year to date. Now see how the other territories are doing against budget for year to date. It's not easy. It would be far easier to work out if the tables followed a consistent layout.

FIGURE 3.59

Chargeable days

North	Actual	Budget	Var'nce
Month	151	160	(9)
Year to date	679	630	49

South	Month	Yr to date
Actual	103	382
Budget	95	420
Variance	8	(38)

West	Budget	Actual	Var'nce
Month	240	214	(26)
Year to date	942	965	23

East	Yr to date	Month
Actual	202	44
Budget	198	43
Variance	4	1

That's the end of the common mistakes. In overview, don't make your data compete for attention. Avoid clutter with your column headings and row labels and with your unwanted brackets, percentages and zero numbers. Do all this and your readers might just be able to see what you want them see.

The next section is the last before the big redo. You may remember that the monthly call centre statistics were in a column, not a row. Next we explain why.

Should data be in rows or columns?

Previously, we showed monthly statistics from a call centre. It was in columns (Figure 3.60), but we could have shown it in rows instead (Figure 3.61).

FIGURE 3.61

Jan	Feb	Mar	Apr	May	Jun	Jul	Aug	Sep	Oct
100	97	100	96	100	93	100	95	100	96

FIGURE 3.60

	%
January	100
February	97
March	100
April	96
May	100
June	93
July	100
August	95
September	100
October	96

Which is best? Somewhat counter-intuitively, even though we read text left to right, we find it easier to scan down a column of numbers than along a row of them. In Figure 3.61, the brain is temporarily distracted by gaps between numbers – these gaps get in the way when scanning the figures. The eye has to read a number, jump a gap, read another number, jump another gap, and so on.

If not convinced, try Figure 3.62. They are the numbers from Figure 3.61 but with perfect scores removed. The leading digit '9' is common to all fig-ures, so readers are now more interested in the

FIGURE 3.62

Feb	Apr	Jun	Aug	Oct
97	96	93	95	96

smallest digits. The eye not only has to jump a gap, but has to ignore a '9' ('ignore a 9, read a 7, jump a gap, ignore another 9, read a 6, jump another gap, and so on'). In Figure 3.63, the brain gets there much quicker. It screens out the 9's that are common to all figures, then scans and com-pares the smallest digits in one quick uninterrupted sweep of the eye: 7, 6, 3, 5, 6. All done.

FIGURE 3.63

	%
February	97
April	96
June	93
August	95
October	96

This is why train timetables usually show times in columns (Figure 3.64). To find a train at about 5 p.m., readers can mentally screen out the minutes and scan down the hours until they reach '17'. Only then do they bother with the minutes – and they read '02'. And it's probably even better than that – readers not only screen out the minutes, they also screen out the leading '1' which is common to all. They just scan the smallest digit of the hour bit: '0, 1, 4, 5, 6, 7 – got it'.

FIGURE 3.64

Here	There
Depart	Arrive
10.08	11.18
11.04	12.14
14.11	15.21
15.02	16.12
16.15	17.25
17.02	18.12
18.15	19.25
19.32	20.42

Compare this to Figure 3.65. To find trains at five in the afternoon, readers wade through everything – the hours, the minutes, the gaps between trains. Also, the brain has to concentrate not just on the size of the number ('Have we reached 17 yet?') but on the type of number ('Are those numbers hours or minutes?').

FIGURE 3.65

Here	Depart	10.08	11.04	14.11	15.02	16.15	17.02	18.15	19.32
There	Arrive	11.18	12.14	15.21	16.12	17.25	18.12	19.25	20.42

FIGURE 3.66

		Unit		
	A	B	C	D
Days	%	%	%	%
>90	12	11	14	18
60-90	22	25	21	20
30-60	32	31	34	30
0-30	34	33	31	32

Let's apply this to business. Figure 3.66 shows a debt-ageing report. Look at the left column of numbers – 12% of unit A's debtors are older than 90 days, 22% are between 60 and 90 days, and so on. Figure 3.67 shows the same numbers but shows them in rows, not columns. Which is preferable?

To answer this, first consider which numbers are compara-ble. Look at Figure 3.66 and run your eye down column A. It is a hotchpotch of numbers ranging from 12 to 34. Not particularly compara-ble. Now run your eye along the '>90' row – all numbers are between 11 and 18. They are comparable. And in the '60–90' row, all numbers are between 20 and 25. They are comparable too.

This is how to decide whether to put number in rows or columns: *Put comparable numbers in columns.*

We find it easier to scan and make comparisons if numbers are in columns than rows. Figure 3.67 is easier to scan and grasp. In the '>90' column, the leading '1' is common to all, so the brain screens out the '1' and just skims down the smallest digit and reads '8, 4, 2, 1' in very short order. Keeping the row height small helps too – remember to keep tables compact.

Compare this to scanning across the top row in Figure 3.66. The smallest digits are interrupted – and the brain temporarily distracted – by other digits and by blank spaces (ignore a '1', read a '2', jump a gap, ignore a '1', read a '1', jump a gap, and so on). It's much more of a chore.

Also, notice two other changes. Firstly, we've assumed readers are most interested in old debt, so Figure 3.67 shows the *most important column nearest the labels* – debtors greater than 90 days. Most debt-ageing schedules have the '>90' column on the far right and readers' eyes constantly flick back and forth to see which units have lots of old debt. Secondly, *its rows are in some order than alphabetical*. They are in descending order of the '>90' column (the column reads down as '18, 14, 12, 11').

Note that neither table has totals. Do you really need to prove to readers you can add to 100%?

Changing columns to rows and vice versa is called 'transposing' a table. And here's a word of caution before you rush off and transpose your own tables: think of your audience. Figure 3.68 is a very popular way to show your monthly summary profit and loss accounts. Figure 3.69 is the same information but transposed. And yes, it follows the principles, it lays out comparable numbers in columns. The first column is the income figures, the second column is the costs. And it's easier to run your eye down a column and see how income or costs or profit change over time. But it is unconventional and unfamiliar. A bit odd, even a bit freaky. If you were to do a table like this, your manager might think you a bit odd, even a bit freaky.

FIGURE 3.67

	Debtors' days			
	>90	60-90	30-60	0-30
Unit	%	%	%	%
D	18	20	30	32
C	14	21	34	31
A	12	22	32	34
B	11	25	31	33

FIGURE 3.68

All £m	Jan	Feb	Mar	Apr	May	Jun	Total
Income	100	90	110	120	95	120	600
Costs	(85)	(85)	(90)	(90)	(95)	(95)	(540)
Trading profit	15	5	20	30	-	25	60
Interest received	6	5	4	3	4	5	6
Operating profit	21	10	24	33	4	30	66
Interest paid	(10)	(10)	(11)	(12)	(11)	(11)	(10)
Profit/ (loss)	11	-	13	21	(7)	19	56

FIGURE 3.69

All £m	Income	Costs	Trading profit	Interest received	Operating profit	Interest paid	Profit/ (loss)
Jan	100	(85)	15	6	21	(10)	11
Feb	90	(85)	5	5	10	(10)	-
Mar	110	(90)	20	4	24	(11)	13
Apr	120	(90)	30	3	33	(12)	21
May	95	(95)	-	4	4	(11)	(7)
Jun	120	(95)	25	5	30	(11)	19
Total	600	(540)	60	6	66	(10)	56

So, even though putting comparable numbers in columns can hugely improve readers' understanding of tables, think of your audience.

Finally, have a look at the TV guides in the newspapers. Some put the TV stations in columns (column 1 = BBC 1, column 2 = BBC 2), others put the times in columns (column 1 = programmes between 6.30 and 7.00 p.m., column 2 = programmes between 7.00 and 7.30 p.m.). Which way works best for you? How do you like to scan the TV guides and see what's on?

That's all the tips and ideas covered. Now you get to apply them – it's the big redo.

The big final redo

Figure 3.70 shows a table of 'provisions for liabilities and charges'. It appears in a company's internal and external accounts. Even though it's got lots of accounting jargon, on my courses I give it to non-accountants to improve – salespeople, HR managers, marketing people, everyone. They apply the principles for tables (and a couple from other chapters too) and they make it far more understandable, far less opaque.

FIGURE 3.70

PROVISIONS FOR LIABILITIES AND CHARGES

	AT 1 JANUARY 2007	Exchange Movement	Utilised in Period	Adj to Gross Basis	Trnsfr from/ (to) P&L a/c	Notional Interest Charge	Companies Acquired/ Sold	AT 31 DECMBR 2007
	£'000	£'000	£'000	£'000	£'000	£'000	£'000	£'000
Vacant Property Provision	12,931	92	(3,726)	0	502	288	0	10,087
Deferred Taxation Provision	22,728	71	1,435	11,872	961	0	0	37,067
Legal/ Litigation Provision	20,010	628	(8,607)	0	0	99	1,628	13,758
Mis-Selling Fine Provision	1,263	0	(97)	0	0	0	0	1,166
Total	56,932	791	(10,995)	11,872	1,463	387	1,628	62,078

Now you have a go. But first some context. This one is part of a board's quarterly information pack and the company has several hundred million pounds of income. It shows the movement in four 'provisions' – see the row labels down the left. The first column of numbers is the value of each provision at the start of the year (January), the last column is the current value (December – this table is from the quarter 4 pack), and the columns in between analyse how you get from January to December. Got that?

I reckon there are 24 changes. How many can you find? Don't worry about two possible changes: (1) don't try to change the esoteric words in the column headings, they are accounting jargon and you're stuck with them; and (2) don't try transposing the table.

Figure 3.71 shows the redone version. We've made the table dramatically better, mainly because (1) numbers are shown to the nearest million and to one decimal place, and (2) we've structured the table much better – when first looking at the table, most readers want to get a feel for it, to see the big numbers. Yet in the first version, they have to look all over for them.

FIGURE 3.71

Provisions for liabilities & charges

December 2007

All £m

Movement made up as follows

	Now	Year start	Inc/ (decr)	Adj to the gross basis	Utilised in the period	Companies acquired/ sold	Transfer from/ (to) P&L a/c	Exchange movement	Notional interest charge
	A	B	C	D	E	F	G	H	I
Deferred taxation	37.1	22.7	14.3	11.9	1.4	-	1.0	0.1	-
Legal/ litigation	13.8	20.0	(6.3)	-	(8.6)	1.6	-	0.6	0.1
Vacant property	10.1	12.9	(2.8)	-	(3.7)	-	0.5	0.1	0.3
Mis-selling fine	1.2	1.3	(0.1)	-	(0.1)	-	-	-	
Total	62.1	56.9	5.1	11.9	(11.0)	1.6	1.5	0.8	0.4

Numbers rounded for clarity, small rounding differences may arise

Commentary

The big movements during the period are as follows: we provided £11.9m extra for the adjustment to gross basis and utilised £8.6m of the legal provision. This was because lorem ipsum est gloriatur expetendis an. Congue contentiones consequuntur et eos, autem vocibus in nam.

The redo arranges numbers so readers can more easily see the big picture. Rows are in descending order. The most important columns ('now' and 'year start') are nearest the labels and we've added a total variance column too. Also, the rest of the columns are in descending order, regardless of whether positive or negative.

Here's the list of all 24 changes. If a change is due to a topic covered in another chapter, I've put the chapter number in brackets after the change.

Table structure
1. Put the most important columns near the labels
2. Put the rest of the columns in descending order, regardless of whether plus or minus
3. Put the rows in descending order

Table format

4. Put a small narrow empty row before the first row of numbers and just before the 'Total' row
5. Made gridlines less intrusive
6. Removed shading from the 'total' row
7. Centre vertically aligned numbers so they don't butt against gridlines
8. Made row height smaller to make the table more compact
9. Put a narrow blank row between the second and third row (note 1)

Numbers

10. Rounded the numbers and put a note on the bottom explaining it. Note how individual deferred taxation movements add up to £14.4m but the total movement is shown as £14.3m (Chapter 6)
11. Stopped brackets misaligning smallest digits
12. Put a light box around the key area of the table to help highlight it
13. Put in a variance column
14. Replaced zeros with dashes

Typography

15. Removed bold on all labels
16. Got rid of upper case on title – all upper case is not easy to read (Chapter 7)
17. Made the title more prominent so it aids reader navigation (Chapter 7)
18. Made the date shorter ('now') – less typographical clutter
19. Right aligned row labels (note 2)
20. Got Rid of Pointless upper Case in labels (Chapter 7)
21. Removed 'provision' from row labels – less typographical clutter

Other

22. Showed the currency once, not eight times
23. Did a commentary, albeit in Latin
24. Put in a decodifier for columns (e.g. A, B, C, D) (note 3)

Three need a bit more explaining.

Note 1: The gap between second and third row Previously I suggested putting a narrow blank row every fourth or fifth row to make tables look less intimidating and to stop readers' eyes losing their place as they scan a row of numbers. This table only has four rows, so why does it need a blank row? It's because the redone table has big gaps between adjacent numbers on rows – which in turn is due to a combination of wide column headings (e.g. 'Exchange movement' in column H) and narrow numbers (e.g. 0.1 in column H). These big horizontal gaps make it all too easy to lose your place when scanning across rows, so the blank row between rows 2 and 3 helps.

Note 2: Right aligning the row labels Earlier, we saw an example where right aligning row labels didn't look good because it created poor alignment (the third version in Figure 3.33). So why have we right aligned them here? It's because it looks good – and that's because there's a vertical line alongside the labels (the one down the left side of the box around the key numbers). The vertical line creates a *natural source of alignment*, and if we were then to left align row labels next to this vertical line (see Figure 3.72), it would create 'trapped space' and that isn't a good thing (Chapter 7 explains why). There you go.

FIGURE 3.72

	Now	Year start	Inc/ (decr)
	A	B	C
Deferred taxation	37.0	22.7	14.3
Legal/ litigation	13.8	20.0	(6.3)
Vacant property	9.7	12.9	(3.2)
Mis-selling fine	1.2	1.3	(0.1)
Total	61.7	56.9	4.8

Note 3: Labelling the columns A, B, C, and so on We've labelled the columns not to help readers see the maths (A less B = C, and C = the sum of D to I), but to help the commentary. If the commentary were to say 'notional interest charge low this year', readers would scan left to right along the column headings to find the 'notional interest charge' – and they won't find it quickly. Eventually they'd land on it. But now the commentary would say 'notional interest charge low this year – see column I', and readers' eyes would go there instantly.

Also notice that column headings are centre aligned. I tried right aligned but it made the text look 'blocky'. This is not a general rule – other tables look better right aligned. Trust your eyes on this. However, study the decimal points: they align down a column – which is fine. Notice that they are near the *centre* of the cells, not near the right of them. This makes the numbers sit more elegantly under the centre aligned column headings.

I could have made the original table even worse – for instance, I could have put gridlines around every number. But if something is too obviously horrible, anyone can make it better. Rather, I wanted you to redo a table that looked complex rather than ugly. I wanted you to improve something that, for many people, was probably already as good as it could be.

And as we've seen, even a complex-looking table can be clarified *considerably* and its contents made more accessible.

Time for the summary.

Final thoughts and recap

The managers want a table of figures by division so you fire up your spreadsheet, pump in some numbers and print off a page. Unfortunately that's all you've done. You haven't structured or formatted the table. It's got gridlines, the numbers are centre aligned, it's in alphabetical order and it shows numbers to the nearest penny. The column headings are simply a download from the main system – what on earth is 'PRM UV'? And as a small final point, the page doesn't say who prepared it and when.

No wonder people say they don't like tables. And what a wasted opportunity to impress the managers.

But next time it will be different. For a start, you know the Big Five Changes that will improve the table your managers asked for. And, if you want to make the table really perfect, you've got the more detailed tips too. But for now, you may wish to keep these in reserve for posh reports and for when you redo your reporting templates.

And when that happens, maybe redo your templates piecemeal rather than all at once. After all, there's a lot of detail in this chapter. When I redid every page of the management accounts at one company, it took me ten months. I did two pages a month. It meant fewer late nights in the office and I had longer to do the exercise. And the board was better able to absorb and appreciate the changes than if it had them all at once. Which meant it better understood what I was doing and why.

But no matter what you do with your tables and templates, one thing's for sure – you now know how to do tables that people will love, not loathe.

Recap

The Big Five

Gridlines

	2008
Smith	450
Jones	200
Total	650

Remove unnecessary gridlines and make the remaining ones faint. Use vertical gridlines sparingly to highlight numbers.

Avoid unnecessarily long gridlines.

Put narrow empty rows above and beneath the main block of data. Make the 'total' row slightly higher. Vertically centre align numbers so they don't butt against gridlines.

Typographical emphasis

DEBT AGEING	Debtors' days		
	0-30	30-60	> 60
	%	%	%
North	50	30	20
South	45	30	25
West	40	25	35
East	35	25	40

Emphasise sparingly – if you emphasise everything, you highlight nothing. Also, avoid shading.

Use sans serif typefaces. Make the font size of the data and row labels about 10% to 15% smaller than the surrounding text. Make the font size of column headings a bit smaller still.

Table structure

Staff numbers	2008
Group total - nos	4,860

Overview
England	2,217
Wales	1,305
Scotland	1,167
Ireland	171

England
London - see below	789
Manchester	568
South West - see below	253
Birmingham	227
Newcastle	121
Sunderland	102
Chester	79
Chilterns - see below	78
England total	2,217

Row order

Put rows in some order other than alphabetical, e.g. numerical. Descending makes it easier for readers to do mental arithmetic.

Should you put the most important rows first? If there are lots of sub-tables that come to a grand total, try starting at the top, i.e. the grand total first, then a table of sub-table totals, then the detailed sub-tables. Use a high-impact font to help readers navigate between tables, e.g. Arial Black.

Also, maybe even strip out small numbers and simply show as 'other' – it will make the important numbers stand out more.

Column order

Put the most important column nearest the labels and consider adding a variance column to save readers from mental arithmetic. Then put comparable columns adjacent to each other. Then put comparable columns in some sort of order, e.g. numerical descending.

Compact tables

Make tables compact, they are easier to scan. Compact tables also help keep gridlines short.

Lead-in titles

Would a lead-in title help either you or the readers? If you do a title, keep it short, don't describe the table in full. Put the literal title underneath. Give a title that is easily supported by the numbers in the table. And always do a title for tables in slides.

Getting them perfect

Put in a narrow empty row every few rows

It helps readers scan a wide row of numbers.

Don't distract from data

Put zeros as a '–' or leave blank. Avoid unnecessary brackets. Try ticks for, say, scores of 100%.

Make column headings clear	When possible, straddle headings across columns to help readers see a table's structure. It also helps avoid acronyms.
Put in 'decodifiers'	Is it clear how the table's subtotals, variances or margins are derived? Small, de-emphasised labels help readers see the maths (E = B to C, P = A/G). They also help the commentary ('see column J'). Remember 'Alt Enter' too.
Be consistent	If possible, keep all row heights consistent and all column widths consistent too (except for the column that describes each row). For reports and slides, keep tables typographically consistent throughout, and, if possible, keep structurally consistent too.
Rows or columns?	Put comparable numbers in columns, we find it easier to skim down a column of numbers than along a row.
Average column or row?	These can help give readers a bit more context and insight.

One final point we've yet to cover in this recap: don't embed lots of numbers in text ('West division grew 10% from £100m to £110m, whilst North went from £72m to £76m, an increase of 6%. Overall, Group income went from £172m to £186m, up 8%'). In text, numbers are more difficult to compare and to refer back to in conversation. Instead, put them in a table.

Chapter **4**

....

Making comparisons

The pros and cons of your list of pros and cons

- > How people often compare alternatives and why it isn't effective
- > Five better ways to compare alternatives and which to use when
- > Decision trees – for weighty strategic issues, not just admin procedures
- > Why you shouldn't work on the presentation as an afterthought

Sally: But I'd like the pie heated and I don't want the ice cream on top, I want it on the side and I'd like strawberry instead of vanilla if you have it; if not, then no ice cream, just whipped cream – but only if it's real; if it's out of a can then nothing.

Waitress: Not even the pie?

Sally: No, just the pie, but then not heated.

Meg Ryan, *When Harry Met Sally*

To help managers reach decisions, they are given notes, reports and presentations that *compare alternatives*. The alternatives could be whether to outsource IT or keep it in-house. Or different ways to enter a new territory: do a joint venture, set up an overseas office or acquire an existing competitor in that country. The presentation might be an internal one, done by the managers' staff. Or it might be done by consultants comparing alternatives for their client.

Regardless, they all have the same objective: to help decision-makers reach informed decisions (ignoring, of course, people's hidden agendas). Yet – as we shall see – many fail to do this effectively. Decision-makers struggle to have informed discussions about the alternatives and often don't even realise it.

This chapter shows how to dramatically improve decisions by bringing *clarity* and *comparability* to your analysis. Firstly, though, here's a quick warning – this chapter *doesn't* look at any of the following:

- How managers *make* decisions, e.g. are they risk-averse or risk-seekers?
- How managers *take* decisions, e.g. behind closed doors or seeking a consensus?
- How accountants *quantify* outcomes, e.g. should they compute an 'NPV' or an 'IRR'?

Such topics are important but a host of other management books cover them. This book is about clarity, so this chapter is too. It looks at the common way of presenting comparisons in business – bullet point lists of pros and cons – then shows five better ways to do it, and which to use when.

And by the end, you will be able to make more informed decisions about how to compare alternatives so your readers can make more informed decisions.

Did you get that?

A table of ticks and crosses

Your managers have asked you to help them buy a camera. They believe there are three alternatives – a cheap compact, a medium-priced one and a pricey fancy one – and they have asked that you do a presentation comparing them.

This scenario is played out regularly at work, albeit not with cameras (at least, not in my experience). Today, though, your managers have asked about cameras, so you do some research. You analyse the pros and cons of each alternative. Is the camera easy to use? Does it give you control over how you can take a picture? Is it compatible with lenses you already own (it would be good if it is, since it saves you having to buy new lenses)? Can it take videos as well as photos? And so on.

What happens next is all too common. In your presentation, you show three slides that look at the pros and cons of each of the three cameras (Figure 4.1): slide 1 on a cheap compact, slide 2 on a medium-priced one, slide 3 on a pricey fancy one.

But because the pros and cons are listed over a series of slides, there is a physical separation between each camera's details; direct comparisons aren't easy. People are unable to compare alternatives unless they have a photographic memory (excuse the bad pun).

Often people do the same in written reports – the pros and cons of the cheap compact are on page 8 of the report, pages 9 and 10 are on the medium-priced one, and page 11 is on the pricey fancy one. Again, readers can't easily make comparisons.

Instead, do a table of ticks and crosses (Figure 4.2). There are even a few double ticks and double crosses for seriously good or bad items.

FIGURE 4.1

Cheap compact

Pros
- Cheap
- Easy to use
- Fits in pocket

Cons
- Cannot control your own settings
- Not good enough picture quality for enlarging
- Cannot do videos

Medium priced

Pros
- Reasonable quality for enlargements
- Tidy size
- Can shoot videos
- Can control some of the settings

Cons
- Existing lenses not compatible
- Controls are a bit intimidating

Pricey fancy one

Pros
- Great for enlargements
- Great flexibility for taking pictures
- Can use existing lenses

Cons
- Expensive
- Needs a suitcase to carry
- Intimidating set of controls

FIGURE 4.2

	Cheap compact	Medium priced	Pricey fancy
Price	✓	–	✗
OK for enlargements?	✗	✓	✓✓
Easy to use?	✓	✗	✗✗
Fits in pocket?	✓	✓	✗
Video'ing available?	✗	✓	✗
Control? How flexible?	✗	✓	✓✓
Compatible with lenses?	✗	✗	✓

There are many benefits to the table of ticks and crosses:

Readers can more easily make comparisons	Not only is the analysis on one page, but the tabular layout aligns items for even easier comparison. Readers can easily compare, say, 'enlargements' simply by running their eye along the second row of the table.
It helps ensure consistency	Tables impose a structure that helps ensure *consistency*, so you are less likely to confuse readers with accidental differences in terminology. With bullet points, people are often casual in their choice of words – our slides said the cheap compact 'can't control' the settings, but then said the pricey fancy one has 'great flexibility for taking pictures'. Do these two bullets refer to the same point? And we said the fancy pricey one has an 'intimidating set of controls' – how does this relate to the other comments that refer to 'control', e.g. 'can control some settings'? The word 'control' refers to two different questions: '*ease* of use?' and '*flexibility* of use?'. With tables you are less likely to have uncertainties from differences in casually chosen terminology.
It is less repetitive	The table has fewer words; each topic such as 'enlargements' is mentioned just once. The slides of pros and cons say it three times.
It helps ensure a more complete analysis	Tables impose a structure that helps ensure *completeness*, bullet points don't. The list of pros and cons never said whether a small compact was compatible with existing lenses. It never said whether a fancy camera could do videos. (Did you spot these omissions?) Because it lacks an underlying structure, a list of pros and cons doesn't help authors or readers see if the analysis is complete. And often the analysis isn't – readers don't get analysis, they get random, incomplete thoughts.

The table imposes a discipline on the analysis. It's obvious if not all questions have been answered – there is an empty cell in the table. (However, neither table nor bullet points can ensure all the right questions have been *asked* in the first place.)

It gives greater granularity	The ticks and crosses give scores out of five (double tick to double cross), whilst the pros and cons divide the answers into just two. How does the list cope if something is neither a pro nor a con but is neutral? A medium-priced camera is neither cheap nor expensive, so is it a pro or a con? However, the list missed it out anyway. In the table, it's easy – it's a dash.
It simplifies and is great for executive summaries	Even for a complex topic that needs lots of narrative, a table of ticks and crosses neatly summarises it clearly and with comparability. The table and narrative complement each other. Alternatively, if there is a comment to add that is brief, cross-refer from the relevant tick in the table to a note below, e.g. if Canon were launching a fancy camera in six months that does videos, the table would have ✓*: *In six months, Canon will launch a fancy camera that does videos.
It is easier to refer back to	The table's structured layout means management can easily refer to it and find items during discussions. They can have a more informed conversation.

You need to ask your questions properly to get all these benefits. If you were to ask about the cheap compact 'Is it easy to use?' and 'Is it *expensive*?', you would get a tick for the first question and a cross for the second, even though both are good news for potential purchasers. Readers would struggle to get a visual overview from the patterns of ticks and crosses. Instead, ensure you phrase all your questions as positives, e.g. 'Is it cheap?'.

Before moving on from cameras, let's look at two other layouts we could have done – a table of pros of cons (Figure 4.3), and a table of numbers that rank (Figure 4.4).

FIGURE 4.3

Area	Pro	Con
Cheap compact	Cheap Easy to use Fits in pocket	Cannot control the settings Poor if you want enlargements Cannot do videos
Medium priced	Reasonable quality enlargements Fits in pocket Can shoot videos Can control some settings	Existing lenses not compatible Controls a bit intimidating
Pricey fancy one	Great for enlargements Great flexibility for taking pictures Can use existing lenses	Expensive Needs a suitcase to carry Intimidating set of controls

Firstly, the table of pros and cons is all on one page so is certainly better than comparing cameras over three slides. But it isn't ideal – check out how good each camera is at enlargements. The eye has to float around the table trying to find references to 'enlargements'. It isn't easy. Comparable items aren't aligned. In the table of ticks and crosses, they are.

And other problems remain too. The table of pros and cons is repetitive, offers little granularity (just a 'pro' or 'con') and has no underlying structure to impose a consistency or completeness.

FIGURE 4.4

	Cheap compact	Medium priced	Pricey fancy one
Price	4	3	2
OK for enlargements?	2	4	5
Easy to use?	4	2	1
Fits in pocket	4	4	2
Video'ing available?	2	4	2
Control? How flexible?	2	4	5
Compatible with lenses?	2	2	4

Then there's a table of numbers (Figure 4.4) that gives scores from 1 to 5 rather than double ticks to double crosses. But take care. Firstly, numbers are not as intuitive – readers have to think more about them than about ticks and crosses. Secondly, with numbers people may be tempted to add them up, and whilst this may help focus the discussion, people might incorrectly read too much into the total scores. The most appropriate camera depends on people's purchasing priorities, not a mathematical sum of the answers to the questions. The box below explains why.

But do replace ticks and crosses with numbers if your audience want even greater granularity. The ticks and crosses effectively score items out of 5, but what if you want a score out of 100? You can't do that with ticks and crosses, you need numbers. *Which?* magazine does this a lot. *Which?* is an association in the UK that sticks up for the consumer and its monthly magazine has articles that compare products. Some of its comparative tables give scores out of 100 and others just show ticks and crosses. But one thing *Which?* doesn't do is make comparisons with a bullet point list of pros and cons.

With the cameras, we had seven questions we wanted answering, so a table worked well. The next section looks at comparing items if there are only two questions. As we shall see, we have more options open to us simply because a piece of paper can show something in 2-D but not 7-D.

Putting an overall score

In the table of ticks and crosses we could put a total score, e.g. if a double tick is +2 and a double cross −2, then a small camera gets a total score of −1, the medium-priced a score of 2 and the fancy SLR 0. However, a simple arithmetic score can be misleading because the most suitable camera could be any of the three – it depends on what buyers want. If buyers want either the cheapest or easiest to use, the cheap compact is best. (Though if you knew someone just wanted the cheapest, you wouldn't do a comparative table, you'd just find the cheapest.) If buyers need one that does brilliant enlargements and all other criteria are irrelevant, the pricey fancy one is best. Or maybe it's a mix of criteria – buyers want reasonable enlargements but aren't fussed whether they are superb, but really want a video. The first criterion rules out the cheap compact, the second rules out the pricey fancy one, so the best is the medium-priced one.

So a simple arithmetic total might be misleading. And if you think it would be good to do a decision tree, we look at that in the last section.

A two-by-two grid

You are reviewing your portfolio of overseas offices. Some are in high-growth countries, some in low-growth ones. Some have a strong ability to compete, others are not so hot. Your report shows these findings as bullet points (Figure 4.5).

FIGURE 4.5

- We are particularly strong in Japan, Argentina, Estonia, Norway, Finland, China, Germany and Australia. However, the first three countries are experiencing low growth, the rest are experiencing strong growth.
- We are less strong in France, Canada and Mexico, albeit Canada and Mexico are high-growth markets.

Even though each individual word makes sense, it's collectively difficult to grasp either the detail or the overview. Study Norway. What is the country's expected growth and our Norwegian operation's ability to compete? Which other countries share Norway's characteristics? The information is embedded deep in wordy paragraphs and is not easy to find quickly during a discussion.

If you were doing a presentation slide, the detail might again be in bullet points, albeit with abbreviated English rather than full narrative (Figure 4.6).

FIGURE 4.6

- Good growth, good ability to compete: Norway, Finland, China, Germany, Australia
- Poor growth, good ability to compete: Japan, Argentina, Estonia
- Good growth, poor ability to compete: Canada, Mexico
- Poor growth, poor ability to compete: France

And the same problems arise – it's difficult to see the detail or overview.

Instead try a two-by-two grid (Figure 4.7). It shows both overview and detail more effectively because of its use of *physical* space. Shapes and groupings are easier to pick out – many countries are top right (and the double tick signals to readers that 'top right' is best), and only one is bottom left (bad news obviously, it's a double cross).

These ticks and crosses make the grid more intuitive – if they weren't included, readers would have to think a bit harder: 'Now . . . which is good – top right or bottom left?'.

FIGURE 4.7

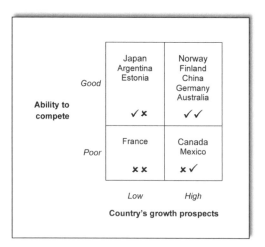

And in the grid, detail is easy to see; it isn't hidden within wordy bullet points.

Of course, if we wanted to score the growth prospects as 'high', 'medium' or 'low' as opposed to just 'high' and 'low', we would do a two-by-three grid. Or we could even do a three-by-three grid. You get my drift.

These grids have limitations though:

They cope if three questions, but not more	If there was a third question, e.g. 'political stability', the grid can still cope if you use a simple typographical signal, e.g. politically stable countries are in darker fonts, unstable ones in lighter fonts (Figure 4.8). (Please don't read anything into how I've shown the countries, it's all just illustrative.)
	If there's a fourth question, don't try yet another typographical signal, it gets confusing. Bigger fonts could signal tight regulatory environments, smaller fonts less tight, so a small light-grey country name means (wait for it, let's get this right) politically unstable with a slack regulatory environment. You're setting tough puzzles for readers to decode. If more than three questions, revert to a table of ticks and crosses. When we compared cameras, we asked seven questions.

FIGURE 4.8

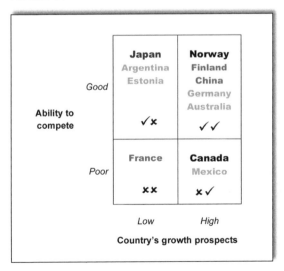

They don't cope well with ranges

Say we wish to give a view on the 'ability to compete' for our China operation – is it 'good', 'average' or 'poor'? What if we have four offices in China and some are good, some are average? Our answer now stretches over two boxes of the grid and the strict divisions of the grid would struggle. This problem also arises when making predictions ('Growth could be anywhere from "average" to "good" – that's as accurate as we can say').

See the next section for how to cope with ranges.

There are three other points to make about these grids.

Quantify the answers? We could quantify our thinking and assign numbers to each country's 'ability to compete' or 'growth prospects'. We could then plot the results on an x–y graph and for each country there would be a dot on the graph that represents its position. However, unless you work for a highly analytical outfit, such an exercise may hinder, not help. To quantify an 'ability to compete' for all operations, you'd need to derive some weighted average score for each of them based on quality of management, their recent financial results, position in market, and so on. There is then a risk that managers would get hung up on the exact scores, weightings and criteria that make up each operation's weighted average score. Management might spend too much time debating whether Canada warrants a score of 65% or 70% for 'quality of management', and too little time on the bigger picture.

FIGURE 4.9

Country	Ability to compete	Country's growth prospects
Norway Finland China Germany Australia	✓	✓
Japan Argentina Estonia	✓	✗
Canada Mexico	✗	✓
France	✗	✗

Do a table of ticks or crosses instead? It isn't bad (Figure 4.9), but isn't as effective or intuitive. The two-by-two grid uses its physical space more effectively.

Don't do the presentation as an afterthought to the report. Occasionally, the report will have the wordy bullet points we started with, but the presentation will have the two-by-two grid. This is because the report is due in first and the presentation not due for another week – and no one works on the presentation until the report's gone in. At which time the authors realise the bullet points lack impact for a presentation, so they dream up the two-by-two grid instead. Unfortunately, it's too late for the report to benefit from the idea.

The moral is: don't work on the presentation as an afterthought to the report, you won't put your best foot forward. Of course, it's easy for me to sit here and give this advice. In reality it's far too beguiling to work on tomorrow's deadline than next week's. There are ways to help this problem, but there isn't space to cover them here.

These grids are an excellent way to make comparisons if asking two or three questions. They also help you look like a consultant. Boston Consulting Group's famous two-by-two grid looked at each business unit's 'Market Growth Rate' and 'Market Share' to see if it was a 'Star', 'Question Mark', 'Cash Cow' or 'Dog'. McKinsey took this a stage further and produced a (wait for it) three-by-three grid (you saw it coming, didn't you?). McKinsey categorised each business unit's 'Market Attractiveness' and 'Business Unit Strength' not as 'High' and 'Low' but as 'High', 'Medium' and 'Low'. And you probably guessed that last bit too.

The tables of ticks and crosses and the grids work well if the answers to questions are *discrete* (e.g. growth is 'good' or 'average' or 'bad'). Next we see how to make comparisons if the answers are a *range*.

A cluster chart

You are looking at which types of company might buy one of your subsidiaries. You categorise groups of potential purchasers according to the following questions:

1   Their strategic fit: What's the degree of overlap with your subsidiary's line of business?

2   Their ability to pay: How easily can potential purchasers get funds to do the deal?

There are two questions, so this is similar to the two-by-two grid example – except here there are *ranges*, e.g. quoted competitors range from those that have a 'good' fit to those where the fit is 'average'. A strictly divided grid won't work, so instead try a cluster chart, one that has ovals or circles to represent the ranges (Figure 4.10).

It shows that unquoted competitors have a good fit with the company up for sale, and they range between those that are rolling in it and those that are as poor as church mice. Quoted competitors are all rolling in it, but some only have a moderate fit with the company for sale. And so on.

The more items to compare, the more these charts effortlessly highlight clusters, patterns, ranges, detail. The chart in Figure 4.11 looks at expected movements in regulatory controls and price changes for 13 different commodities (OK, it's not the most realistic of examples, but it is just illustrative).

FIGURE 4.10

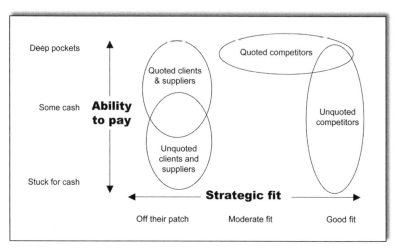

FIGURE 4.11

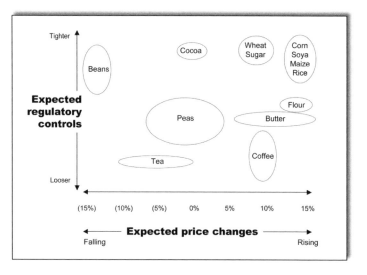

They say a picture paints a thousand words, and this cluster chart does. If we tried showing this information in words, it would be awful. Readers would struggle with detail and overview. Comparability would be almost impossible.

We could try showing the information in a table – for tea's expected price change, the table would say '(10%) to 0%'. It wouldn't be as intuitive, though, because the table would put quite a strain on short-term memory if readers wish to compare across different commodities. Because the cluster chart uses its physical space to show the information, it's far less of a strain. The cluster chart really is ideal when answers to questions are not discrete but in ranges.

Even though we've seen several ways of making comparisons, we haven't yet covered all the bases. For instance, what if we added a third question and the answers are in a range? We do this in the next section – and as it's one of the tougher bits of the book, you'll probably need your thinking cap on a bit more.

Are these Venn diagrams?

The oval shapes in Figures 4.10 and 4.11 may remind you of the Venn diagrams you learnt at school, ones that showed who was wearing a blazer, who was wearing a tie, and who was wearing both (Figure 4.12). However, as the table below explains, cluster charts and Venn diagrams are very different:

FIGURE 4.12

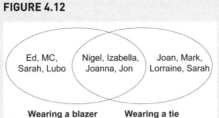

Function	Venn diagram	Cluster chart
What it does	The Venn diagram is to *categorise*.	The cluster chart is to show relative *position*.
The overlap of the ovals	Some ovals must overlap. The Venn diagram exists so people can see which items are in the overlap area and which aren't.	It doesn't matter if there is no overlap.
The size, shape and position of the ovals	So long as their content and overlaps are correctly stated, the size, shape or position of the ovals isn't significant.	The size, shape and position of the ovals is critical.
The number of ovals	The Venn diagram is confusing if there are too many ovals – see below for a real-life horror.	The cluster chart works even better if many ovals – it visually summarises something that would be awful in words.

If these differences aren't crystal clear, you might end up doing a real turkey – you might unwittingly use oval shapes to categorise instead of show relative position, like the one in Figure 4.13 which categorises companies by activity. For instance (see bottom left of the chart), Forsyths Ltd is in Transportation and Financial Services but not in Utilities, Mining, and so on. And, in case you are wondering, not only did this really exist, but the original looked exactly like this one. It really was this bad.

▶

It would be better as a table of ticks and crosses.

FIGURE 4.13

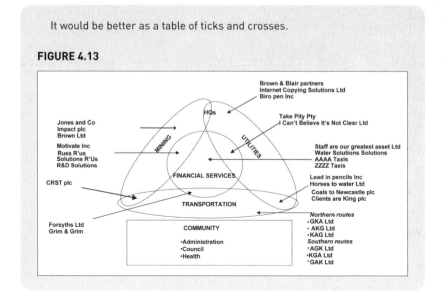

Covering the bases

Right, take a breath, here goes. Let's revisit a previous example (shown again in Figure 4.14), the one about potential purchasers for your subsidiary, and add a third question: how keen are we to sell to these groupings of companies?

FIGURE 4.14

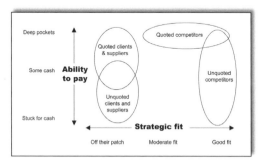

What happens next depends on how this third question affects existing groupings. If we are willing to sell to one group, less willing to another, and not willing at all to the other two, the third question doesn't affect existing groupings at all. We had four different groupings before we added the third question, and we still have the same four different groupings after.

To show the answer to the third question, we can then simply signal it typographically. That is, we show each grouping's name ('quoted competitor') in a darker or lighter font – dark means 'OK to sell to', light means 'less willing to sell to'. We explain this distinction in a note to the chart, and all is fairly clear (Figure 4.15).

FIGURE 4.15

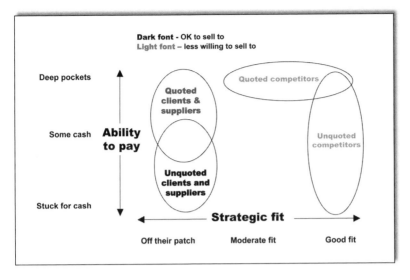

But what if our 'willingness to sell to' *changes within a grouping*? What if we don't mind selling to some quoted competitors but do mind selling to others? We can't simply signal answers to the third question typographically because there are both types of 'willingness' within the 'quoted competitors' category.

It's probably best to revisit the groupings so as to simplify. We could create more ovals and, for instance, have two ovals for quoted competitors: one for those companies we are willing to sell to and one for those we aren't. We could then typographically signal them with light and dark fonts, but it's a bit useless to have an oval that says 'quoted competitors we want to sell to'. It's as useless as saying 'I've done an analysis of people we want to promote, and there are two main groupings: people we want to promote and people we don't' – but then not giving names. (Also, when I tried doing it with this chart, it didn't work because the two ovals lay on top of each other. It wasn't visually effective.)

So instead make the analysis more granular. Give names. Look not at *groupings* of companies but at individual companies – look at competitor ABC, supplier DEF and client GHI, and so on. If you know each company's ability to compete, strategic fit and your willingness to sell to them, you no longer have ranges. You can do a table of ticks and crosses, or a scattergram of names (Figure 4.16). This chart has only a few names on it to illustrate. Dark font means 'OK to sell to', light font means 'less willing to sell to'.

FIGURE 4.16

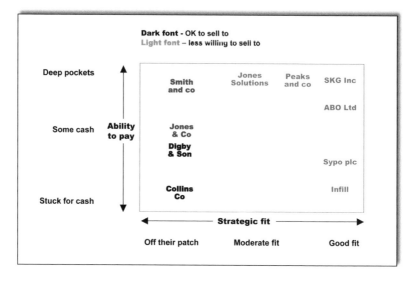

This assumes we can get rid of ranges by drilling down from groups of items and looking at individual items. But what if there's a range because we just *don't know*, because we are predicting the future and all we can say is 'between good and excellent' (such as in the example about commodities' expected regulatory controls and expected price changes). If that's the case, we're back to doing a table. Not ideal but probably as good as it gets.

To summarise, if you've three questions whose answers are ranges, the best way to show the information depends on *why* the answers are in ranges. If it's because we're assessing a grouping of items, then split the grouping up until you no longer have ranges for one or all of the answers – at which point you can clearly show the information. If, however, it's a range because we just can't quantify the future precisely, then we are more limited in what we can do – it's pretty much a table.

The next section is the last before we summarise the chapter and it's a bit different. It's about decision trees. These help readers make choices by leading them through successive stages until they reach their preferred choice. We look at decision trees because, if people are making comparisons, they probably want to reach a decision. And they might think that comparing answers to questions means they are asking the right questions to reach that decision. As we will see, they are not necessarily. But they would be with a decision tree, which is why trees deserve a mention.

An accountant's decision tree

Accountants use something called 'decision trees' but they are different to the ones here. Theirs are for computing net present values of projects. The trees in this section are about communicating and clarifying, not computing.

A decision tree

If your slides or notes have bullet points that start 'if this, then that, if that, then the other', a decision tree will probably be better. Bullet points such as these often arise when people explain procedures. The slide in Figure 4.17 explains how much discount to give. It depends on the value of the sale, the day of the week (there are bigger discounts on Monday), whether its cash or credit, and whether the manager has signalled a 'Special Week'.

FIGURE 4.17

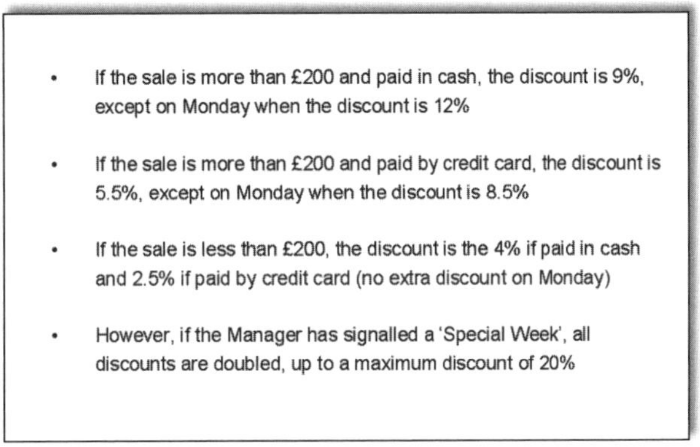

- If the sale is more than £200 and paid in cash, the discount is 9%, except on Monday when the discount is 12%

- If the sale is more than £200 and paid by credit card, the discount is 5.5%, except on Monday when the discount is 8.5%

- If the sale is less than £200, the discount is the 4% if paid in cash and 2.5% if paid by credit card (no extra discount on Monday)

- However, if the Manager has signalled a 'Special Week', all discounts are doubled, up to a maximum discount of 20%

At first glance, the bullet points seem fine for explaining the discounts. But hidden within them are 12 different discount rates, so when you use the bullets to work out a discount, they suddenly seem less innocuous, more impenetrable. They set readers a puzzle to decode and require a fair amount of concentration. Try using the bullets to work out the discount for a £150 credit card sale on Thursday that's also a Special Week. And when you've eventually worked it out, there's that nagging feeling you might not have got it quite right. Also, there's the kicker at the end that can be easily missed: the doubling of discounts if a Special Week. And there's the kicker in the kicker – the doubling is subject to a maximum discount of 20%.

Figure 4.18 shows the discount rules as a decision tree. At first glance, it may look a bit more intimidating than its bullet point equivalent, but it is much easier to follow. People follow the path that is relevant to them and read only what they have to read until the tree gives the discount rate to apply. It is an easy-to-refer-to guide.

FIGURE 4.18

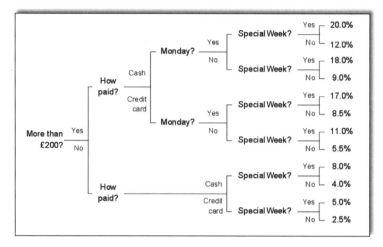

I once did a decision tree to help a client explain industry changes to its staff. It was only then that the client realised they hadn't properly understood the changes – they had drafted bullet point slides to explain them, but the slides were wrong. And because the bullet points were a bit impenetrable, no one had noticed. Thankfully, the decision tree was so clear, it highlighted the error.

FIGURE 4.19

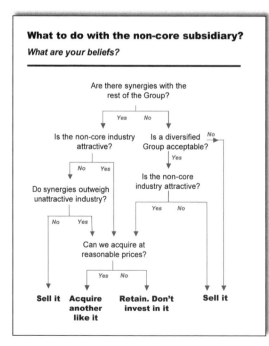

Decision trees aren't just for procedures, though, they are for big strategic decisions too. They allow managers to spend less time struggling with confusing wordy descriptions of the issues and more time discussing them intelligently from a position of knowledge. A new CEO is wondering what the board should do with a non-core subsidiary that is a marginal player in its industry: (1) flog it, (2) hang on to it but let it carry on unchanged, or (3) give it money to make a big acquisition so it becomes market leader? The decision tree in Figure 4.19 shows the issues and arranges them in order.* The CEO can quickly see how different assumptions lead to different outcomes, because it shows the tipping points. Also, it's easy for the board to refer back to it during a conversation. (To simplify this example, I've assumed the CEO doesn't care if there's a big loss on disposal, it can be blamed on the previous CEO.)

To see how much the tree simplifies, here's the tree in words (Figure 4.20 – hold on to your hats, it's quite a ride):

FIGURE 4.20

- If we believe a diversified group is acceptable, but the industry is unattractive, we should sell.
- If we believe a diversified group is acceptable and the industry is attractive, we should retain the subsidiary – or even invest in it if we can acquire similar companies at reasonable prices.
- If there are synergies but the industry is not attractive, we should sell the subsidiary if synergies don't compensate for the unattractiveness of the industry.
- Conversely, if the industry is unattractive but synergies more than compensate for this unattractiveness, we should retain the subsidiary – or even invest in it if we can acquire similar companies at reasonable prices. (Are you still with me?)
- If there are synergies and the industry is attractive, then we should retain the subsidiary – or even invest in it if we can acquire similar companies at reasonable prices. (Almost there.)
- Finally, we should also sell the non-core subsidiary if we believe a diversified group is not acceptable, regardless of how attractive the industry is. (Phew, made it.)

It's awful, it would send a glass eye to sleep. It's dense, repetitive, confusing and a huge strain on short-term memory. Try referring back to it quickly during a conversation about the subsidiary.

Of course, if you can establish someone's beliefs, you can dispense with this long list of alternatives and simply state the one outcome that best fits those beliefs. I can almost hear the boss saying 'Stop all that intellectualising, just give me the answer – what do you recommend?' But with issues like this, there are many decision-makers and you don't know all their beliefs – and often there isn't any great consensus amongst them. Some think diversification is bad, some think it good. Some think there is synergy, some don't.

And this is the decision tree's strength – it works for all these people. It doesn't just give *an* answer, it gives *the* answers. Everyone can quickly establish the course of action that best fits their own assumptions.

But often, the board doesn't even get the turgid bullet points, it gets something far less evolved – a list of issues (Figure 4.21). This is lazy thinking. It doesn't identify the hierarchy of these issues nor relate them to

* Some of this tree is based on Michael Porter's three tests for diversification. These are reproduced in Chapter 12 of *Managing the Multibusiness Company*, a collection of essays edited by Michael Goold and Kathleen Sommers Luchs. Chapter 12 is one of the most fascinating reads I have ever seen in business.

FIGURE 4.21

> Whether we sell, retain or invest further in the non-core subsidiary depends on the answer to four key questions:
>
> - Is there synergy between the subsidiary and the rest of the group?
> - Is it in an attractive industry?
> - Can we buy competitor companies at reasonable prices?
> - Do we believe it is acceptable to have a diversified group?

possible *outcomes*. For instance, if the board thinks a diversified group is unacceptable and believes there aren't synergies, it should sell the subsidiary regardless of industry attractiveness and whether companies can be bought at reasonable prices. But the list of issues makes no attempt to work this out. Also, the person doing the list hasn't shown how the outcome sometimes depends on the *trade-off* between two issues – do synergies more than compensate for the unattractiveness of the industry (assuming there are synergies and assuming the industry is unattractive)?

Decision trees are a huge help for complex issues because they identify these hierarchies and relate them to outcomes. *They ask questions in the right order.*

And they ask the *right* questions. Cast your mind back to cameras – even after answering all the questions, we can't say which camera would be best for someone because we don't know what matters to them. If price is most important, then the cheap compact is the best, and so on. So even after comparing cameras in detail, we still can't choose a camera.

And that's because we didn't ask the *right* questions – which means we can't use the list of answers to work out outcomes. (I've seen various Internet sites try and fail to do a tree for cameras. It's obvious they've failed, they ask questions like 'Do you take sports photos?' and have no line to follow if the answer is 'no'.)

Decision trees do such a lot. They ask the right questions in the right order, and for each set of questions they identify the outcome. They give the answers, not an answer. They present the information clearly, concisely and in a way that can easily be referred back to and which doesn't put a strain on short-term memory. That's quite a few good reasons to use them when you can.

Finally, if you've seen *When Harry Met Sally*, you may remember Meg Ryan's speech that's reproduced at the start of this chapter. She bangs on about 'if this, then that, if that, then the other'. It needs a decision tree. So here it is – and because Meg had such well-defined priorities, Figure 4.22 was easy to do.

FIGURE 4.22

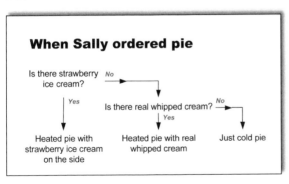

There are tips on constructing trees, on checking them, on making them look neat (e.g. tricks to avoid criss-crossing lines). I drafted a 25-page chapter on the topic but don't have room for it here, other than to give a final thought: remember your audience. Some people love decision trees, others hate them. In particular, don't use decision trees on the young or old – research has shown they struggle with them.

Final thoughts and recap

I did think of summarising with a bullet point list of the pros and cons of bullet point lists of pros and cons. It would have had a certain irony to it – but I couldn't. When I dummied it up, it was lopsided – no pros, all cons.

Which shows just how bad bullet points are at making comparisons. They are unnecessarily wordy and repetitive. They suffer from inconsistencies and differences in terminology that confuse. They have no underlying structure to impose a discipline on the analysis, so the analysis is often incomplete – and often neither author nor reader spot this. Also, the physical separation between the pros and cons makes it difficult to compare.

We've looked at several better ways to make comparisons. I don't doubt there are other ways too, but this chapter covers enough for most situations. And it's not just business situations either. All of us constantly compare alternative ways of doing something, be it different ways of renewing a passport or different courses we might do at college. No matter what you are comparing, the ideas in this chapter will help.

Also, to see how to make numerical comparisons (e.g. productivity or staff utilisation by department), see Chapter 3.

Recap

The *three-by-two grid* in Figure 4.23 shows which is the best way to make comparisons.

FIGURE 4.23

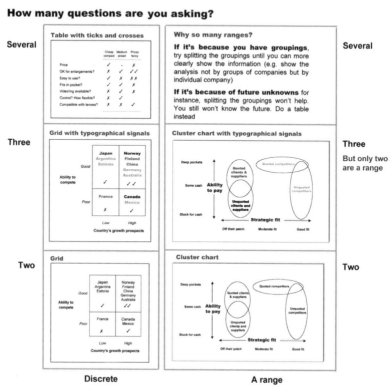

To help readers reach decisions rather than make comparisons, try a decision tree like the one on the left. Decision trees ask the right questions in the right order, and for each set of questions they identify the outcome. They give *the* answers, not just *an* answer.

Whichever way you choose, think about the strain on readers' short-term memory. Think about how their eyes move around to compare items. Are you giving puzzles to decode? Ask yourself how effectively you show both detail and overview.

And at last you can now make more informed decisions about how to compare alternatives so your readers can make more informed decisions.

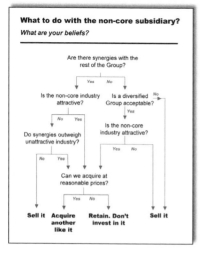

Applying Figure 4.23 to itself

Let's apply the grid to itself (Figure 4.23). We want to know the best way to show different ways of making comparisons and we are going to use the grid to help us decide.

See the question at the top left of the grid: 'How many questions are you asking?' Well, to decide how best to make comparisons, we *know* there are two questions that help you decide: one of the questions is down the left, the other is along the bottom.

Now see the question along the bottom: 'Are the answers discrete or a range?' We can see they are discrete – in Figure 4.23, nothing sprawls over two or more adjacent parts of the grid.

So we have *two* questions, and *discrete* answers. Now look on the grid, and see the best way to show the information – and lo, according to the grid, it's a grid. Which is what we've done. Which is reassuring.

Chapter **5**

Slides

Slides that inform and influence

> How to do slides so people remember your messages
> Great alternatives to bullet points – a reminder of ideas from other chapters
> Getting the audience to listen to you, not read your slides
> Presenter's props – if you have fewer bullet points, how will you remember what to say?
> For the bullet points you want to keep: how to do them better
> Doing better handouts

People talking without speaking, people hearing without listening.
Simon and Garfunkel, 'The Sound of Silence'

You're presenting your six-point action plan at a get-together of senior managers. Or maybe you're presenting your new investment proposal to the board. Or you're pitching for a new account, one you've been stalking for some time, and you have at last got the undivided attention of key decision-makers. Either way, you are at the front of the room, you have your big moment, your chance to inspire, inform, influence, motivate, impress. And you put up slide after slide of bullet points and read them to the audience.

What a wasted opportunity. Often there are better alternatives to bullet points – which is what this chapter is about. Next time you're preparing a presentation, dip into this chapter for inspiration and ideas, for better ways to reinforce, engage and remind, better ways to influence, impress and make an impact. And to do them, you don't need to buy any fancy new software or attend Advanced PowerPoint courses.

As for your slides that rightfully stay as bullet points, we see how to do them better. Also, if bullet points are your script and you can't imagine how to cope without them, we cover that too.

Two last points. Firstly, this chapter is *not* a triumph of style over content, about making your slides look groovy and sexy with fancy arrows and icons. It's about communicating your information more clearly and effectively. In common with the rest of this book, it's about *clarity and impact*.

Secondly, a lot of this chapter relates to other chapters. Slides have *bullet points*, *graphs* and *tables*. People use slides to *make comparisons* and show *numbers*. Also, people want slides to be *designed*. Given that the italicised words are other chapters, we'll be referring to them fairly regularly, as you'll see.

The first section looks at ideas that not only get your message across but also help ensure it's remembered.

How to get your message remembered

Sometimes, you want your audience not only to understand your message but also to remember it, to have unprompted recall of it. Maybe it's because you want to win over not just your audience but your audience's audience too. If you can give your audience something they can use in *their* conversations, you will help them to help you in your cause.

And the answer isn't bullet points. Of all the bullet points you've seen over the years, how many can you remember? Bullet points don't win hearts and minds. At best, they lay out an argument in a linear, sequential, logical way. At worst, they bore into submission.

So here's some alternatives, four ways to do slides your audience will remember: be big, use an acronym, use a memorable quote, or find a picture that *reinforces* (i.e. *not* clipart).

The first is: **BE BIG**.

Be big

You are launching a new product to the sales force and want to reassure and excite them with just how much time and money you've spent developing it. So you show them some bullet points which spell out the numbers along with some boosterish catch phrases ('It must and will succeed') – see Figure 5.1.

FIGURE 5.1

FIGURE 5.2

Our major new product

• A major commitment to our future
• A total of £10m invested in it
• Five years to develop & research
• A market waiting for it to be launched
• It must and will succeed

£10m
5 years

But the two points you really wish to convey are hidden deep undercover, submerged by the words and bullet points. If you want the sales force to remember '£10m' and 'five years', try the slide in Figure 5.2 instead.

Also, this approach helps create an air of seniority for the presenter. There is something quite confident, almost cocky, about keeping slides this minimalist and being so 'big picture' and in-your-face with the two numbers. The slide is more likely to be done by a senior manager than a middle one.

People often hide key numbers deep in slides. To show how a company has grown 15% a year for the last five years, I've seen slides with five years of profit and loss accounts, each with about 10 numbers (income, cost of sales, gross profit, overheads, etc). Fifty numbers, but the one number that was important – '15%' – wasn't even shown. Instead, do a slide with a massive '15%' on it. That spells it out.

Be big with words too – it makes it impossible for the audience to misunderstand you. Often, bullet points don't engage. People don't give them sufficient critical thought, especially after the 100th bullet point appears on the screen. Also, people often ponder each bullet in isolation from the others, and even in isolation from their own values and beliefs. They accept each bullet individually but still walk away from the presentation rejecting them collectively. A presenter can show the six steps to manage a project, and the audience will nod along with it all, and yet still go away and do exactly what they did before – dive into a project without doing a timetable.

Instead, be *big*. Confront the audience in a way that ensures even a dulled set of faculties will hear the message. Don't bother with all the steps for managing a project, just put this on a slide (Figure 5.3) – it won't be misunderstood or forgotten:

FIGURE 5.3

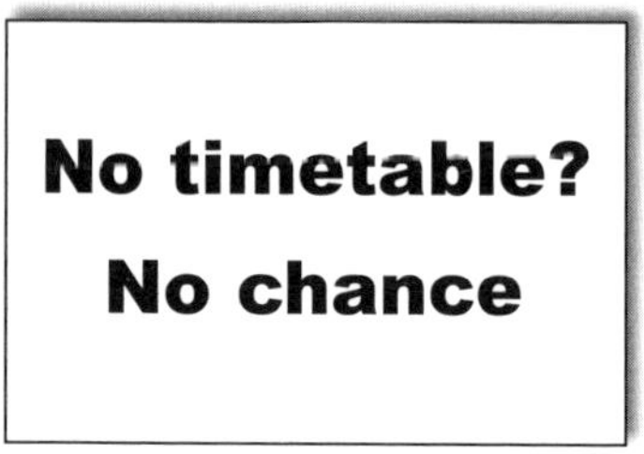

> # No timetable?
> # No chance

This is simply following one of the principles of communicating: 'Avoid too many messages – if you try to get too many across, you will get none across.' In Figure 5.3, we've ignored all the more minor tips on project planning and instead have gone for the jugular, the one point we fear everyone will nod along to but then ignore – doing a timetable. Which is also following another of the communicating principles: 'What outcome do you seek?' Here, we want people to do a timetable, and the slide has been utterly single-minded in emphasising that.

There is one problem with these 'big' slides, though: they don't make a good stand-alone handout. I discuss this later.

Next we look at the second way to get your slides remembered: it's 'DANA' – Do A Neat Acronym.

'Never have more than five bullets or four numbers on a slide'

You can read this advice on the Internet. Given that I've just been saying 'be big', you might think I agree with it.

I don't. Even though we've all seen a bad slide with 50 numbers on it, it doesn't mean all slides with 50 numbers are bad. All dogs are animals, but not all animals are dogs. It depends on what the presenter wants to say and what the audience are interested in and hope to hear.

If I was a knowledgeable football pundit, and if the audience were keen football fans, I could show the latest Premiership football table on the screen and talk about it for 30 minutes. I could highlight how City are currently above Rovers on goal difference simply because United got whipped 5–0 by City a month ago. I could talk about how last year's promoted teams are doing. And the table of numbers on the screen would act as a backdrop, a reference point for my comments. And everyone would have a great time.

But there would be over 200 numbers on the slide, so that can't be right, can it? Yes, it can. Sometimes 200 numbers can be fine, sometimes just 10 is too many. It depends. The key is not 'How many numbers should be on a slide?', but 'What are you communicating, to whom, why, and which way works best?'

An acronym

You want your audience to remember the four stages of a receivership so you put up a slide with four bullet points (Figure 5.4).

They will not be remembered. Instead, try a slide with the acronym 'HELP' – Hold, Evaluate, Liquidate, Pay (Figure 5.5).

FIGURE 5.4

FIGURE 5.5

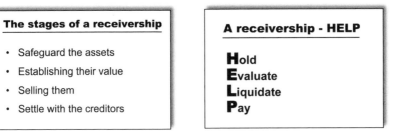

As anyone who has sat exams knows, a good acronym is a great way to remember things. 'Every Good Boy Deserves Food' for music, 'CRAP' for document design (if you haven't yet looked at Chapter 7, this last one will confuse you). And I will always remember the stockbroker's report on Robert Maxwell's empire before it went bust: 'Can't Recommend A Purchase'.

If you want your staff to remember the five key action points for the year, don't expect your bullet point list to stick in their brains. Try an acronym. One of my clients was presenting its five action points that were going to knock the competition into a cupped hat. By marginally changing one word in the list, the five points created an acronym: 'FIRST'.

These acronyms work because they are a bit different. I do wonder, though, about ones like the 7Ss (for strategy) and the 5Ps (for marketing); they seem to have an air of contrivance about them. It's too much of a coincidence that every important bit of strategy starts with an 's', and every important bit of marketing starts with a 'p'.

Next, we look at a third way to get your audience to remember your message: use a good quote. After all, 'You can't always get what you want, but if you try sometimes, you just might find you get what you need'. Mick Jagger sang that.

A memorable quote

You wish to tell staff why marketing is vital. You can do bullet points that intellectualise about its importance. Or maybe you could recite case studies of marketing successes and sound like some business school lecturer. But neither are likely to win hearts and minds. Neither gives your audience much they can use on *their* audience and repeat on your behalf.

FIGURE 5.6

> "He was a strange man.
> He wasn't very good
> at marketing."

FIGURE 5.7

> "It's just called The Bible now
> We dropped the word 'Holy'
> to give it more mass
> market appeal."

FIGURE 5.8

> "Practice doesn't make
> perfect, it makes permanent."

Instead, find a memorable quote. The one in Figure 5.6 is neat. It was said by the auctioneer about Van Gogh after his *Sunflowers* painting had been sold in 1987 for $40m, despite being considered worthless in his lifetime.* Or maybe try the quote in Figure 5.7. This was said by a spokesperson from Hodder & Stoughton, the publisher of *The Bible*.† Finally, if trying to convince people of the need to train properly and learn from professionals, don't bore with bullet points ('You learn best practice, you learn from other people's mistakes, etc.'). Instead, put up a memorable quote – see Figure 5.8 for a pithy comment from Warren Buffet's golf pro.

A decent quote gets remembered – as does a decent cartoon, and this is the next and final idea for getting your audience to remember your message.

A cartoon that reinforces

Don't get me wrong, I am not advocating clipart. I hate the stuff. Some pictures may paint a thousand words, but clipart isn't one of them. It doesn't help your audience *internalise* your message, it is just colouring for a dull bullet point.

You are in charge of the office relocation that's happening next week and are telling staff the timetable. Your real objective, though, is to plead for patience, to manage the audience's expectations and to ask for tolerance with any teething troubles. You could put up a slide with lots of typographically bad bullet points, bad grammar ('its') and clipart of a man smacking the computer (Figure 5.9).

No one will remember the bullet points. As for the clipart, at best it doesn't help your message, at worst it hinders if your audience hate clipart (many do). So instead show something like the cartoon in Figure 5.10, I found it on a birthday card.

It's a striking cartoon, one that sticks in the brain. It reinforces your message and does it memorably – it doesn't even need a title. Also, it gives a vocabulary for the future. If someone asks how it's going, you say 'A bit like Moses and his Red Sea – it's a bit muddy'. With luck, it might even become part of the lexicon of the company, so that if people moan that

---

*Quote taken from *The Business Book of Quotations*, compiled by Eugene Weber and originally printed in *Fortune*, 27 April 1987.

†Taken again from *The Business Book of Quotations*, compiled by Eugene Weber and originally printed in the *Financial Times* list of 'Quotes of the Year', 30 December 1989.

FIGURE 5.9

The office relocation progress report

- A massive undertaking that touches all parts of our business
- Much detailed planning – but nothing ever always goes right
- There may be teething problems
- Please be patient, we will do our utmost to ensure its seamless

FIGURE 5.10

"What do you mean 'It's a bit muddy'...?"

'A bit muddy' by Steve Best, © Paperlink 2007

their computers take longer to fire up, their peers will say to them 'What do you mean . . . "It's a bit muddy". . .?' Their peers will go into bat for you, since you have given them the means to do so.

We have found an image that is so apposite, it doesn't just 'liven' up bullet points, it replaces them.

There are a few points to watch, though. Don't breach copyright. Also, think of your audience, some of whom may think cartoons trivialise presentations. And avoid pictures of trite metaphors and parallels – to emphasise the need to change, people show an ostrich with its head in the sand, and to emphasise teamwork, they show a tug-of-war. Trite pictures like these aren't memorable or engaging, they are clichéd and overworked.

Never hang your entire presentation on a metaphor, it is tedious and contrived. Yes, refer to a good metaphor once or twice or three times, but don't contort every section of the talk to fit the metaphor.

Also, don't confuse a memorable cartoon with 'PowerPoint Paraphernalia', the stuff and fluff that people put on slides to appear sophisticated. The 'jigsaw' slide (Figure 5.11) probably once seemed sophisticated, but it's now overused, clichéd and passé (and it's not only the PR department that does this sort of thing). I suppose people think it pads out an empty slide, surmising that if the slide simply had four words on it, it would be a bit dull.

And fancy intriguing arrows (Figure 5.12) are often a sign of flabby thinking or a paucity of decent ideas. If someone hasn't got much to say, if they're a bit short of decent content, no worries – just do a few groovy arrows, that'll fool the audience . . . won't it?

Next are ideas we've seen in other chapters. We saw them then because they are great for reports, and they briefly reappear here because they are great for slides too.

FIGURE 5.11

The PR jigsaw

Message
People
Media
Strategy

FIGURE 5.12

Pointless graphics
3-D shapes
Intriguing arrows

Other better alternatives to bullet points

In other chapters, we've seen alternatives to bullet points that are better because they achieve greater *clarity* or *comparability*. This section quickly reminds us of five that are great for slides too: 'WiT', two-by-two grids, decision trees, cluster charts, and tables of ticks and crosses. See the other chapters for the full details.

'WiT' – Words in Tables (Chapter 1)

In Chapter 1, we showed how powerful and versatile 'WiT' (Words in Tables) is. Below is another 'WiT' slide example – to present the five key strategies to your management team, you do the following bullet point slide (Figure 5.13):

FIGURE 5.13

The five key points

- To focus on products and markets where we are or can be in the top three
- Growth – organic, not by acquisition, unless an opportunity arises to do a deal at acceptable risk–reward levels
- Building a portfolio of businesses in which we believe there are or will be sustainable and identifiable synergies between them
- Businesses to be invested in selectively in order to strengthen and build them in their chosen areas of expertise
- Our client-facing operations are to be kept on-shore

Instead of listing the points out with visually indistinct bullets, try doing 'WiT' (Figure 5.14):

FIGURE 5.14

What we will do

Market leadership	We will focus on products and markets where we are or can be in the top three
Organic growth	We will grow organically, not by acquisition, unless we see a great acquisition opportunity
Synergies	We will only include companies in our group if they have synergies with other parts of the group
Investment	We will invest selectively to strengthen and build into our business
On-shore locations	We will keep our client-facing operations on-shore

The difference is dramatic. The slide has much more impact – the key points lift from it. Also, by putting 'Words in Tables', we use the slide's white space more effectively, which makes it more visually interesting. However, there are two other reasons why the 'redo' is better. Firstly, the slide is typographically more interesting – there is *contrast*. The heading is no longer bland and indistinct, it is bold and confident – as is its underline at the top.

Secondly, the writing has much more impact. The first version was grammatically inconsistent – one bullet started with an imperative, the next with a noun, the next with a gerund, and so on. The second version is more consistent – and this doesn't just keep grammatical pedants happy, it creates impact. The redone slide is all in the active voice, which is engaging, humanising and action oriented. And it benefits from the power of repetition: all the points start 'We will'. It is emphatic, like the middle bit of Winston Churchill's famous speech in which the phrase 'We shall fight' ran through it repeatedly. Listeners are left in no doubt as to what is being said:

We shall fight with growing confidence and growing strength in the air, we shall defend our Island, whatever the cost may be, we shall fight on the beaches, we shall fight on the landing grounds, we shall fight in the fields and in the streets, we shall fight in the hills . . .

Imagine how this might've been done in a slide:

FIGURE 5.15

Our four key objectives and fighting locations

- Growing confidence and strength in the air
- Defend our land whatever the cost
- Primary fighting places: beaches, on the landing grounds
- Fields, streets, hills: secondary places to fight

Ridiculous.

'WiT' is a dramatic improvement, but doing tables in PowerPoint can be fiddly. If doing your slides on a train to the presentation, you probably won't want to muck about creating 'WiT'. To overcome this, set up a template, it saves doing 'WiT' from scratch. Also, maybe keep 'WiT' for important slides, the ones you wish to make an impact with or that you will reuse a lot.

And plan your work better so you don't have to do it on the train.

The next four ideas are all from Chapter 4. Presenters often need to compare alternatives, and here are quick reminders of ways to do this.

Two-by-two grids (or three-by-three, etc.)

You are reviewing your portfolio of overseas offices. Some are in high-growth countries, some in low-growth ones. Some have a strong ability to compete, others are not so hot. Figure 5.16 is a bullet point version of your findings. Figure 5.17 is a two-by-two grid which is far better at showing both overview and detail. Groupings are easier to pick out – many countries are top right (and the double tick signals to readers that 'top right' is best), and only one is bottom left (bad news obviously, it's a double cross).

FIGURE 5.16

- Good growth, good ability to compete: Norway, Finland, China, Germany, Australia
- Poor growth, good ability to compete: Japan, Argentina, Estonia
- Good growth, poor ability to compete: Canada, Mexico
- Poor growth, poor ability to compete: France

FIGURE 5.17

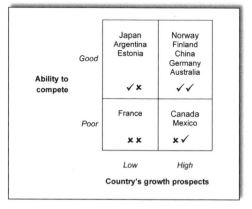

Decision trees

You are explaining to staff the rules for discounts. Figure 5.18 shows the rules as bullet points. It takes a fair amount of concentration to work out the discount to give. Figure 5.19 is a decision tree of the same rules. Staff can easily use it to work out the right discount.

Decision trees are not just for administrative points such as working out discounts, they are great for big strategic decisions too – see Chapter 4 for a decision tree on the options a CEO has for his non-core subsidiary: sell it, just hang onto it, or give it money to make a big acquisition so it becomes a market leader?

If your slides have lots of bullet points that say 'if this, then that, if that, then the other', try a decision tree instead.

FIGURE 5.18

- If the sale is more than £200 and paid in cash, the discount is 9%, except on Monday when the discount is 12%

- If the sale is more than £200 and paid by credit card, the discount is 5.5%, except on Monday when the discount is 8.5%

- If the sale is less than £200, the discount is the 4% if paid in cash and 2.5% if paid by credit card (no extra discount on Monday)

- However, if the Manager has signalled a 'Special Week', all discounts are doubled, up to a maximum discount of 20%

FIGURE 5.19

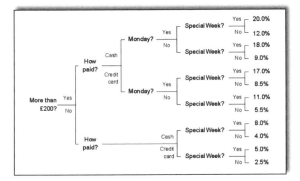

Cluster charts

You are looking at which types of company might buy one of your sub-sidiaries and you categorise groups of potential purchasers according to two questions: (1) strategic fit: the degree of overlap with your subsidiary's line of business; and (2) ability to pay: the ease with which a potential purchaser can get the funds to do the deal.

Bullet points are wordy and make it difficult to spot interrelationships (Figure 5.20). The cluster chart is far better (Figure 5.21). It shows both overview and detail and helps readers make comparisons – the information visually lifts from the page. Cluster charts really can paint a thousand words. Use them instead of two-by-two grids if your analysis gives ranges rather than specific answers (e.g. the 'strategic fit' for quoted competitors ranges from 'good fit' to 'moderate fit').

FIGURE 5.20

- Most likely acquirors: a number of the quoted competitors and a few of the unquoted competitors

- In particular the ones for whom the deal would be a good strategic fit and who have the funds to do the deal

- Many quoted clients and suppliers have the funds for a deal but it would be off their patch

- Unquoted suppliers and clients: both lack funds and the deal is not a good strategic fit for them

FIGURE 5.21

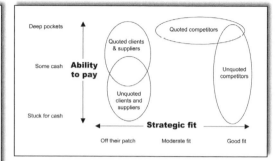

FIGURE 5.22

Cheap compact

Pros
- Cheap
- Easy to use
- Fits in pocket

Cons
- Cannot control your own settings
- Not good enough picture quality for enlarging
- Cannot do videos

Medium priced

Pros
- Reasonable quality for enlargements
- Tidy size
- Can shoot videos
- Can control some of the settings

Cons
- Existing lenses not compatible
- Controls are a bit intimidating

Pricey fancy one

Pros
- Great for enlargements
- Great flexibility for taking pictures
- Can use existing lenses

Cons
- Expensive
- Needs a suitcase to carry
- Intimidating set of controls

Ticks and crosses

You are comparing three different cameras – a cheap compact, a medium-priced one and a pricey fancy one. Figure 5.22 are bullet point lists of the pros and cons spread over a series of slides. The slide in Figure 5.23 is a table of ticks and crosses. The table is better because readers can more easily make comparisons. Also, the analysis is less repetitive and more likely to be consistent and complete. It allows a greater granularity and is easier to refer back to.

These five ideas helped us achieve far greater clarity and comparability than their bullet point equivalent and should be part of every presenter's toolkit.

The next section is a bit different and based on an obvious premise: to stop people reading slides when you don't want them to, make it difficult to read or don't give them anything to read . . .

FIGURE 5.23

	Cheap compact	Medium priced	Pricey fancy
Price	✓	-	✗
OK for enlargements?	✗	✓	✓✓
Easy to use?	✓	✗	✗✗
Fits in pocket?	✓	✓	✗
Video'ing available?	✗	✓	✗
Control? How flexible?	✗	✓	✓✓
Compatible with lenses?	✗	✗	✓

Getting the audience to listen, not read slides

A haphazard layout

You want to tell your audience that acquisitions fail more often than they succeed. To support your conjecture, you show a list of companies who have done reports showing this (Figure 5.24).

FIGURE 5.24

Because you've gone to the trouble of writing the bullet point list, your audience will feel obliged to read it – which sets up a conflict: do the audience read the words or listen to you? And if they read the words, the presenter and audience get out of sync – people read faster than they can speak.

Yet this is all so unnecessary. You actually don't *want* people to read the names, you just want to give the impression that quite a few companies say acquisitions fail.

So instead do a slide that gives that impression but which doesn't set up a conflict, one which doesn't invite people to read it so much. Lay the words haphazardly around the page, rather than linearly down the page (Figure 5.25). At a glance, readers get the general impression that eminent names have said acquisitions fail. Then, rather than twisting and turning their necks one way then another to try to read it, there is a good chance that the audience will give up and instead *listen to your words*.

Which is what you wanted them to do all along.

FIGURE 5.25

Show nothing

If a slide helps bring across your point more effectively, do one. If not, don't bother.

When giving training, I start by saying the course is one-third tables, one-third graphs, one-third words. Then a little while later, I return to this comment and say that it might have confused some people – after all, I merely *said* it. Maybe some people would grasp the comment better if I showed a bullet point slide – and then I click to the one shown in

Figure 5.26. Then I say that some people like to grasp their information visually – 'the trend is their friend'. So to help them, I show another slide, this time of two graphs (Figure 5.27).

FIGURE 5.26   **FIGURE 5.27**

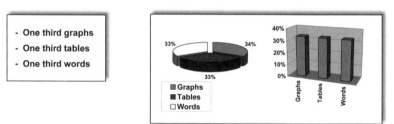

Of course, both slides are preposterous. Neither was necessary – the comment was fine on its own. You don't need to accompany every comment with a bullet point, you don't need to plot a graph or do a table every time you have some numbers.

Some presenters or audiences might prefer *something* other than a blank screen or the previous slide that's still sitting up there. So, if talking about why the company is restructuring, just show a slide that says 'Why restructure?' and then talk over it. The slide will remind people what you are talking about if their minds wander off for a bit.

Also, writing 'Why restructure?' keeps your presentation flexible. If your points change just before you give the talk, you don't have to change your bullet points. And keeping the slide so minimalist is similar to just showing two big numbers ('£10m', 'five years') – it's a confident, 'big-picture' approach to presenting and, again, it helps you look like a senior manager. (Maybe you are.)

We've now seen many different ways to show information in slides, ways that help you achieve your goals more effectively than bullet points. But if we get rid of bullet points, how will presenters know what to say? The next section explains how.

'Let's just talk about your business'

A corporate buyer once told me how he wanted companies to pitch for business by having a conversation with him. He didn't want to sit and passively listen to a presentation and read some slides. He wanted to explore how two companies could work together as client and supplier. His sentiments are echoed in a book by Louis Gerstner who describes his early days as President of IBM.

> One of the first meetings I asked for was briefing on the state of the main-frame computer business . . . At that time, the standard format of any important IBM meeting was a presentation using overhead projectors

and graphics that IBMers called 'foils' (projected transparencies). Nick was on his second foil when I stepped to the table and, as politely as I could in front of his team, switched off the projector. After a long moment of awkward silence, I simply said, '*Let's just talk about your business*'.

I mention this episode because it had an unintended, but terribly powerful ripple effect. By that afternoon, an e-mail about my hitting the Off button on the overhead projector was crisscrossing around the world. Talk about consternation! It was as if the President of the United States had banned the use of English at White House meetings.

Source: From *Who Says Elephants Can't Dance? Inside IBM's Historic Turnaround* by Louis Gerstner Junior (2002, HarperCollins page 43) – and thanks to Edward Tufte's book for bringing it to my attention.

'But the bullets are my script . . .'

Bullet points are often for the presenter's benefit, not the audience's. They are to remind the presenter what to say. In which case, is it possible to replace lots of bullet point slides with cartoons, acronyms, cluster charts, tables of ticks and crosses, and so on? Without bullets, presenters will have to remember the script, and whilst this might be OK for trainers who present the same thing week in, week out, is it practical for business people doing one-off presentations to client targets? Also, having the script on the screen does help presenters who are a little nervous.

Life with fewer bullets needn't be a problem, though. Presenters may even find it easier without them, not harder, and because of the different dynamic it creates between slide, presenter and audience, you will be seen to be a better presenter. The table below explains why:

You *will* still have your script	Your full script or notes will be in your hand, you aren't being asked to do the presentation from memory. You're just sparing the audience from seeing your script on screen.
Many 'alternative' slides are your script too	If you show a two-by-two grid, you'll need to explain the axes, the content, the clusters. When you do, the slide is no longer a transcript *of* your words, it's a prop *for* them. The chart provides you with your script.

And as for remembering what to say if the words aren't on the screen, this isn't an issue with some alternative slides – an acronym helps the audience remember, so it will help presenters remember too.

The 'alternative' slides help connect you with the audience	With a cluster chart, you give a more *dynamic* talk. Such charts almost invite presenters to wander to the screen and use their hands to point out axes, different clusters. Presenters are no longer standing rigidly at a podium reading a script. They come alive, they move, they gesticulate – and they talk seemingly without script or bullet points. It humanises the presentation and creates a connection between presenter and audience.

Yes, it may be intimidating for presenters when they first move away from a slide show designed almost entirely around bullet points. But it's also amazingly liberating, both for presenter *and* audience. And it's a virtuous circle. The more you do it, the more you crave to do again. Once the genie is out the bottle, once contact has been made with the audience, it's difficult to go back to how it used to be.

Having encouraged you to try something different to bullet points – or even do without them – the next section tells you how to do better bullet points.

Better bullet points

The section starting on page 32 explained when bullet points are acceptable, and its comments apply to slides as well as reports. Bullet points are a way of showing a list of brief items (sounds obvious, doesn't it?). To tell your audience the five topics that the presentation will cover, five bullet points pretty much do it. To remind the audience of the six countries that are struggling, six bullets do the trick. In the middle of a complex presentation, bullet points are easy on the brain and your audience might appreciate the mental break from more unusual slides.

However, even though bullet points have a valid part to play in presentations, below are some dos and don'ts. The first few apply to all bullet points, be they in slides or reports, whilst the rest are more just for slides. Also, remember the caveats listed on page 32, they apply to slides too:

➤ Use bullet points in moderation.

➤ Use them to denote only a single hierarchy, not multiple ones (use 'WiT' if multiple hierarchies).

➤ Don't expect too much from them – they aren't memorable nor visually lift points from the slide.

(Bracketed numbers cross-refer to other chapters and sections for more detail.)

Tips for all bullet points

Start at the end and maybe start at the end for each bullet? And make the summary typographically different from the rest of the bullet	Put the overall conclusion as the lead-in to the bullet points, it gives readers context and helps the skim reader. It makes it easier to refer back and find information (step 1, page 7).
Segment, order, maybe strip out	Sort between good and bad, important and unimportant, recurring and non-recurring or whatever. Then put in some order other than merely alphabetical. Also, strip out less material items, they lessen the impact of the comments that really do matter (step 2, page 8).
Maybe number your points instead	If you number them, you are more likely to think about their order. Also, it's easier to refer to a particular point in a numbered list.
Put in columns	Readers struggle with wide rows of text (see page 198).
Avoid just one bullet	It looks silly and is pointless:

They have offices in:
• Marlow

Is that it? Just the one? Has the author forgotten to mention a couple?

Indent *all* the text in the bullet, not just the first line

Compare the following – the top one looks smarter and is easier to read.

> • Compare the following, the top one looks smarter and is easier to read
> • It's one of the four design principles in action

> • Compare the following, the top one looks smarter and is easier to read
> • It's one of the four design principles in action

Ensure grammatically consistent

Each bullet is grammatically different to the others. It's similar to the example on page 159 – remember Winston Churchill's speech done in PowerPoint? It's unprofessional. Also, poor writing is a sign of poor thinking – if the authors can't be bothered to correct the grammar, they probably haven't sorted, grouped or clustered either. The underlying analysis is probably suspect too.

> We will do the following:
> • Establish procedures
> • Implementation of procedures
> • We will report back afterwards

Avoid numbering as well as bullets

This is what I mean by 'numbering as well as bullets':

> • 1. There might be a bullet point.
> • 2. Then another bullet point.
> • 3. But each bullet is also numbered.

Very weird. Very freaky.

More relevant for slides

Use a sans serif typeface

Fonts such as Arial are legible, so are better for readers to glance at on a screen. Compare this to Times New Roman which is readable and better for continuous text on a page (page 197).

Use the active voice 'we' and 'you'

Don't do a slide that says:

Action points this year
- Major new product developed
- Key acquisition undertaken
- Group organisation restructured

Instead, write this, you will engage and inspire more:

We've been busy this year
- We launched a new product
- We did a big acquisition
- We restructured our Group

If appropriate, give the slide a decent lead-in title*

To tell people how well the new product is doing, don't head up the slide 'New product update'. Say 'A fantastic first year for the new product'. If telling people how busy this year's been, don't head up the slide 'Key initiatives undertaken'. Say 'A busy and productive year'. Maybe even try the 'we' word – 'We've been busy and productive'. See above about using the 'we' word.

Also do this if reporting conclusions. If you've researched which countries to enter and a slide says it's Australia, don't head it up 'Which country to enter?' Say 'Australia is best to enter'.

Do a decent lead-in title* for all slides other than deliberately cryptic or kooky ones such as the massive '£10m' (page 153) or 'He wasn't good at marketing' (page 156) or the cartoon of Moses (page 157).

*But remember your audience: some people don't like this. Also, I haven't done lead-in titles for slides in this chapter because I want you to compare the 'before' and 'after', rather than be distracted by my choice of lead-in title.)

Avoid pidgin English, it can confuse	The slide says 'ABC used to reduce errors'. Is this saying that ABC is a way to reduce errors? Or that ABC once reduced errors, but no longer does? Is it 'yoozd' or 'yoost'? The slide says 'Competitor Z may be differentiated with new products'. Again, what does it mean? That Z has released new products already, but we aren't sure if they've helped Z differentiate itself? Or Z *could* differentiate itself if it were to release some new products?
Avoid Random upper Case, it's distracting and Changes meanings	On bullet Points, some People Use 'upper case' whenever They want, Especially on Slides. Don't, upper case isn't A lifestyle Choice. It's mandatory When you should use It and Not an option When you shouldn't. I'm Not being pedantic, Worrying about 'correct Usage'. Rather, upper Case creates 'defined' Terms that Have particular meanings. Also, it Is Distracting. Like This. A closer look at the itinerary revealed that this was not to be our third world tour but a Third World Tour. And, really, there's not a lot of logistics involved except 'Where's the electricity?' *This is Spinal Tap, The Official Companion* (2000, Bloomsbury, page 189)

Also on bullet points in slides, how should you punctuate them? Personally, I don't think it matters hugely so long as the punctuation is consistent. But if you need some guidance* try this:

> If there is a comma or semicolon at the end of each bullet, the next bullet should start 'lower case', and the last bullet should end with a full stop.

> If there is a full stop at the end of each bullet, the next bullet should start 'upper case'.

> If there is nothing at the end, start the next bullet how you want, either in 'upper' or 'lower' case – but Avoid random Upper case.

My personal preference is to start each bullet in 'upper' case and have no punctuation at the end. It is more minimalist, and for slides, less is definitely more.

* If you've read Chapter 4, you'll realise how this guidance should be shown. Because it says 'if this, then that, if that, then the other', it should be in a decision tree. But if I were to do a decision tree for punctuating bullet points, you'd think I'd gone mad.

Finally, for a more hard-line view of bullet points, read Edward Tufte's fascinating 32-page pamphlet that pretty much argues for a worldwide ban on PowerPoint. It's interesting and thought-provoking stuff. See the Bibliography for more.

The next section looks at which tips in this book can be ignored when doing slides.

When to bend 'rules' for slides

The dynamic for a presentation is different to that for a report. With a report, readers can go at their own pace. If they find something tough, they can skip and go back later, or they can read it again and again until they've got it. If they're a bit bored, they can take a break. With presentations, though, the audience has to go at the same pace as the presenter, so presenters need to be a bit more *flexible*. Which is a euphemism for 'for slides, ignore some of the ideas in the rest of this book'.

Mix it up a bit – maybe do a gratuitous graph	Assume you have lots of numerical information to present over, say, 20 slides, and assume the tips in this book indicate it's best to show it all in tables. So you'll have 20 slides and 20 numerical tables – and an audience driven to despair by slide after slide of tables. So mix things up a bit. Do a 'big number' or a quote or something. Think about how to ring the changes so as keep your audience with you. 'Mixing it up' applies less to written reports. Many long reports have no graphs but lots of tables and they are still excellent.
Use a bit of gratuitous colour	Don't go overboard, just put a nice shade of blue as the slide background for instance. It won't take long to do, audiences expect it, and a bit of colour can help lift the mood. But resist the urge to overcomplicate. Don't then experiment to see how the slides look with the bottom line in yellow, for instance. If you do, it will spiral quickly out of control – your boss will want a dark yellow, whilst the marketing department will want a red line. You'll then waste a whole day looking at different colours for that footer.

Remember your audience	People can have strong opinions about presentations. Some like the opening to be arresting whilst others think it a bit gimmicky and prefer it to be more linear (tell 'em what you are going to tell 'em, etc.). Some people like a degree of formality, others like a lighter presentation that stands less on ceremony. Each to their own. Remember your audience.

Finally, before we summarise, we look at handouts. They are often done badly and we explore how to do them better.

How to do a great handout

Remember this slide (Figure 5.28)? It doesn't make a good handout – it isn't much of a reminder of a presentation's content. It also isn't much use for those that didn't attend the talk – what exactly is the slide saying?

FIGURE 5.28

The answer is not to change the slide but to change the handout. To better understand this, let's step back and see how slides are created. Someone decides they want to put a few bullet points on a slide. Then someone realises the slides are to be printed off and handed out as a reminder of the presentation and to provide the detailed support for some of the presentation's comments. So the presenter crams more detail on the slide, e.g. a table of figures, or more explanatory words or whatever, and, yes, the slides now give the detail.

Which means the slides end up too detailed to be a decent presentation and not detailed enough to be a decent stand-alone report. Because the slides have tried to serve two masters, they have failed in both.

The answer is to produce two different documents: slides that work as a presentation, and a report that works as a stand-alone document. This is not the answer you want to hear: people never have enough time to prepare the slides, let alone prepare two separate documents. But it is a trade-off: do you wish to fail on both counts, or put in a bit of extra effort and succeed on both?

Anyway, when preparing slides and reports, many jobs go to the wire not because insufficient time was allowed to do the job, but because of poor project planning and control – everything gets concertinaed into the last week. So with better project planning and control, you should be able to do a handout that is more than just a printout of the slides. (It's easy for me to sit here saying this.)

If you do, you'll have slides that work as slides and a handout that works as a handout. Which is a target worth aiming for.

Final thoughts and recap

Bullet point slides aren't evil, it's what people do to them and expect of them that makes them sometimes seem evil. People use too many, show 50 bullet point slides on the trot and the audience end up inwardly screaming for it to end. Others use bullet points as their script with slides crammed full of words that the presenter reads out. When done to excess, the presenter isn't even needed, because the audience could simply read the slides themselves. Others believe bullet points possess magical powers to visually lift points from slides, to explain complex interrelationships, to inspire audiences or help people remember things.

They don't. But there are ways to do these and this chapter has given a few ideas. Flick through them when next preparing a presentation. Use them to help you achieve your goals. Use them to reinforce better. Use them to give more impact, interest and *variety* to your presentation.

Recap

Try 'WiT' (Words in Tables) or two-by-two grids.

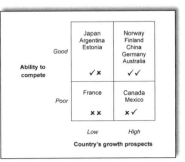

What we will do	
Market leadership	We will focus on products and markets where we are or can be in the top three
Organic growth	We will grow organically, not by acquisition, unless we see a great acquisition opportunity
Synergies	We will only include companies in our group if they have synergies with other parts of the group
Investment	We will invest selectively to strengthen and build into our business
On-shore locations	We will keep our client-facing operations on-shore

Or maybe decision trees, tables of ticks and crosses or a cluster chart.

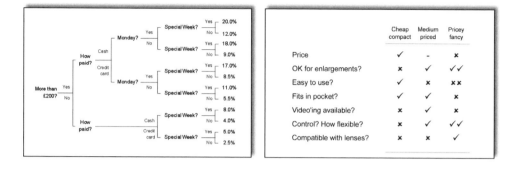

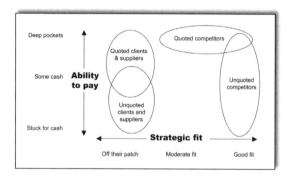

If you want your audience to remember your message, to have unprompted recall of it, try a quote, an acronym, a cartoon or just show one or two really big numbers or words.

If you want your audience to listen to you rather than read your slide, don't give them a slide to read. Lay items around the page haphazardly or just show nothing. It's surprising how often this last one is best. If a slide helps bring across your point more effectively, do one. If not, don't.

FIGURE 5.23

Along the way we stumbled across other points and tips:

Avoid PowerPoint paraphernalia	Avoid clipart, trendy arrows and 'jigsaws'. Don't let style triumph over content.
Never have a metaphor run through the entire presentation	Don't contort all your points to fit a particular sporting metaphor, it becomes tedious and contrived.
Build a library of ideas	Look out for interesting cartoons, images or acronyms. Look out for decent quotes. Crib ideas from other people's presentations.
Ring the changes to keep your audience on board	Mix up your slides a bit. Don't have too many similar slides one after the other (e.g. 20 bullet point slides one after the other, or 20 graphs, etc.). Use a bit of colour. And remember your audience.
If using bullet points . . .	Start at the end. Segment, order, maybe strip out. Maybe number the points (but don't use bullets as well). Put in columns, not wide rows of text. Avoid just one bullet. Indent all text, not just the first line. Ensure grammatically consistent. Use a sans serif face. Use the active voice, use the 'we' and 'you' words. Give slides a decent lead-in title. Avoid pidgin English. Avoid Random upper Case.
Try to avoid using your slides as a handout	Do a handout that is more than just a copy of your slides. If not, you will be asking your slides to meet two different objectives and they can all too easily fail at both.

If this sounds a lot of work, it isn't all bad news – sometimes it can save work. Try this question: Which of these takes more time to edit and get everyone to agree on the words:

> A slide with six bullet points, each with about 12 words?

> A slide that simply says 'He wasn't very good at marketing'?

If the detailed points change, which slide takes longer to edit to reflect the changes?

And with the quote, not only will you save time, but you will inform, influence, engage, reinforce and internalise.

Which is not bad for just six words on a slide.

Chapter **6**

Numbers

How to make sure your numbers clarify, not confuse

- ➤ Why numbers confuse
- ➤ Why you should round your numbers – and how best to round them
- ➤ Problems with percentages
- ➤ Lonely numbers

A difference is only a difference if it makes a difference.
Darrell Huff, *How to Lie with Statistics* (page 56)

This chapter gives the tips and principles for making numbers clearer and so have greater impact and influence.

The ideas are relevant for both accountants and non-accountants. Accountants will benefit from them. Even though they spend their lives dealing with numbers, they don't get taught these tips and principles. If in any doubt on this, study your management accounts pack – it will probably be far more impenetrable and indecipherable than it need be. Alternatively, look at the 2005 Annual Report of the European Commission, which shows operating revenue as €107,890,098,965.56.* Yes, you read that right, 100 billion euros – and 56 cents. More on this later.

And non-accountants will benefit too. Everyone shows numbers, be they in sales, HR, IT, strategy, compliance, or whatever.

Before we start, though, let's address two possible misconceptions. Firstly, this chapter isn't about Excel rounding to one or no decimal places, it's about *variable* rounding, something that Excel can't easily do. Secondly, it isn't about how to crunch the right numbers. Many other books will teach you about data integrity and different ways of working out your 'payback period', 'net present value' or 'internal rate of return', and so on. This is about how to *show* numbers so they are understood.

Before looking at how to show numbers clearly, we first need to see why they confuse.

Why numbers confuse

We present numbers constantly. In reports, presentations, updates, KPI packs, brief notes, and so on – and we assume readers understand these numbers and grasp their significance.

But often they don't. One company had £250m income and its monthly accounts showed every number to the nearest pound – income for the first 10 months was shown as £182,392,967. After I'd redone the pack and showed numbers to the nearest million with one decimal place (£182.4m), a long-standing director said of a particular page: 'I've never understood this financial schedule. Could you talk me through it please?' He'd stared at that schedule every month for 10 years without ever engaging with it.

But you can understand why he hadn't. Every figure was shown with up to nine digits and the pages were a blur of intimidatingly long numbers. They weren't for mere mortals, they were pages only accountants could grasp. The pack looked so impenetrable that the director hadn't ever tried to penetrate it. When I shortened the numbers, it looked much simpler and more

* If you can't believe this really happened, visit www.jmoon.co.uk/downloads for a link to the Report.

accessible. So after 10 years, the director no longer had an excuse for his confusion, and he at last made an effort to understand what it was saying.

There are several reasons why long numbers confuse, why they stop people from engaging with them:

They are daunting for the reader	It is intimidating to be confronted with a dense page filled with long numbers. Readers engage more with shorter, rounded numbers.
They are difficult to remember	If I said income was up £119,491,234 to £624,112,645, an increase of 23.67938%, you would struggle to remember it. The extra digits hinder clarity, not help it. You are more likely to remember that income grew £120m to £625m, a 24% rise.
They are difficult to do sums with	Mental arithmetic is how people make sense of numbers. When readers look at a sports league table, they compute that the top club is (cue mental arithmetic) seven points clear of the second club, which in turn is (more mental arithmetic) just one point clear of the next club. With shorter numbers, readers can easily work out distribution and make comparisons. With longer numbers, they can't. If income grew from £658,291 to £962,755, readers could only work out the increase in income by rounding to say £658 and £963 (both in thousands) – or more likely, to £660 and £960 (again in thousands).
They give a false indication of accuracy	If there was about £355k income from 17 sales, the average sale is computed as £20,822. But it is a bit nonsensical to show a computed number more accurately than the numbers from which it was derived. The average sale is actually about £21k.

Even though there are benefits to rounding, many people don't. Next we see why.

Why people don't round

Far too often, people show income as £62,364,834 or staff turnover as 10.364%. It doesn't occur to them to show approximate numbers – why on earth would someone do that? Surely management want the most accurate information available. Management don't though, they want the *clearest* information and would willingly sacrifice accuracy for clarity.

However, for some people, it *does* occur to them to round numbers – and they choose not to. They actively reject rounding for two reasons:

They don't understand the numbers	People aren't sure of the significance of staff turnover being 10.364%, so they report all digits just in case.
They don't know how management will use the numbers	They fear management might make a wrong decision if given a rounded number. If told that staff turnover is 10.364%, management will do something different than if told staff turnover is 10% or 10.5%.

This second concern is misguided. Management rarely make decisions based on a single statistic: 'Staff turnover is 10.364%'. Management make decisions based on numerous inputs, both qualitative and quantitative, e.g. staff turnover for this year and last year, the underlying economy, the impact of the new IT system, competitors' staff turnover, and so on.

People should round. Next we see how best to do it, and it isn't just showing numbers to one or no decimal places.

Examples of unnecessary accuracy

The European Union's revenue	It is €107,890,098,965.56. That's 14 digits, including the point 56 at the end. Some accountant must have a very big calculator. Yet this level of accuracy is inappropriate, given that auditors have qualified the accounts for 12 years running (double postings, material errors, irregularities, and so on).

The investment banks' competitor analysis	When a top investment bank showed a table of income for a client's competitors, it showed figures to the nearest $100,000. Which doesn't sound bad, except the biggest competitor had almost $5 billion income – the table said it was $4,891.2m (that's five digits). The lowest income was $24.7m – which I believe is roughly $25m. The report also said average revenue in the industry was $999.7m for the top 10 players and $98.7m for players 11–20. The numbers would have had more impact if shown as $1,000m and $100m instead.
The acquisition's income per client	I've seen a board report for a £45m acquisition that showed annual income from each of the target's clients – and each client's income was shown to the nearest cent (and the clients were in alphabetical order). All a bit idiotic really.
Projections to the nearest pound	At least the numbers above were not projected figures but historic ones, so they were 'accurate'. For really spurious accuracy, you can't beat projections to the nearest pound. Preposterous.

How to round – variable rounding

The table in Figure 6.1 shows competitors' income figures ranging from £3.6bn to £23m. Columns A and B show the companies and their income figures to the nearest pound. Columns C to G show different ways to round the figures when showing them to the nearest million.

Let's look at each column in turn:

Column C: this shows figures to one decimal place (just like the investment bank report did) and for all companies we retain too many digits. The top two rows of column C show Briggs' and Davids' income as £3,623.1m and £1,092.2m. This is five digits – too many to easily do mental arithmetic, too many for the figures to be easily understood and remembered. With one decimal place, even the smallest company gives too much detail – Grahams' income is £22.9m. We don't need the extra accuracy from the third and final digit – after all, this is a summary table of competitor figures

FIGURE 6.1

Company	Income (£)	1 decimal place	No decimal place	Max 3 digits	2 digits	Variable rounding	Rounding error
			Showing to the nearest £m				
A	B	C	D	E	F	G	H = B to G
Briggs Ltd	3,623,145,794	3,623.1	3,623	3,620	3,600	3,600	0.6%
Davids Ltd	1,092,194,346	1,092.2	1,092	1,090	1,100	1,100	(0.7%)
Arms Inc	753,419,756	753.4	753	753	750	750	0.5%
Corey Pty	297,261,732	297.3	297	297	300	300	(0.9%)
Evering plc	123,759,456	123.8	124	124	**120**	124	(0.2%)
Fireshort Inc	115,643,179	115.6	116	116	**120**	116	(0.3%)
Harveys Ltd	45,055,067	45.1	45	45	45	45	0.1%
Grahams Inc	22,876,431	22.9	23	23	23	23	(0.5%)

(Column G annotations: Briggs Ltd to Corey Pty — 2 digits; Evering plc to Fireshort Inc — 3 digits; Harveys Ltd to Grahams Inc — 2 digits)

that merely gives a broad order of magnitude. Just saying £23m would have been sufficient.

Column D: this shows figures to no decimal places and is a little better. Grahams' income is now shown as £23m. Short, simple, easy to understand. But the big companies are still not right. Briggs and Davids are now shown as £3,623m and £1,092m, so, again, they retain too many digits.

Column E: like column D, column E shows figures to no decimal places but then shows a maximum of three digits and it's a bit better still – Briggs' income is now £3,620m, not £3,623m as in column D. However, we are still showing three digits, which is too many for most of us to do mental arithmetic. And do we need to know that Arms' income is £753m? Surely it would be sufficient just to say £750m?

Column F: this shows figures to two digits, and it's clearer for some figures, but introduces big rounding errors for others. Arms' income is now shown as £750m, not £753m, and Corey's as £300m, not £297m. We've made numbers easy to understand, remember and internalise. But study Evering's and Fireshort's income in column E: they are almost 10% different to each other, but when we show them to two digits in column F, they are shown as the same, £120m. It is an unacceptably large rounding error. (What is 'acceptable'? See later.)

So what should we do? Rounding to three digits retains too many digits. Rounding to two digits solves this problem but creates another – big rounding errors.

Column G: this is the answer, namely *variable* rounding. Some numbers are shown to two digits, except when big rounding errors creep in, in which case we show numbers to three digits.

Column H: this is the rounding error for the numbers in column G. The biggest error is less than 1%, which for a schedule of competitor income figures should certainly be acceptably small. I once read that rounding errors of up to 1 in 30 are acceptable. I don't know why it's 1-in-30 as opposed to say 1-in-50, but at least it puts a stake in the ground.

Finally, the mathematically minded will spot that these rounding errors aren't the maximum we could get from the numbers in column G – but we look at that soon.

(As an aside, we could view rounding another way – that is, we round numbers to two *effective* digits. 'Effective' digits are *those that vary within a data set*. For example, assume we had the following: 142, 153, 159, 168, 173, 187. The leading '1' is common to all, so isn't 'effective'. Hence, to do *effective* rounding, we would show all three digits. And we'd also show all three digits if we did *variable* rounding – showing two digits would give us 140, 150, 160, 170, 170, 190, which is too much rounding. Therefore, rounding to *effective digits* produces similar results to *variable* rounding.)

Now for a reality check. Getting Excel to variable-round is a bit tricky. It can be done, but needs some pretty weird formulae to do it, stuff that I don't understand but I can see works. See page 271.

Variable rounding in PowerPoint slides and Word documents is dead easy, though. In fact, it's easier than *not* rounding. It's easier to type '3,600' into a table than '3,623'. It's easier to type 'the income of our competitors ranges from £3.6bn to just £23m' than to type it as ranging 'from £3,623,145,794 to just £22,876,431'. It's easier for you when preparing the work, and it's easier for your audience when they see it. Variable rounding is great for showing numbers.

But variable rounding can cause people grief. This is discussed next.

When to round small numbers more than big numbers

This is a counter-intuitive oddity that warrants passing mention. To avoid rounding errors, sometimes round the bigger number more than the smaller number (Figure 6.2)

For example, you have a table that shows the percentage of calls in a call centre that were answered within the target time over a six-month period, e.g. in January, 83.72% of calls

FIGURE 6.2

Month	Result	Rounded
	%	%
Jan	83.72	84
Feb	88.21	88
Mar	91.56	92
Apr	94.83	95
May	98.16	98.1
June	99.22	99.2

▶

were within target time. In the right column of the table, we've rounded the smaller numbers more, e.g. 83.72% is rounded to 84%, whilst 99.22% is only rounded to 99.2%. This is because we are interested not in the number that the table shows but the *difference* between that number and 100%.

At 99.22%, the call centre was 0.78% short of perfect. If shown as 99%, it would seem one percentage point short, which is a rounding error of 28% (i.e. 1% is 28% more than 0.78%). This is an unacceptably large rounding error. And by the same logic, if 83.72% is shown as 84%, the rounding error is less than 2%, an acceptably small rounding error.

Here it is best to round small numbers more in order to avoid rounding errors.

(A way around this is for the table to show not the percentage of calls answered (98.1%), but the percentage *not* answered (1.9%). If showing clients how good your call centre is, you probably would want to 'accentuate the positive' and show the 98.1% figure. If negotiating bonuses with the call centre managers, you might wish to show the 1.9% figure.)

Dealing with objections to variable rounding

Rounding numbers – and in particular variable rounding – causes more grief on my courses than any other topic (I've even had people tell me it's illegal to round numbers – and that was for internal reports). Below I explore people's objections, and there is a pattern to them: people that object aren't the ones reviewing the numbers, they are ones preparing them. I've never had a manager or board director or client object to rounding. I think this is all we need to know.

The numbers aren't accurate	Welcome to the real world. Showing income as £3,623m isn't accurate, the real number is £3,623,145,794 – and a few pence. Yet even that isn't 'accurate' – all accounts include some pretty big estimates and provisions. The question is not: Should you present inaccurate numbers? It is: How inaccurate is acceptable?

Variable rounding is inconsistent

Surely rounding some figures to three digits and some to two is inconsistent in how we show numbers? Interesting, but wrong. Consider the biggest and smallest competitor figures we saw earlier and the rounding errors that arise if showing numbers to no decimal places. For a number shown as £3,623m, the maximum rounding error is about *140* parts in a million (when actual income is £3,622,500,001). The maximum rounding error for a figure shown as £23m is *22,000* parts in a million. That's a big difference. Showing to no decimal places produces very inconsistent maximum rounding errors.

With variable rounding, the maximum rounding error for a number shown as £3,600m is *14,000* parts in a million, which is substantially closer to the 22,000 parts in a million error for a £23m figure. Now that's more consistent.

There are two objections you do need to address: (1) 'the numbers look estimated' – a figure of £3,600m can look made up whilst £3,623m looks more definitive: and (2) 'the numbers won't add up'. So, when presenting numbers, head these off at the pass by putting a small note at the bottom:

Numbers rounded for greater clarity; small rounding differences may arise; exact numbers available.

It lets people know you're sacrificing accuracy for clarity, that you have *thought* about how to show the information rather than just regurgitating it blind. Does this caveat work? I presume so, because no one has ever accused me of making up my numbers, asked me for exact figures or banged on about figures not adding up.

And if the numbers don't add up in an internal report, *does it matter?* If we put a total figure in the income table (Figure 6.1), it would be £6bn, not £6,073,355,761. Yes, it wouldn't add up, but, again, clarity comes before accuracy. What do your managers really want from you – proof you can add numbers or information to run the business?

There are times when you shouldn't round and we look at these next.

Another benefit to rounding numbers: it hides errors

There is another benefit to rounding numbers I haven't yet mentioned: it helps hide your errors. Most spreadsheets that crunch routine monthly information are correct; they've been going so long, any errors have been ironed out. But if doing numbers for a project, most spreadsheets have glitches somewhere and these get spotted as the analysis progresses. If you report unrounded numbers, however, readers will spot that numbers have changed ('Hey, you're saying the result is £8.832m – previously you said it was £9.267m. What's changed?'). Your mistakes and errors may be rumbled. But if you show rounded numbers, the first projection said the result was £9m – and so did the second projection. Spreadsheet error? What spreadsheet error?

This tactic works for small errors. I once found a £400m error in the spreadsheet printout reproduced in a publicly circulated investment bank report – it overstated the share price by 40%. Errors that big are trickier to explain away. (I spotted it because I wanted to reuse the bank's spreadsheet model for something I was working on, but struggled to recreate it. Eventually I realised why – the £400m error. I often wonder if anyone else spotted it.)

When not to round

Don't round under the following circumstances (the first four are all from *A Primer in Data Reduction* by Professor Ehrenberg):

If dealing with small differences	If you were a foreign exchange dealer, you'd lose lots if you rounded.
If doing repeated multiplications	Don't round if in the middle of compound interest computations, otherwise large rounding errors accumulate. Do your computations, then round numbers when presenting them.
If you have a control check to make	If accountants round their numbers too soon, their trial balance won't balance. Make sure it balances first, then round the numbers afterwards when presenting.

If the numbers are to be used by others for analysis	People use the figures from the Office of National Statistics (ONS) to produce 'derived' numbers (e.g. they take the household and headcount figures to compute people per house). Because of this, the ONS can't show numbers that are too rounded otherwise it would render the derived numbers too inaccurate.
If you have an audit trail to follow in which case show both rounded and unrounded alongside each other	In a fraud report, I wanted readers to be able to cross-refer a lot. I wanted them to see that the figure in this section is the same as the one in the previous section but different to one in the section before that. Yet if I'd shown numbers rounded to the nearest thousand, all three would have been shown the same – £123k. So whenever I showed a table of numbers or a reconciliation, I always showed two columns: a rounded column for ease of understanding (£123k), and an unrounded column so readers could make correct cross-references between numbers ('Ah, I see, that £123,125.78 is not the same as the £123,104.32').
If you wish to confuse your audience	Rounded numbers are easier to grasp. If you don't wish your audience to grasp your numbers, leave in as many digits as you can.

That's all on rounding numbers. I will summarise fully at the end, but for now the message is: present rounded numbers – people can better understand and remember them.

The rest of the chapter looks at other problems when showing numbers, e.g. how to show numbers in text, problem percentages, and so on.

How to show numbers in text

Some of the 'rules' for showing numbers in text come down to personal preference and house style (e.g. is it £10m or £10mn or £10 million?). In the meantime, below are four quick principles that are more than just house style, they are best practice:

Write the number in full if ten or less	Example: we have six product lines. But if we had more, we'd have 12 product lines. Use numbers even if less than 11 when they are part of series, e.g. 'the scores were 15, 6, 2 and 11'. Or if a reference – see section 2, chapter 3 and version 4. Also it's different with percentages – unemployment is 5% rather than five per cent.
Don't start a sentence with a number	Don't say '12 days ago, they finished.' Either type out the number in full, 'Twelve days ago, they finished', or restructure the sentence to avoid the problem, e.g. 'They finished 12 days ago.'
Don't omit the leading zero in text	The exchange rate was 0.5 to the pound, not .5 to the pound. We received replies from just 0.8% of people, not .8%. There are exceptions to this – you shoot someone with a Colt .45, not a Colt 0.45.
How to show a range of numbers	'Income grew from £10m to £12m', *not* 'from £10m–£12m'. Also, 'the forecast income is £10m–£12m', *not* '£10–£12m'.

Problems showing percentages

Take care if computing variances between say 'actual' and 'budget' or 'actual and 'last year'. Firstly, readers get confused by percentage changes that are big (2,178%). Secondly, spreadsheets often get it wrong if one number is negative (e.g. what's the variance if profit was £2m but it's now a loss of £3m?).

Each is discussed in turn below.

Big percentage changes

Firstly, do a little test. Ask people to answer this quickly and without using a calculator: if a number goes from 100 to 350, what is the percentage change? I do this a lot, and often get given the wrong answer. The popular answer is 350%. The right answer is 250%.

I've seen this sort of error in a company's marketing brochure and in the final draft of a plc's statutory accounts. In both cases, the percentage increase was more than 100%.

It's because people struggle with large percentage increases. Assume a company achieved a decent profit after being near break-even (Figure 6.3). Trading profit has gone from £2m to £50m (columns A and B), which gives a computed percentage increase of 2,400% (column C) – and a percentage figure like that really doesn't mean much to many people. It confuses, not clarifies.

So don't make people struggle with such a number. Instead, do a variance like the one in column D – show it as

FIGURE 6.3

	Last yr	This yr	Incr/(decr)	
	A	B	C	D
	£m	£m	%	%
Income	1,000	1,100	10%	10%
Costs	(998)	(1,050)	5%	5%
Trading profit	2	50	2,400%	>99%

'>99%' (and if the figure was minus 133%, show it as ('<99%').)

This avoids cluttering up the page with nonsensical numbers. By putting '>99%', we are flagging to readers that the increase is a bit different to the others, it isn't a 'last year plus 5 or 10%' figure. And we aren't forcing our readers to grapple with 2,400%. Instead, they spot the flag ('>99%'), then refer to the actual figures and see the story instantly – profit has gone from £2m to £50m.

Getting Excel to compute percentage changes

It's easy to compute percentage variances, isn't it. It's just:

[(This Year)/(Last Year) minus 1] per cent

If 'This Year' is 110, and 'Last Year' is 100, then we get 10%. Simple.

OK, let's try another, this time with some negative figures. If last year's result was a £4m loss, and this year's was a £2m profit, the formula above gives a variance of minus 150%. Minus? But we improved the result in the year, didn't we?

And if 'Last Year' was nil because it's a new line of business, we get a nasty-looking '#DIV/0!'. Get a few of those on the page and it looks a mess.

And, of course, we've got problems if variances are greater than 100% or less than 100%. The Appendix shows 17 different variants of profit or loss changes (going up, down, staying the same, loss to profit, profit to loss, etc.), and the above formula gives a decent variance only 4 times out of 17. That's not a good hit rate.

Do you still think computing variances is easy?

I mention this in case you put variances into your Excel schedules – there are many pitfalls for the unwary. I've cracked it, but only with some horrible-looking Excel formulae (seven nested IF functions within a cell). That's in the Appendix too.

The next section looks at the problem of 'lonely numbers', numbers that have no friends.

Why numbers need friends

On their own, numbers are lost and aimless. The monthly 'Marketing Report' shows a pie chart of this month's marketing spend by activity, but it doesn't mean much unless readers can remember other numbers that give it context. What was the split by activity last month? What is the budget split? What do competitors spend by activity? And then there's the next level of analysis: how many leads does each activity generate? What sales come from those leads? Numbers need comparatives.

And don't assume people know the comparatives and context. The CEO of a big company told me his second biggest division would make a trading margin of 15%, and as I stood there thinking vainly of something intelligent to say, he said rhetorically, 'Mmm . . . is that good? I know, let's see what it made last year.'

Worse than lonely numbers are no numbers. An accountancy practice spoke to a company's management and sent me a report (we were looking to buy the company). The report had a section on client wins and losses over the past year, but didn't give a single figure – it just listed names of wins and losses. It didn't say whether a particular win was huge or tiny. What a pointless report.

When you mention numbers in reports, make sure you give them context.

Next is the chapter summary.

Final thoughts and recap

When I ask bank staff for my balance, they say the figure to the nearest pence: 'Your balance is one thousand, nine hundred and eighty-seven pounds and sixty-three pence.' I always get them to say the number twice because I can't work it out first time. I scribble it on a piece of paper, '1 . . . 9 . . . 8 . . . 7 . . . point . . . 63', then shorten it and finally understand. 'It's about two grand.' Rounding numbers helps in conversations too.

The final word on rounding goes to a friend of mine. A few years ago, he was asked his age in a job interview. He was 54 at the time, so somewhat sheepishly admitted, 'I have to confess, I am nearer 50 than 40'. That's one way to round, I suppose.

Next is the recap which includes a couple of new points we haven't seen before – how to show negative numbers.

Recap

Round your numbers	Sacrifice accuracy for clarity – unnecessarily long numbers are difficult to understand, remember and do sums with. Shorter numbers have greater impact and help readers engage with the data, not be intimidated by it.
How to round	Variable round for greatest clarity. Show some numbers to three digits, some to two. If doing a table of rounded numbers, warn readers with a comment at the bottom, e.g. 'Numbers rounded for greater clarity; small rounding differences may arise; exact numbers available.' See the Appendix for formulae to variably round in Excel.
When not to round	Don't round if doing control checks or repeated multiplications. Don't round if others need accurate numbers for their own number crunching. Don't round if dealing with small differences.

Numbers in text	Don't start sentences with a number. Write it out instead, or restructure the sentence. Also, the exchange is 0.5 to the pound, not .5 to the pound.
Percentage variances	Avoid showing big percentage changes (3,623%), they confuse. Take care if computing variances with numbers that go from positive to negative or vice versa – your variances can easily go wrong. The Appendix has an Excel formula that gives the right answers.
Put numbers in context	Numbers need friends if they are to make sense. I got a £5,000 bonus last year. Was I pleased or disappointed by it?
Negative numbers	Put negative numbers in brackets, not with a leading minus sign. It is all too easy to miss the minus sign or think it just a smudge or line on the page.

Never only signal a number as being negative by putting it in red. When the document is printed or copied into black and white, the number will incorrectly become positive.

Never have the minus sign way over on the left (Figure 6.4), a crazy formatting option that Excel offers and some people accept. It's all too easy to miss the minus sign and read the figure as positive.

FIGURE 6.4

-	1,903
-	1,845

Finally, if the document is important, consider shunting brackets on negative numbers slightly to the right – it ensures digits align properly in a column of numbers. The text box on page 110 gives an example whilst the Appendix gives the Excel formula that does the shunting.

Chapter **7**

··

Document design

Tips, principles and ideas for notes, reports, packs and slides

- ➤ Simple, accessible, easy-to-apply design principles for smarter documents
- ➤ Redos – a report front cover, a slide, a CV, a client meeting note and more
- ➤ Ideas and inspiration – for circulars, for reports in landscape and more
- ➤ Common formats that hinder readability
- ➤ Checklists for colour – should you use colour, and, if so, how?

Your scientists were so preoccupied with whether or not they could, they didn't stop to think if they should.

Jeff Goldblum, *Jurassic Park*

This chapter is for people that design documents – and that means *you*. When you prepare a note, report, slide or information pack, you *are* designing. There's not much difference between you and those creative people down the corridor who work on Apple Macs. Except they know how to do sharp-looking documents.

Which is a shame because you want your work to look elegant, you want to put your best foot forward. You've worked hard to collate numbers, do analysis, reach conclusions. But your final document seems a let-down – it doesn't look smart enough to do justice to your work. So you tinker. You try some bold here, a flash of red there, you justify some text. But to no avail. It still looks amateur, nowhere near as smart as other documents you've seen.

But what else can you do? You don't want to send your work to the design department for it to polish. You don't want to do a design course – you want sharper looking documents, not sit with creatives learning about posters. You don't want to learn fancy design software. All you want are simple design tips that work in Excel, Word or PowerPoint.

This chapter gives you just that. Instead of tinkering and making no difference, learn how to turn your documents into something to be proud of. Applying the tips needn't take long either. Later, you'll see how it takes just one minute to turn a bland front page of a report into something more professional – when you know how.

Learn how to transform the slide in Figure 7.1 into the one in Figure 7.2. The words are *exactly* the same on both slides, but the 'before' is amateur, the 'after' elegant and professional. Granted the redo uses 'WiT' (Chapter 1), but it does more than that, it *designs* the slide. And good design not only makes documents sharper, it also makes them *clearer*. Good design makes points visually lift from the page.

FIGURE 7.1

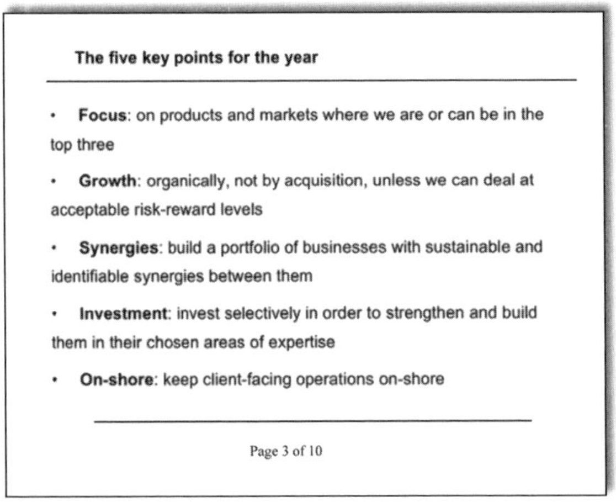

The five key points for the year

- **Focus**: on products and markets where we are or can be in the top three

- **Growth**: organically, not by acquisition, unless we can deal at acceptable risk-reward levels

- **Synergies**: build a portfolio of businesses with sustainable and identifiable synergies between them

- **Investment**: invest selectively in order to strengthen and build them in their chosen areas of expertise

- **On-shore**: keep client-facing operations on-shore

Page 3 of 10

In this chapter, we see four design principles and apply them to several common but uninspiring documents. It's fun and eye-popping stuff because, when we redo them, the change is *dramatic*. We also see ideas for your documents – different front covers, different headings, ideas for landscape reports. Dip into them for inspiration.

There are typographical tips such as which font to use when, and when to justify and when not to. OK, it doesn't

FIGURE 7.2

> ## The five key points for the year
>
> | | |
> |---|---|
> | **Focus** | On products and markets where we are or can be in the top three |
> | **Growth** | Organically, not by acquisition, unless we can deal at acceptable risk-reward levels |
> | **Synergies** | Build a portfolio of businesses with sustainable and identifiable synergies between them |
> | **Investment** | Invest selectively in order to strengthen and build them in their chosen areas of expertise |
> | **On-shore** | Keep client-facing operations on-shore |
>
> Page 3 of 10

sound sexy but they are important – many documents are hard to read because the writer doesn't know these details.

We also look at colour and at in-house templates and style guides. Firstly, though, here are some thoughts and caveats:

This chapter is just a brief introduction	Design and typography are big topics – and some people might think a little learning is dangerous. If flying planes or building bridges, I'd agree. But for design, a little learning is incredibly empowering.
This chapter is not breaking new ground	More than for any other chapter, this one's a collection of well-known principles or other people's ideas. In particular I am indebted to Robin Williams, the American designer. It's her four principles I talk about and examples I adopt and adapt. See the Bibliography for more details.
Design isn't a panacea	It makes a well-written document even better but won't make a badly written document good (though it might at first sight seem like it has done).
Design 'rules' often get broken	There's lots of well-designed work that doesn't follow the tips and principles in this chapter – experts know when it's OK to break 'rules'. Also, design is an art, not a science, and not all designers will agree with everything here anyway.

You may need to learn a new Microsoft trick or two	On the whole, though, most tips aren't hard to do. If something is tricky, the person at the next desk should be able to help. Or try the IT department. Don't do any 'Advanced Computing' courses just yet, though – first find out what you should do, then afterwards think about how to do it on a PC.
You may want to change work practices	You'll probably realise you need to think of design at the planning and writing stage and not leave it as a last-minute tarting-up exercise. OK, if you leave it until then, you will probably get by – but you create a lot of extra work.

Let's start. We need to quickly review three typographical topics before we can get into the four design principles. Firstly, we review fonts.

Which fonts to use when

Let's define terms. For most day-to-day purposes there are two main categories of typeface: serif and sans serif. For those unfamiliar with these two categories, the table below gives details. Note that Arial is a typeface, a family of fonts, whilst 'Arial Black, 10 points' is a font.

Serif typeface S	These are typefaces like Times New Roman or CG Times. They are traditional looking with thick and thin bits (that's how quill pens wrote them) and squiggly bits. The 'serif' is actually the bit at the end of the letter, its 'tail'.
Sans serif typeface Arial	These are typefaces like Arial. 'Sans' is French for 'without' – so there aren't any tails at the end. There are no thick or thin bits, they are *monoweight*.

There is a popular myth that serif typefaces like Times New Roman are awful, traditional, dull. Not true. As the table below explains, Times New Roman is readable and good for continuous text, Arial is legible and good for glancing at.

Typeface	Its strength	When best to use	Example
Serif, e.g. Times New Roman – like this one	Readable	**Continuous text** Best to avoid for bullet point text on slides.*	Look for it in books and newspapers.
Sans serif, e.g. Arial – like this one	Legible	Text that will be glanced at, e.g. report **headings and subheadings**, graph labels and titles, table labels and data.†	Look for it on estate agents' boards and road signs.

* This may be why some people hate Times New Roman. They see it on a slide and rightly hate it, but incorrectly assume that Times New Roman is always bad. It isn't – it's bad on a slide.
† Sans serif can work for continuous text – look for it in magazines. Keep line lengths short, though, and have few typographical tricks, e.g. not too much bold etc.

If unconvinced that Times New Roman is easier to read, dummy up a page of text in Arial and again in Times New Roman, then compare. The page in Arial may look like it should be easier to read as there are less twiddly bits to fight past. But try it – you should find the Times New Roman page easier. If wondering why this book's continuous text is a sans serif typeface, I can't fully explain it, other than to say it's the publisher's design.

Finally, avoid more than two typefaces on a page unless you know what you're doing and have studied design and typography in detail (I haven't). With three different typefaces, two are probably either sans serif or serif – and similar typefaces can set up a conflict and look unprofessional. Also, readers might think two similar but different typefaces is an accident, not a design.

The next section is the first round of typographical tips and are on line length and white space. Then we will be ready to get into the four principles.

Quick and effective typographical tips, part 1

Two quick tips: avoid long lines of text, and use and create white space. Each is explained further in the table:

Avoid long lines of text: this is a long line of text (way more than the optimum 12 words width) and the eye gets weary going all the way along it – and on reaching the end eventually, the eye takes too long to flick back to the start. Also, it is easy to lose one's place and have the eye track all the way back to the start of the wrong line. The most common offenders of text width that is too wide are the 'consultancy' type reports done in landscape. They have notes at the bottom of the page or slide that stretch all the way across the landscape width . . . like this.

Avoid long lines of text

Long lines of text are difficult to read, the eye gets weary chuntering along them, then loses its place when making the long journey back to the start of the next line. The optimum width of text is 70 characters (i.e. about 12 words). Except if on a computer screen, when it is about 50 characters. Or in a reference manual when it is about 40 (from *Dynamics of Document Design*, page 263).

Newspapers lay out text in columns. Try it for a one-page note, or maybe selectively for some pages in your reports. It has three advantages. It's visually different, which helps maintain reader interest. It gets closer to optimum text width. And it introduces white space down the middle of the page – which is the next point we look at.

Use and create white space

White space creates visual interest and helps things stand out. See how the note on the left halfway down really stands out, even though it is not bold, underlined, nor even a big font size. But it has lots of white space around it.

Also known as 'blank space'

Beginners fear white space. Experienced designers love it, and they know it's not how much white space there is, it's how you use it. Soon we'll see a great example of this.

In the meantime, an easy tip is: don't take your words right to the paper's edge, it looks awful. Leave a margin round the outside.

We're now ready to move on to the four principles. It's a long section, but it's fun. We apply the principles to several typical but uninspiring documents and see how easy it is to make dramatic improvements.

Introducing the four principles

The principles are contrast, repetition, alignment and proximity. When Robin Williams coined them in the 1990s, she noted they create an interesting acronym.

FIGURE 7.3

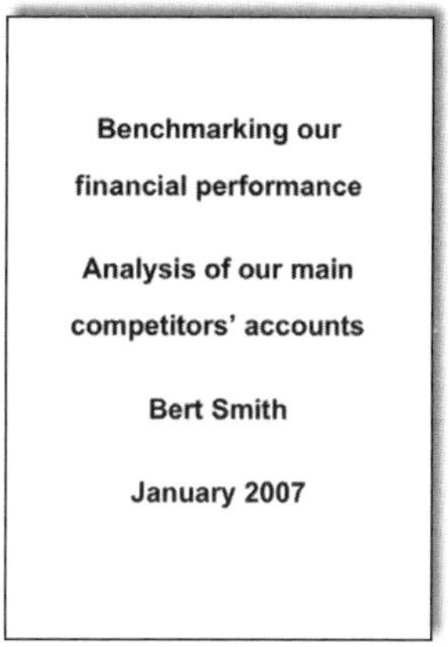

Benchmarking our

financial performance

Analysis of our main

competitors' accounts

Bert Smith

January 2007

FIGURE 7.4

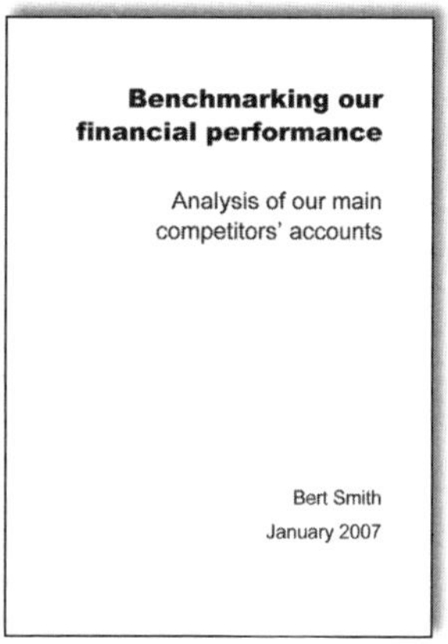

Benchmarking our financial performance

Analysis of our main competitors' accounts

Bert Smith
January 2007

Firstly, let's see three of the four in action for a typical front page of an internal benchmarking report (Figure 7.3). The layout is bland, a bit like a school project by a student. In Figure 7.4, we've redone it and it is far more professional looking. It has better contrast, alignment and proximity, each of which is explained in detail below.

Also, notice the white space. Both pages have similar amounts, but the redone version uses it better. It's not how much white space you have, it's how you use it. Figure 7.3 uses it badly, it's broken up. It's in places it shouldn't be, like between the first and second lines. When white space is 'trapped' like this, it tends to visually push elements apart, even when you don't want them apart.

Redoing the page took less than one minute. Sometimes, smartening documents can be that quick and easy when you know how.

The first principle is contrast, and it is gloriously simple to do.

Principle 1: Contrast

Create typographical contrast in your work, it makes a page look visually interesting and helps readers see the hierarchy of a report and navigate around documents easily.

Below are four different headings for the speech from *Hamlet*. Version 1 is Times New Roman in bold and in the same size as the text beneath it (font size 7) – and it looks weak, timid, diffident. Times New Roman doesn't do good 'bold'. Version 2 is Arial in bold (and again the same font size as the text). It's a bit better but still lacks impact and confidence. Beginners do this with headings – a bit of bold, and that's it.

Version 1	Version 2	Version 3	Version 4
Poor Yorick	**Poor Yorick**	**Poor Yorick**	**Poor Yorick**
Alas, poor Yorick! I knew him, Horatio: a fellow of infinite jest, of most excellent fancy: he hath borne me on his back a thousand times; and now, how abhorred in my imagination it is!	Alas, poor Yorick! I knew him, Horatio: a fellow of infinite jest, of most excellent fancy: he hath borne me on his back a thousand times; and now, how abhorred in my imagination it is!	Alas, poor Yorick! I knew him, Horatio: a fellow of infinite jest, of most excellent fancy: he hath borne me on his back a thousand times; and now, how abhorred in my imagination it is!	Alas, poor Yorick! I knew him, Horatio: a fellow of infinite jest, of most excellent fancy: he hath borne me on his back a thousand times; and now, how abhorred in my imagination it is!

Version 3 is Arial in bold, font size 8.5. Having headings a couple of points bigger helps lift them visually. It's pretty good. Version 4 is font size 9 and Arial Black, a typeface that has strength, impact (and it isn't even emboldened, it doesn't need to be). It gives the heading even more contrast – this helps readers navigate and makes the page look more arresting. It's that easy.

The next principle is repetition, something many people have a passing familiarity with.

What word dominates the page in your information pack?

In many internal information packs, the biggest word on each page is the company name: **Smithers Group plc** sits proudly astride each page in big letters that have lots of white space around them and are easy to see.

Yet readers know this anyway, since the entire pack is Smithers Group plc. But the description of each page is in a smaller font, fighting for attention with lots of other words nearby such as 'April 2007', 'monthly information pack', 'private and confidential', 'final version' and so on. Again, most of this other stuff is known and common to all pages in the pack. Finally, hidden deep amongst this stuff, readers eventually see what they are looking for – the description of the page: 'staff turnover: cumulative to date'. At last, readers know where they are.

Help readers quickly navigate around the report. Make the biggest words on the page: '**staff turnover: cumulative to date**'. Contrast. It helps people navigate.

Principle 2: Repetition

Use typography and design to make all parts of your documents look unified and coherent and to help readers more easily navigate the document.

Firstly, let's look at *consistency*. Most people realise a document should be typographically consistent – all headings should look like other headings, all subheadings should look like all other subheadings. Most of us know this helps readers – just by glancing at a page, the typography indicates to readers the level of importance of the text they are reading (a heading, a subheading, a text box, etc). I've read that documents are similar to a road map in a car – people need the symbols on the map to be consistent if they are to read the map accurately and get to the right place quickly.

However, this consistency often breaks down with management accounts or KPI packs. Typographically, each page of the pack looks different to the rest. Different typefaces and font sizes, different looks to the graphs, page numbers in different places on the page, and so on. The pack looks like it was prepared by six different people – and that's because it probably was. It seems thrown together, incoherent, amateur.

If you make all the pages consistent, the pack will *start* to look professional, unified. But it is only a start – consistency is not enough. We've all seen reports where the typist has diligently made the headings the same, the subheadings the same, and so on. Yes, it is consistent. No, it isn't smart looking. It still looks bland, uninspiring.

What helps is *repetition*. Repetition is *actively* looking for elements of design that will help create a unified look. It could be an alignment of the text, a heavy line at the top, a strong font for headings, a flash down the side, or whatever – something that doesn't just ensure consistency but *creates* repetition. Look out for repetition in newspapers, magazines, annual reports.

We'll see examples of repetition later.

Meanwhile, after contrast and repetition, we have alignment (C–R–A – yup, that figures). And it's the longest subsection of the four principles because here the devil is in the detail. But when you get the alignment just right, your work will really start coming together.

Principle 3: Alignment

Line up the constituent parts of a page properly, both horizontally and vertically. It helps make reports, notes and slides look sharp and tight.

There are many different parts to a page: the header, the rule under it, the text, the graphs and tables, the rule at the bottom, the page number and so on. In many documents they are thrown around the page haphazardly and it looks messy. Instead, align items horizontally and vertically.

The page shown in Figure 7.5 has tight alignment and looks sharp. It's aligned down the right and in the middle. (Arguably, vertical alignment

FIGURE 7.5

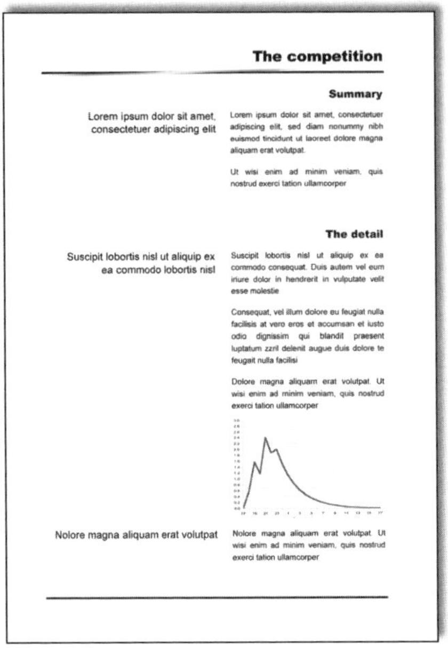

might be even tighter if the words in bold were not right aligned but left aligned in line with the left edge of the main text.) And, horizontally, each pull quote on the left is aligned with the start of the related text on the right.

Study the one-page notes done by investment banks on a company's year-end results, they have very strong alignment and look smart.

Next are five small examples of vertical and horizontal alignment. In each case, getting proper alignment won't make much difference. Collectively, it will make a big difference to the look of the page.

Vertical alignment

Align the edges of your Word tables

FIGURE 7.6

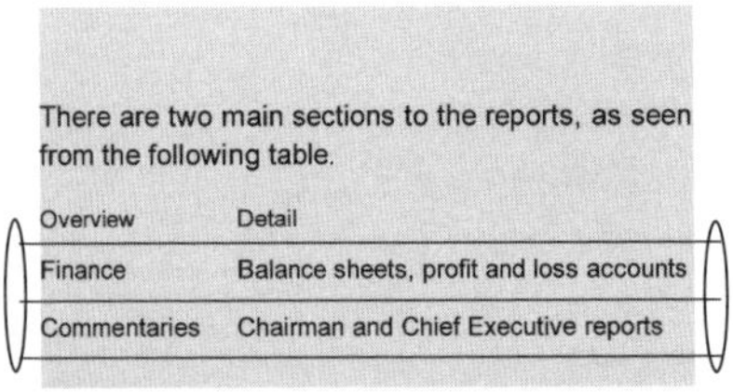

FIGURE 7.7

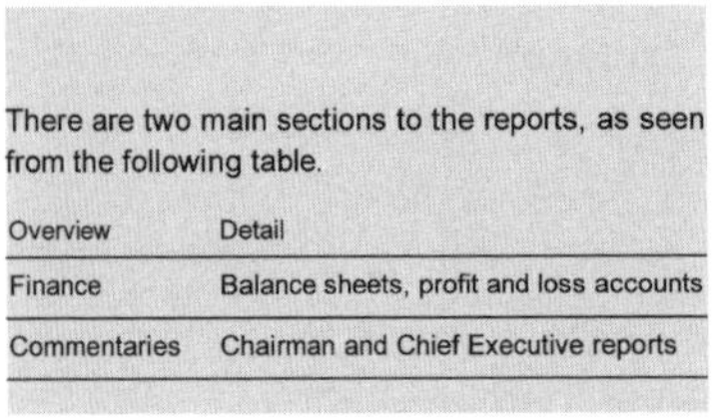

As a default, Microsoft Word horizontally extends its tables' gridlines beyond the text boundary. The shaded area in Figures 7.6 and 7.7 represents that boundary, and in Figure 7.6 the horizontal grid goes beyond it. The left and right edges of the grid don't align with the text in the table nor with the introductory text and heading above it. It looks a bit untidy.

In Figure 7.7, we've used the indent markers at the top of the Word screen to get a better vertical alignment. It looks sharper. Obviously, doing this would look bad if we had vertical grids, since the left-aligned words would butt against them.

But why would you want vertical grids?

Align numbers too

Microsoft Word does the same for numbers too (Figure 7.8). Again, correct them using the tab markers at the top of the screen (Figure 7.9).

FIGURE 7.8

North	110
South	20
Total	130

FIGURE 7.9

North	110
South	20
Total	130

I haven't worked out how to do this in Excel, though – it leaves a small gap between the left or right edge of a cell and its contents.

Align quote marks and full stops
This is known as 'hanging the punctuation'

(This is getting detailed, but if you've a lot of quotes in, say, a market research report, this helps make it look professional.)

"In this paragraph, the opening quote marks misalign the first letter on line 1 with the first letters on lines 2 and 3, and so on"

"But with these quote marks, we've slightly indented them so as to retain alignment of the first letters of each line. Much better"

"Also, if a perfectionist, align closing quote marks for right-aligned text. Like this"

Do it with full stops too, like this paragraph. But aligning the stops and closing quotes is tricky in Word because you have to *force* a line break before the last line.

Horizontal alignment

Align tops of columns of text

Unaligned column tops look careless – see Figure 7.10 below.

FIGURE 7.10

Lorem ipsum dolor sit amet, consectetuer adipiscing elit, sed diam nonummy nibh euismod tincidunt ut laoreet dolore magna aliquam erat volutpat. Ut wisi enim ad minim veniam, quis nostrud exerci tation.

Duis autem vel eum iriure dolor in hendrerit in vulputate velit esse molestie consequat, vel illum dolore eu feugiat nulla facilisis at vero eros et accumsan et iusto odio dignissim qui blandit praesent.

Align labels in tables

FIGURE 7.11

	East	South West	Total
Product A	10	30	40
Product B	20	20	40
Total	30	50	80

FIGURE 7.12

	East	South West	Total
Product A	10	30	40
Product B	20	20	40
Total	30	50	80

In Figure 7.11 below, labels along the top are vertically top aligned, so the words 'East' and 'Total' are somewhat strangely dangling in space a bit above the gridline. It looks weird. In Figure 7.12, labels are bottom aligned, there are no weird spaces. All labels sit nicely just above the border beneath them. Much better. (To do this in Word, shade the cells you wish to align with the bottom of the row, select 'Table', 'Properties', 'Cell', then 'Bottom'.)

Many routine business documents are poorly aligned, when, with just a bit of effort, they can be aligned tighter than a snare drum and look much better for it.

Time for the last of the four principles: proximity. We've come across it briefly before, when it created the 'trapped' white space on the report front cover (Figure 7.3).

Where jargons clash — computing meets design

You get *horizontal* alignment by moving things *vertically* on your computer. Look at the last example above that says 'Align labels in tables'. In Figure 7.12, the words 'East', 'West' and 'Total' are aligned along an imaginary *horizontal* line – they are *horizontally* aligned. But to do this, we got the computer to align the words vertically within the table's cells. In fact, if the table had been in Excel, our computer instructions would have been: 'Format', 'Cells', '*Vertical*', 'Bottom'. Which pretty much spells it out. You horizontally align items by moving them vertically.

Principle 4: Proximity

Typographically cluster related items together and separate unrelated items to help create visual distinctions between parts of a page. It helps readers see structure and gives them 'breathing space' when reading.

Many documents, especially slides, have poor proximity between items – the typographical clustering is poorly done. In Figures 7.13 and 7.14, each page has a heading, then two bullets, then another heading, then two more bullets.

That's the logic, but in Figure 7.13 the spacing doesn't reinforce that logic. The proximity is poor. The gap between lines is about the same as the gap between bullets and the gap between sections. They all run into one.

These equal gaps give incorrect signals to readers – a new section is a new idea, a new start, so the page needs a decent break between sections. Also, each bullet is a new thought, albeit linked by

FIGURE 7.13

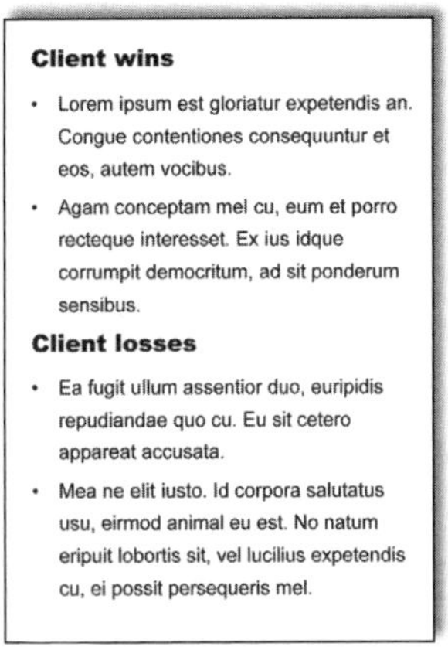

Client wins

- Lorem ipsum est gloriatur expetendis an. Congue contentiones consequuntur et eos, autem vocibus.
- Agam conceptam mel cu, eum et porro recteque interesset. Ex ius idque corrumpit democritum, ad sit ponderum sensibus.

Client losses

- Ea fugit ullum assentior duo, euripidis repudiandae quo cu. Eu sit cetero appareat accusata.
- Mea ne elit iusto. Id corpora salutatus usu, eirmod animal eu est. No natum eripuit lobortis sit, vel lucilius expetendis cu, ei possit persequeris mel.

FIGURE 7.14

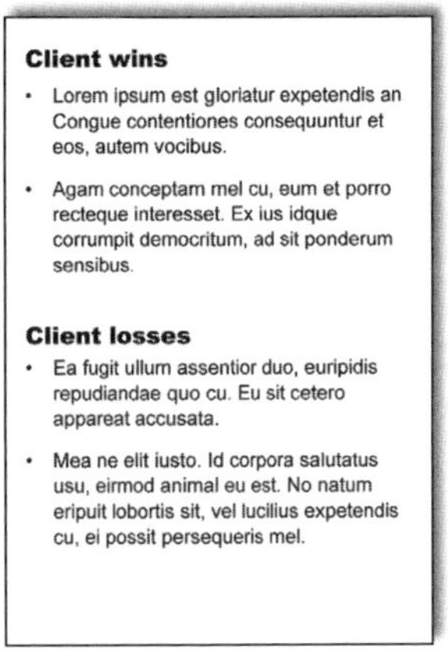

Client wins

- Lorem ipsum est gloriatur expetendis an Congue contentiones consequuntur et eos, autem vocibus.
- Agam conceptam mel cu, eum et porro recteque interesset. Ex ius idque corrumpit democritum, ad sit ponderum sensibus.

Client losses

- Ea fugit ullum assentior duo, euripidis repudiandae quo cu. Eu sit cetero appareat accusata.
- Mea ne elit iusto. Id corpora salutatus usu, eirmod animal eu est. No natum eripuit lobortis sit, vel lucilius expetendis cu, ei possit persequeris mel.

association with its other bullet, so we need a gap between bullets too, albeit slightly smaller than the one between sections. All these gaps are like the pauses by presenters just before starting a new slide – they give the audience breathing space and signal to readers that something new is on its way. And without these pauses readers get no respite, no rest from the seemingly continuous outpouring of text until they reach the bottom of the last bullet point.

Figure 7.14 correctly gives these typographical cues. It has good proximity.

Let's see how the four principles can make a huge difference to three routine documents: a PowerPoint slide, a CV and a client meeting note.

Applying the principles: slides, CVs, meeting notes

A PowerPoint slide

Figures 7.15 and 7.16 are the PowerPoint slides we saw at the start of the chapter. When you saw them earlier, you could see Figure 7.16 was better but, I suspect, you couldn't put your finger on why. You didn't have the vocabulary or design concepts to express why – which means you wouldn't have known how to do a similar page.

FIGURE 7.15

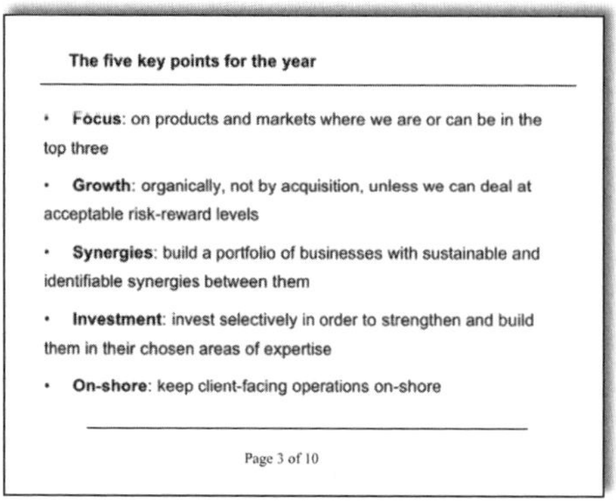

The five key points for the year

- **Focus**: on products and markets where we are or can be in the top three
- **Growth**: organically, not by acquisition, unless we can deal at acceptable risk-reward levels
- **Synergies**: build a portfolio of businesses with sustainable and identifiable synergies between them
- **Investment**: invest selectively in order to strengthen and build them in their chosen areas of expertise
- **On-shore**: keep client-facing operations on-shore

Page 3 of 10

FIGURE 7.16

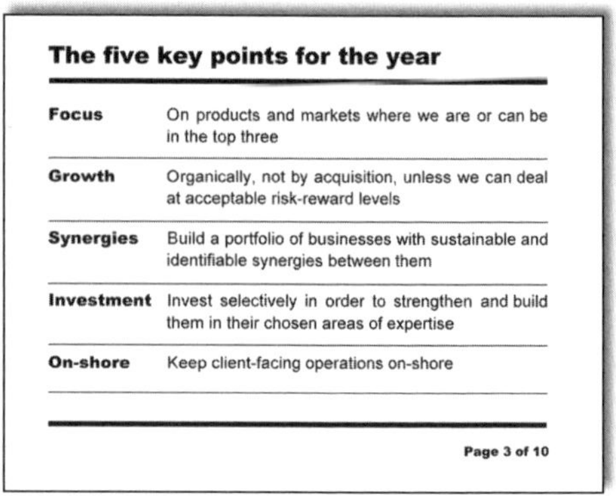

The five key points for the year

Focus	On products and markets where we are or can be in the top three
Growth	Organically, not by acquisition, unless we can deal at acceptable risk-reward levels
Synergies	Build a portfolio of businesses with sustainable and identifiable synergies between them
Investment	Invest selectively in order to strengthen and build them in their chosen areas of expertise
On-shore	Keep client-facing operations on-shore

Page 3 of 10

Now you know why it's better. It has contrast, repetition, alignment and proximity. Study the poor proximity in Figure 7.15 – the gap between lines is similar to the gap between paragraphs. (Also note how the redone version is another example of 'WiT'.)

And you now know how to redo a similar page – like the CV that follows next.

A curriculum vitae

Figure 7.17 is a typical-looking CV. Its author has tried to tart it up – a bit of underlining and the like, but it's dull, uninspiring and looks amateurish. (It could have been worse – it could have been done in 'monospaced' typefaces `like Courier which make the text look like it was done on a typewriter.`)

Now see Figure 7.18 – and here we haven't even done 'WiT'. Much is the same as before. All the words are the same as before. For the continuous text, the typefaces and font sizes are as before. Both pages have the same items in bold, albeit the right version drops the underlines and we've got rid of the bullet points. But the right version looks completely different – and you now know why, don't you? It's got contrast, repetition, alignment and proximity. It has impact and makes the person look more professional. (And its design is cribbed from *The Non-Designer's Design Book*, page 57.)

It again illustrates that it's not how much white space you have, it's how you use it. The two versions have almost identical amounts of white space (the redo actually has slightly less because its bold items are bigger), but the redo looks so much more airy, less cramped. It must surely be a miracle of design.

FIGURE 7.17   **FIGURE 7.18**

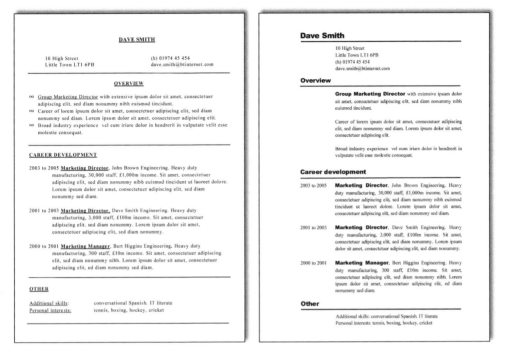

Before anyone says it, a good CV is of course not just about positions, it's about achievements. Also, in Chapter 1, didn't I suggest doing the career history bit of a CV as a 'WIT'? To see a CV that uses the four design principles *and* has 'WIT', visit www.jmoon.co.uk and click on 'Downloads'. It's in Microsoft Word too, so you can download and adopt and adapt it.

A client meeting note

Figure 7.19 shows a client meeting note (minutes of a meeting, if you prefer), the sort of note that gets typed up, then sent to the client for review, signature and return to confirm that it agrees with the note.

It looks amateurish. The page is redone in Figure 7.20 and looks much better.

Firstly, there is now contrast. The heading and the line under it are visually more interesting, more confident and bold.

Secondly, there is much better alignment. In the first version, bits of the page are all over the place – the date and time of meeting are on the right at the top, the page numbering is centred at the bottom, as is the verbose disclaimer/request at the bottom. In the redo, alignment is tight. Study the right alignment of the 'Action' column and the left alignment of the numbers in the left column. The text in the 'Subject' column is justified to

FIGURE 7.19

Client meeting note

Record of meeting with	Multiconglomerate plc	
Held at	Multi Offices, Huddersfield	8 March 2007 at 10.30am
Attending from client	Fred Smith	
ABC personnel	Dave Jones, Fred Brown	
Purpose of Meeting	Catch up and golf	

	Subject	Action
1	In respect of the potential financial claim, Lorem ipsum dolor sit amet, consectetuer adipiscing elit, sed diam nonummy nibh euismod tincidunt ut laoreet dolore magna aliquam erat volutpat. Ut wisi enim ad minim veniam, quis nostrud exerci tation ullamcorper suscipit lobortis nisl ut aliquip ex ea commodo consequat.	
2	The renewal questionnaire was discussed and ut wisi enim ad minim veniam, quis nostrud exerci tation ullamcorper suscipit lobortis nisl ut aliquip ex ea commodo consequat. Duis autem vel eum iriure dolor in hendrerit in vulputate velit esse molestie consequat, vel illum.	ABC
	2.1 Lorem ipsum dolor sit amet of the main site disposal, consectetuer adipiscing elit, sed diam nonummy nibh euismod tincidunt ut laoreet dolore magna aliquam erat volutpat.	ABC
	2.2 Ut wisi enim no incidents to notify, ad minim veniam, quis nostrud exerci tation ullamcorper suscipit lobortis nisl ut aliquip ex ea commodo consequat. Duis autem vel eum iriure dolor in hendrerit in vulputate velit esse molestie consequat, vel illum.	FS
3	"Lorem ipsum dolor of the flood cover sit amet, consectetuer adipiscing elit, sed diam nonummy nibh euismod tincidunt ut laoreet dolore."	ABC
4	Regarding other insured risks, lorem ipsum dolor sit amet of the renewal terms and options, consectetuer adipiscing elit, sed diam nonummy nibh euismod tincidunt ut laoreet dolore magna aliquam erat volutpat. Ut wisi enim ad minim veniam, quis nostrud exerci tation ullamcorper suscipit lobortis nisl ut aliquip ex.	DJ
5	"Lorem ipsum dolor sit amet of environmental liability, consectetuer adipiscing elit, sed diam nonummy nibh euismod tincidunt ut laoreet dolore magna aliquam erat volutpat."	
6	"Lorem ipsum dolor sit amet on the terrorist cover, consectetuer adipiscing elit, sed diam nonummy nibh euismod tincidunt ut laoreet dolore magna aliquam erat volutpat."	

Signed ....
F Smith
9 March 2007

Page 1 of 1

We Believe this Document Accurately Records the Points Discussed at our Meeting and We will Proceed Accordingly Unless We Hear from you to the Contrary Within the Next 7 days.

FIGURE 7.20

Multiconglomerate plc

Client meeting note

Multi Offices, Huddersfield, 8 March 2007 at 10.30 am

Person(s) seen: Fred Smith

ABC personnel: Dave Jones, Fred Brown

Meeting objective: catch-up and golf

	Topic	Subject	Action
1	**Potential financial loss claim** (notified approximately twelve months ago)	Lorem ipsum dolor sit amet, consectetuer adipiscing elit, sed diam nonummy nibh euismod tincidunt ut laoreet dolore magna aliquam erat volutpat. Ut wisi enim ad minim veniam, quis nostrud exerci tation ullamcorper suscipit lobortis nisl ut aliquip ex ea commodo consequat.	
2	**Renewal questionnaire**	Ut wisi enim ad minim veniam, quis nostrud exerci tation ullamcorper suscipit lobortis nisl ut aliquip ex ea commodo consequat. Duis autem vel eum iriure dolor in hendrerit in vulputate velit esse molestie consequat, vel illum.	ABC
2.1	*Main site disposed of*	Lorem ipsum dolor sit amet, consectetuer adipiscing elit, sed diam nonummy nibh euismod tincidunt ut laoreet dolore magna aliquam erat volutpat.	ABC
2.2	*No incidents to notify*	Ut wisi enim ad minim veniam, quis nostrud exerci tation ullamcorper suscipit lobortis nisl ut aliquip ex ea commodo consequat. Duis autem vel eum iriure dolor in hendrerit in vulputate velit esse molestie consequat, vel illum.	FS
3	**Flood cover**	"Lorem ipsum dolor sit amet, consectetuer adipiscing elit, sed diam nonummy nibh euismod tincidunt ut laoreet dolore."	ABC
4	**Other uninsured risks**	Lorem ipsum dolor sit amet, consectetuer adipiscing elit, sed diam nonummy nibh euismod tincidunt ut laoreet dolore magna aliquam erat volutpat. Ut wisi enim ad minim veniam, quis nostrud exerci tation ullamcorper suscipit lobortis nisl ut aliquip ex.	DJ
5	**Environmental liability**	"Lorem ipsum dolor sit amet, consectetuer adipiscing elit, sed diam nonummy nibh euismod tincidunt ut laoreet dolore magna aliquam erat volutpat."	
6	**Terrorist cover**	"Lorem ipsum dolor sit amet, consectetuer adipiscing elit, sed diam nonummy nibh euismod tincidunt ut laoreet dolore magna aliquam erat volutpat."	

Signed ....

F Smith, 9 March 2007

Please check and confirm correct, we'll start actioning this in 7 days further strengthen alignment (albeit with a trade-off in readability, as we will soon see). The bits at the bottom are left aligned ('Signed', 'Please check, etc'.). Even the quote marks in sections 3, 5 and 6 have been indented slightly.

Also, there is repetition – the thick line at the top is at the bottom too.

Proximity has been improved. The meeting details are all clustered together at the top more effectively than before.

Also, note two other points. Firstly, section headings are Arial (legible) but continuous text is Times New Roman (readable). Secondly, the page has been put as 'WiT'.

There is a postscript to this example. It's actually based on a redo I did as a quick favour for a friend. It took me just 30 minutes, and his company then approved and adopted it in six city-based offices in the UK. Which shows that it doesn't take long to smarten a document when you know how.

We've now seen the four principles and are in a better position to correct any poor design and typography. But sometimes getting a document right is not about correcting what's there but about adding something that isn't. Documents sometimes look uninspiring simply because people can't think of what else to do. People don't have *ideas*.

This is next – ideas to add to your toolkit when working on documents.

Ideas for your documents

If looking for inspiration for your documents, see if any of these meet your needs. The first few apply to any document: newsletters, reports, slides, and so on. After that, there are ideas for particular documents, e.g. reports done in landscape.

Some ideas take more time and effort to do, e.g. pull quotes. For certain documents, though, it is still surely worth doing them, e.g. for client pitches or widely distributed reports or ones that go to senior people or regular reports. Also, if good design means people are more likely to read and remember the document, then it's worth it.

For any document

Front cover For one idea for the front cover, see the one we redid on page 199. Also, see Figure 7.21 – it's another possible layout. It has contrast, alignment, proximity. Note the grey font for the words 'For business people' – it's to create a bit of visual interest, to make the page look less black and white. Note also the big capital D at the top – it's something different (albeit it's also the sort of trick that comes and goes in design fashion). Finally, all text has been shunted slightly to the right so it's not just a simple left alignment. The line down the left helps emphasise this.

FIGURE 7.21

These ideas are simple, quick and easy. There are fancier covers that can be done, ones with client logos (cor!) and fancy colours (double cor!). We discuss these later.

'Pull quotes' 'Pull quotes' are important statements within the text that are shown again separately for further emphasis. To do them, align the main report down the right and have the pull quotes down the left (Figure 7.22). This creates both white space and narrower columns of text that are easier to read.

FIGURE 7.22

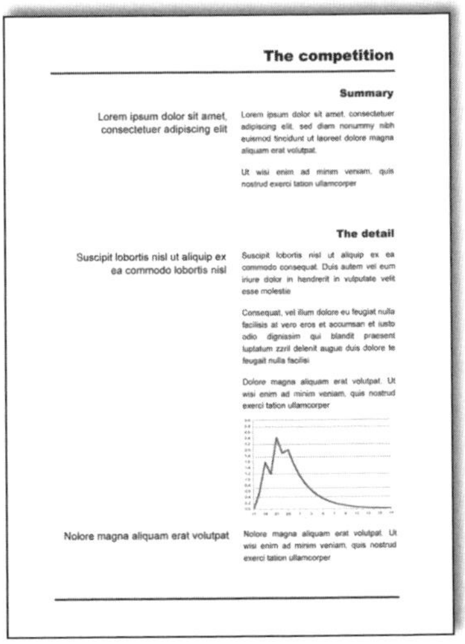

Section headings

As well as giving your headings contrast, there are other ways of doing them, of ringing the changes. Figure 7.23 shows a few simple ideas.*

FIGURE 7.23

The toy market	2.9
The toy market	2.9
The toy market	2.9
The toy market	2.9
The toy market	2.9

Note how the section number is on the right – this is to help readers find the page. Most reports have the section number tucked in by the binding, either on the left for a portrait report or at the top of a landscape report. It's not easy to find. Compare these to the Telephone Directory, which puts its index in a much easier to find place – on the right side of the right page and the left side of the left page.

* The computing bit
The first four headings were done as tables in Word (the first three are two columns wide, the fourth is three columns). However, if you use the 'style' features in Word, doing headings in tables can create extra work. The last one was done with a text box laid over a table.

'WiT'

Remember that 'WiT' is a great way to lay out documents. See Chapter 1.

For particular documents

Landscape reports

Consultancies and investment banks often do reports in landscape (Figure 7.24) which they then hand out and 'talk to' around a table of managers. The reports are rather smart looking (albeit they have their critics – see text box below). Here are ideas for their design.

Firstly, have a title that concludes ('Australia is best market to enter'), not merely introductory ('Review of markets we could enter'). Also, in the main part of the page, try writing text – you don't have to do pidgin English bullet points.

FIGURE 7.24

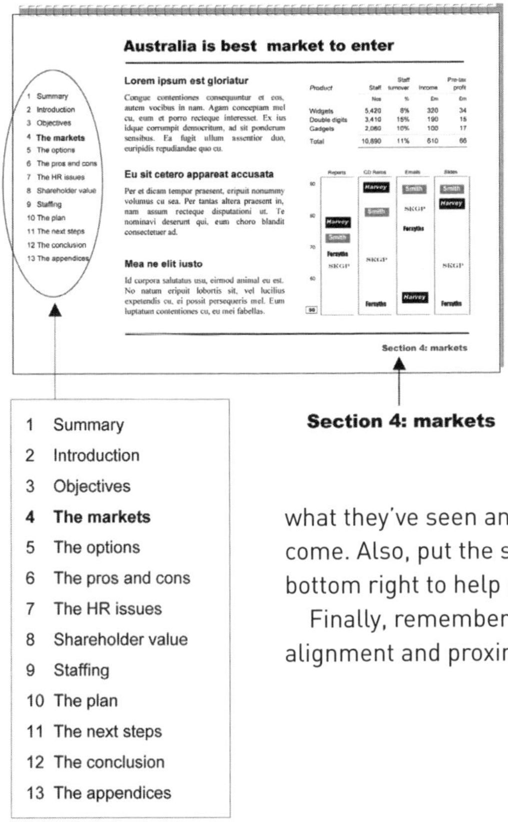
Australia is best market to enter
Lorem ipsum est gloriatur
Eu sit cetero appareat accusata
Mea ne elit iusto
Section 4: markets
1 Summary
2 Introduction
3 Objectives
4 The markets
5 The options
6 The pros and cons
7 The HR issues
8 Shareholder value
9 Staffing
10 The plan
11 The next steps
12 The conclusion
13 The appendices
Section 4: markets

Divide the page into columns – don't have text stretching across the page. Maybe have a recurring structure if possible: text on the left, table or graph or flowchart or whatever on the right. It can be very effective.

Have the index in a small de-emphasised font down the left but with the current section a bit bolder than the rest. It reminds readers what they've seen and tells them what's still to come. Also, put the section number and title bottom right to help readers navigate.

Finally, remember contrast, repetition, alignment and proximity.

Circulars or reports

A flash down the side creates visual interest and helps brand a document. On the front page, the flash can be big and bold – see Figure 7.25. But make it smaller and more subdued if alongside the main text in the report – see Figure 7.27.

The top and bottom of the flashes are tightly aligned with other parts of the page. Also, in Figures 7.26 and 7.27 the grey font makes the flash less visually dominant.

You might think the text for Figures 7.25 and 7.26 should be aligned to the right, not the left, so as to avoid 'trapped space'. Here it's not a problem, though – there are only two lines, which is not enough to create much of a weird, ragged, white 'trapped space' pattern between text and flash.

FIGURE 7.25 **FIGURE 7.26** **FIGURE 7.27**

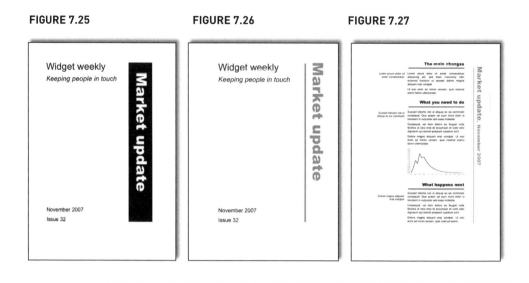

Thoughts on landscape reports

Landscape reports certainly make life easier for authors, it's usually far quicker to write a document in landscape than portrait. Portrait documents seem to demand proper prose, a continuous narrative, and that takes time to construct. In landscape, readers seem more willing to accept broad sweeping comments in pidgin English and are more forgiving if some are a bit imprecise ('The authors are mostly right when they write *"it's a growing market"*, so let's not get too pedantic with them – after all, it's just a discussion document').

But landscape reports have their critics. Because the layout seems to encourage simple, short bullet points, it can dumb down. (It doesn't have to, though.) Also, not everything can be put into bite-sized explanations that last just one page – no more, no less.

I would occasionally do landscape, for both fair reasons and foul. I would do them if I felt readers wanted some prompts to help the discussion – documents in landscape seem more like discussion documents than the portrait equivalent. I would also do them if short of time or if the report was a box-ticking exercise that nobody was particularly interested in – I could get the reports off my desk that much quicker. Finally, I would do them if writing for someone who was impressed with consultants and investment bankers – landscape reports helped me look like one.

We've now seen all the redos this chapter has to offer. The rest is more detailed typographical tips, some thoughts on colour and a look at templates and style guides.

Quick and effective typographical tips, part 2

Avoiding mistakes when emphasising

Computers can format text in many ways: upper case, underline, etc. There's much advice on the Internet that says these formats give 'visual interest and help highlight points' – but they're wrong. Many formats hinder clarity and readability. The table below explains which formats to avoid and why.

Avoid underlining	Don't use underlines (Ctrl U). The underline merges letters, hindering readability, and also bumps into 'descenders' (e.g. on letters like q, y, p, g).
Avoid upper case	AVOID UPPER CASE FOR CONTINUOUS TEXT, IT REDUCES READING SPEED BY BETWEEN 13% AND 20%.* WE ABSORB WORDS NOT JUST BY THEIR LETTERS BUT ALSO BY THE SHAPE THOSE LETTERS CREATE. WORDS THAT ARE ALL UPPER CASE DON'T HAVE A DISTINCTIVE SHAPE, THEY ARE ALL BOX SHAPED. ALSO, UPPER CASE LOOKS AS IF YOU'RE SHOUTING (AND THE BIGGER THE FONT SIZE, THE LOUDER YOU SHOUT). It's acceptable to use upper case for a small number of words in headings because the words are surrounded by space, which helps readability – but keep upper case to a minimum. The London Underground map got rid of most upper case in 1960.[†]
Avoid Random upper Case	It's Distracting and changes Meanings. Chapter 5 looked at This in More detail.
Avoid italics	*Avoid whole paragraphs or long sentences in italics (especially if the font size is small) – it slows reading speed 'substantially'.* Information packs and slides often have notes at the bottom in a small font and in italics, and they are very difficult to read.*

Take care with
white on black

Also known as
'reversing'

It's effective for highlighting, but use sparingly – it is visually dominating. Also, avoid for continuous text, because it slows reading speed by up to 15% and readers might dislike it.* Use sans serifs like Arial, ones with thick strong strokes; avoid serifs like Times New Roman, which have thin bits that don't work well with a strong background.* Also, avoid all upper case – the shape of the letters forms a box and a box in a box looks odd.*

* *Dynamics of Document Design* (pages 274 and 275).
† *Mr Beck's Underground Map* (page 50).

You can really slow down reading speed if you put it all together. Like this:

NEWSPAPERS SOMETIMES DO TEXT LIKE THIS. THEY PUT THE STORY ON TOP OF THE DARK PART OF A BIG PHOTO – AND IT'S ALMOST ILLEGIBLE. IT'S A SERIF TYPEFACE IN CONTINUOUS TEXT, WHITE ON BLACK – AND WITH POOR PRINT QUALITY, SO IT'S LIGHT GREY ON DARK GREY. IT COULD BE WORSE, I SUPPOSE. THE NEWSPAPER COULD USE UPPER CASE AND UNDERLINED TOO – LIKE THIS.

How best to align continuous text

The table below gives examples and details, but the headline is this: centre aligned is rarely best for continuous text. Justified text gives strong alignment but can hinder readability if the text is narrow – gaps between words are not uniform and can be distractingly big. Also, remember your audience – some people detest justified text. I know one person who hates it so much that, whenever she's emailed a Word document with justified text, she left aligns it before printing and reading.

In the table, the comments apply to *continuous text* rather than to brief headings (e.g. notice I say 'avoid right alignment' but then right align all the headings in the left column).

Fine to use

Left aligned Left margin aligned	Routine, normal.	Alas, poor Yorick! I knew him, Horatio: a fellow of infinite jest, of most excellent fancy: he hath borne me on his back a thousand times; and now, how abhorred in my imagination it is!
Justified Both margins aligned	Justified strengthens alignment and looks smart. Take care with very long paragraphs of continuous text, it can look block-like. Justified isn't suitable for narrow text widths – see next example.	Alas, poor Yorick! I knew him, Horatio: a fellow of infinite jest, of most excellent fancy: he hath borne me on his back a thousand times; and now, how abhorred in my imagination it is!
When's too narrow to justify?	Generally, you should be able to justify if the line length in inches is bigger than the font size divided by 3. (Got that?) If the font size is 9, you'd need a line length of at least 3 inches.*	*Too narrow – big gaps appear* Alas, poor Yorick! I knew him, Horatio: a fellow of infinite jest, of most excellent fancy;

* *The PC is Not a Typewriter* (page 46).

Ones to avoid

(remember this is for continuous text)

Right aligned Right margin aligned	It can make reading difficult because the eye has to hunt for the beginning of lines.	Alas, poor Yorick! I knew him, Horatio: a fellow of infinite jest, of most excellent fancy: he hath borne me on his back a thousand times; and now, how abhorred in my imagination it is!
Centre aligned	It's formal, dull, not easy to read. And *never* centre align the stream of bullet points in your slides.	Alas, poor Yorick! I knew him, Horatio: a fellow of infinite jest, of most excellent fancy: he hath borne me on his back a thousand times; and now, how abhorred in my imagination it is!

Finally, we have the last lot of typographical tips. And the usual mantra applies: individually the tips won't make much difference; collectively they make a huge difference.

Other detailed typographical tips

Line spacing

Continuous text – set to about 1.2×	Go for line spacing of '1.2×' (one point two times). Let me explain. Microsoft Word usually defaults to 'single' line spacing, i.e. '1×'. Don't worry about what it is multiplying by 1, that's a story for another day and involves history lessons on leading and hot metal. What you need to know is: single line spacing looks a bit cramped, and typographers suggest using 1.2×. You can change line spacing in Word and PowerPoint, but not Excel. For narrower rows of text, use slightly less line spacing – 1.1× for instance.

Headings – set to, say, single, not 1.2×	If headings wrap over more than one line and are set to 1.2× line spacing, consecutive lines often look too far apart, too fragmented. Headings don't need as much space around them, they are surrounded by white space anyway.
# 0.8 for big headings?	For big headings, set the line spacing even smaller – maybe 0.9× or even 0.8× (though make sure the ascenders and descenders don't clash).

Other

Beautiful borders and lines	Avoid thick and visually distracting text borders that visually compete with text for attention. Also, they look ugly, like the health warning on a cigarette packet.

Also avoid thick lines that visually compete with headings they sit under

Avoid borders and lines that butt up to words – again, it looks like a health warning on a cigarette packet. Give words room to breathe, so they look and read much better.

Now we're making progress. A visually unobtrusive border. Room for the words to breathe. Much better.

But why's a thick line OK here then?

It's because the font of the text is big and brash enough to compete back. The thick line is *appropriate* for the big font. A thin line would look weak and timid next to it.

Break headings where *you* want, not where the computer tells you	She lived in a tee-pee
	Don't give headings a bad break. Decide where you want the break to be, don't let the computer decide for you.

| **Avoid typographical clutter** | In the first column of Figure 7.28, the '/' adds clutter to the page and is visually distracting. The full stop is less intrusive – see the second column. The gap is neatest of all. Removing clutter like this makes a big difference if a page has many dates on it.* |

FIGURE 7.28

12/05/09	12.05.09	12 05 09
23/06/08	23.06.08	23 06 08
19/12/06	19.12.06	19 12 06
25/07/05	25.07.05	25 07 05

Railway timetables often miss out the full stop and simply show the time as 14 05.

Government statisticians often omit commas on pages of statistics, e.g. 10,220 is shown as 10 220. Again, if there's many numbers on a page it helps.

* Take care with how you show dates, because they differ throughout the world. What is 02.01.07? In the UK it is 2 January 2007. In the USA it is 1 February 2007. And in military date format in UK it is 7 January 2002 (i.e. it is YYMMDD). This last format is great for filenames on your PC because everything stays in strict date order.

That's enough detailed typography. Let's move on to colour.

Avoiding mistakes with colour

Colour is an emotive topic. Some hate reports that aren't in colour, some hate reports that have gratuitous colour. So if wondering whether to use colour, really think about your audience.

Let me pin my own colours to the mast – excuse the pun. When in corporate life doing internal reports, I never once used colour in a report (I don't count grey as colour, though typographers may disagree with me). Below, I explain why. And I am not alone: a 400-page book on document design mentioned colour once, and that was to say it wasn't going to mention colour.

Yes, good colour can help a document, but often colours are done badly. Rather than helping, they actively hinder. When people see a vast array of kaleidoscopic colour in reports and presentations, they condemn it and are suspicious of it – how much time was wasted in preparing them? What is the author trying to misdirect us away from with all those groovy colours?

So the first question is: should you use colour? The table below gives questions to help you decide. And if you decide you should, the table then gives some dos and don'ts. If you shouldn't, there are tips to help you in your black and white world.

Should you use colour?

Will you court controversy?	Everyone thinks they know the right shade of blue for that pie chart slice. Also, someone will tell you your choice of green for the heading was wrong. Do you want people to discuss your work or your choice of colours? Also, people in different countries prefer different colours –what's right for one is wrong for another.
For whose benefit is the colour – yours or the audience's?	Putting colour into reports is a great waste of time, you can tinker with it for ever and a day, the options are endless and the playing around is fun too. It beats real work. As for your audience, remember that 5% to 10% of people are colour blind or colour deficient so your fancy colours will be lost on them. (These first two reasons are why I've never done colour in internal reports.)
Does your audience expect or need it?	Colour can help motivate. Also, audiences expect presentation slides to be in colour. But don't go overboard, just put a nice shade of blue as the slide background, for instance. It won't take long to do and a bit of colour can help lift the mood. (Related to this question is: does your *manager* expect colour? Some people do reports in colour not because they want it or because the audience wants it, but because the person's manager *thinks* the audience wants it. This often happens with client proposals – the business producer insists the report is done in colour because he or she thinks it will impress the client and help win the account.)

Will your audience resent it?	Too much style is as disturbing as too little – will people think you've been wasting your time being overly creative? Earlier we saw some black and white front covers, and for the more routine internal reports they tread a good middle ground between looking amateurish and looking over-designed.
How good is the colour copier or printer?	If the printers or copiers aren't good, poorly printed black and white work is often less obnoxious than poorly printed colour.
Will the document end up in black and white?	Many reports and slides are copied on black and white copiers or printed on black and white printers. Not only are your colours lost, but any charts that rely on colour to understand them become indecipherable (e.g. graphs with legends). Also, it is *much* more expensive and time consuming to print or copy in colour.

If doing colour

Colour is more expensive to print and difficult for colour-blind people. Many comments below relate to these two problems.

If distributing soft copies that people will print	Check how the document prints in black and white and choose colours accordingly. Don't burden your readers and audience with the extra time and cost of always having to print it in colour.
Soft or harsh colours?	Vivid colours are overpowering and emotive – avoid them for routine parts of your documents. Use instead muted colours such as soft brown, soft green, soft blue, etc. Use vivid colours sparingly for emphasis. But see next point on colour blindness.

Avoid codes that rely solely on colour – they will be lost on people that are colour blind	People that are colour blind can more easily distinguish vivid colours so *avoid colour cross-references that use soft colours*. So if doing a line graph, use soft colours so they look good for those who aren't colour blind, but then label lines directly so they can be understood by those who are colour blind.

Also, RAG reports (Red, Amber, Green reports) are all very trendy but are lost on people that are colour blind if the code is merely a different-coloured circle. There are two ways round this. Firstly, avoid colours – use a tick, cross or dash. Or if you use double ticks to double crosses, you score performance out of 5, not 3 – this greater granularity may be preferable.

Alternatively, if you really want to retain colour, have a coloured tick or cross (green tick, amber dash, red cross). Or a green 'G', an amber 'A' and a red 'R'.

See http://jfly.iam.u-tokyo.ac.jp/html/color_blind/text.html for more on colour blindness. It's on how to do work that is accessible to colour-blind people. It talks about different types of colour blindness and how to design charts accordingly. It also has other interesting ideas, e.g. when presenting, don't refer to items purely by their name ('see the red line'), refer to their location too ('see the red line at the top').

But still choose colours people can name	It makes conversations and commentary easier. Don't have people struggling to describe something ('Can you talk me through the greeny-blue, sort of jadey, turquoisey line please?').

Use colours consistently	If doing a series of coloured graphs on divisional performance, ensure a division is the same colour throughout.

Send to the design department?	For certain reports, colour is expected (e.g. client reports). In this case the report should probably be done properly in a fancy package like InDesign. So send it to the marketing or design department, they will know about colour and probably have a colour template they must follow too.
If colour is needed and you don't have a design department	Copy someone else's work. Hunt out a few reports that have colours you like, pass them around your colleagues and bosses and ask which ones they like. Then copy the one that the most senior person likes or go for the majority vote. Alternatively, reinvent the wheel. Learn about different colours, how they work together or clash, how they affect mood, maybe do an evening class and read a few books, then dummy up lots of different alternatives based on your new-found knowledge. Eventually, after all your hard work, the bosses will then hand you something else they've seen and like, something done by a client or maybe done by their kids at design class in school. And they'll ask that you do something similar. The choice is yours. I recommend the first way.

If not doing colour

Use grey for visual interest	Colour doesn't mean just black and white. Try grey for flashes down the side or for creating visual interest or typographical cues. Until only quite recently, newspapers couldn't do colour but people still bought and read them.
Change the Excel default palette	Excel's default colour palette gives you only four shades of grey. This isn't enough if you are limited to black and white, so do 'Tools', 'Options', 'Colour', 'Modify' to change the palette and get more shades of grey. Take care if moving the sheet to another workbook, because the modified palette doesn't travel with it.

Next we look at the practical problem of style guides and computerised templates.

In-house design templates

Quite a few companies have style guides or computerised templates that people must adhere to or use when preparing documents. And they have their benefits. They can help work look good and save time – people don't waste time reinventing the design wheel, discussing with their colleagues which shade of blue is best. They also help compliance, and can ensure bases are covered and administrative best practice followed. They help create and maintain a brand, an image. They project a unified, consistent quality of product to the world. And so on.

That's the theory – and sometimes it works in practice. But not always. The templates might not be any good. Some designers do 'decent' stuff not because they know what they are doing, but because they copy 'decent' stuff done by others but haven't necessarily understood why it's decent. Without this understanding, their designs won't always work. Would you let someone operate on you if they didn't know why an operation worked but had simply seen someone do a successful operation like it? Alternatively, sometimes the designer's idea of 'decent' is misguided. I've seen style guides that tell people to underline or put in italics for emphasis, to do pie charts if they have numbers, and so on.

And even if the template and rules are fine, people still often populate templates with rubbish or in a way that looks rubbish. To draw another metaphor, an automatic car ensures you are in the right gear, but won't on its own make you a good driver.

To get the most out of your templates and style guides, ask the following:

1   What is the *standard* of the templates and style guides? Do they follow the principles of decent design and information? Or do they tell staff to underline words and do pie charts?

2   Do staff receive training that is appropriate to the *flexibility* of the templates and style guides? Flexible templates require more training because users have greater opportunity to mess things up. If the slide template is just a Slide Background, plus some rules on which fonts to use, users should be told not to stretch text all the way from one side of the slide to the other but to create columns where possible. But if a stricter template or style guide forbids long lines of text, users wouldn't need this training.

To judge *flexibility* and *standard*, simply review the documents people produce from the templates. How consistent are they with each other? And if consistent, are they *consistently good*?

If this review highlights problems, the answer is not simple. Try to change the system by negotiating with whoever has the power. If you do try, ensure you have some good alternatives up your sleeve. Hopefully this chapter has given you some.

Final thoughts and recap

When it comes to design and typography, everyone has an opinion but very few learn anything before offering that opinion. So they say that light blue is best, Times New Roman is awful, underlined words give emphasis.

This ignorance makes even less sense, given how people increasingly obsess about style rather than content. I once attended a talk on a new information database on thousands of companies, and the only question from the audience was: can we download company logos from it to put on reports to clients? Putting a logo on a report seems to be what business is about nowadays: we have the computing power to do it, so, by George, we are going to.

I guess I'm being a bit disingenuous. I suspect people put logos on reports because they want to make the reports smart, accessible, inviting, but don't know how to, other than by putting the client's logo on the front page.

Well now you do know. This chapter has given numerous, quick and easy ideas and tips, ones that help make documents dramatically clearer, easier to navigate, more inviting to read. They aren't tricky, you don't have to go on a design course or learn fancy new software, and they will save you time.

Also, to see more examples of these tips and ideas in action, the next chapter uses them to radically improve pages from monthly information packs. They really will be clearer than you ever thought possible.

Recap

Typographical details

Fonts	Serif typefaces like Times New Roman are readable – use them for continuous text. Sans serif typefaces like Arial are legible – use them for headings (try Arial Black), PowerPoint slides, tables and graphs. Don't have more than two typefaces on a page: one serif, one sans serif. For continuous text, avoid upper case (though it's acceptable for short headings) and avoid italics, especially with small font sizes. To emphasise, choose a different **font** instead. Avoid random Upper case on Slides. And <u>don't underline</u>.
Aligning text	For continuous text, avoid centre or right alignment. If you justify text, it's a trade-off between look and readability. Don't justify text that is too narrow – as a minimum, font size divided by 3 (in inches) should be OK.
Line length	Avoid long lines of text, the eye gets weary reading them – 12 words long is about right. Remember this for your PowerPoint slides.
Line spacing	Use 1.2× spacing for continuous text. Use smaller spacing for headings that stretch over more than one line, and smaller still for big headings.
White space	Create white space – and it's not how much white space you have, it's how you use it. Also, don't take text to the edge of the page.
Borders	Don't butt words up to lines and text box borders. Also, make their thickness appropriate to the text they are near – use thick lines only with big fonts.
Headings	Don't give your headings a bad break.

The four design principles

Contrast	Use contrast to create visual interest and help readers navigate a document.
Repetition	Make documents look unified, coherent. Actively look for elements of design that will help create a unified look. Repetition helps navigation.
Alignment	Align the separate bits of a document with each other, both horizontally and vertically. Also correct the default alignment for tables in Word.
Proximity	Cluster and group items to create visual distinctions between parts of a page, it helps readers see structure, plus gives readers 'breathing space'.
Before and afters	Remember the CV, the slide (both shown again below) and the client meeting note. Also, see the next chapter for a few more decent layouts.

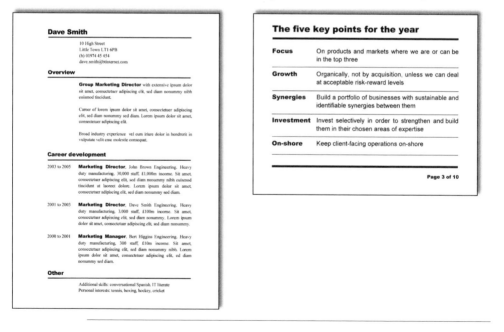

Using colour

Should you use colour?	Think before proceeding. Will people comment on your colour, not your work? Will your colour be wasted on the 5% to 10% of people that are colour blind? Will people resent you wasting time on colour? Will they print soft copies on bad colour printers? Will they print them in black and white? But is colour needed to help lift an audience? And will your audience expect it (they probably will for slides)? Remember, it is much more expensive and time consuming to print or copy in colour.
If using colour	If distributing soft copies, use colours that reproduce well in black and white. Avoid cross-references that rely on colour – that way, you can use soft colours, not harsh ones. Choose colours people can name. Use colours consistently. Maybe send the work to the design department if colour is needed. If you don't have such a department, copy someone else's decent colours.
If black & white	Grey is a colour, use it for visual interest. Also, change the Excel default palette to get more shades of grey.

Ideas

Try these	Flashes help branding, and pull quotes bring out key messages.

If you want a front cover for your internal report that's smart but not over-designed, and is quick and easy to do, try this one.

Landscape reports Have a title that concludes. Write text, not bullet point pidgin English. Put text in columns. Have an index down the left. Remember the four design principles.

Finally, in this long recap, if you have in-house templates or style sheets, check out their *standard* and *flexibility*. If the documents they produce aren't good, the system isn't working.

And if you still want the client's logo on the front cover

I'm reluctant to give a view on this topic for two reasons. Firstly, just as everyone knows the best shade of blue for that pie chart slice, so everyone has a view on the best position for the client's logo. Secondly, it's rather sad if putting client logos on front covers makes a difference to your winning the account.

But we are where we are, so here are my views (and that's all they are because I haven't managed to find a consensus on this topic – I've seen so many different ways of doing it).

Put not just the client's logo on the front cover but your logo too. Next to each logo put the company name for that logo so you have two logo-and-name *sets*. Make both sets quite small, certainly not the dominant feature of the page. Make each set roughly the same size as each other. Put one set in one corner and the other set in an *adjacent* corner, e.g. if one set is bottom left of the page, have the other either top left or bottom right. If one set is top right, the other is top left or bottom right. Get the picture? (I haven't been too prescriptive on exactly which corners to go for – that's because it depends a bit on what else you have on the page.) Align each set with the other and with other parts of the front page. There you go.

Chapter **8**

....

Variances, KPIs and 'flashes'

Great layouts that management can understand and act on

> Great layouts for variances, KPIs and 'flashes'
> Easier-to-understand balance sheets

Not all that glitters is gold.
Proverb

In this chapter, we draw together many of the tips on graphs, tables, numbers, 'WiT' and document design and turn base metal into gold. We start with routinely unpleasant-looking pages from information packs, and turn them into jaw-droppingly good schedules that will leave your readers impressed and informed.

If you review schedules or packs rather than prepare them, still read this chapter. It will show you how much better they can be. Get the people that prepare them to redo them as shown and your life will be so much better.

And if you are the person redoing them, you need to be comfortable linking Excel to Word. The Appendix gives a few quick tips.

Also, yet again this chapter assumes you know what to show and why – you just want help showing it more clearly. If that isn't the case, there are many other books that will help you decide content. They ask you: 'What are your objectives?', 'What information drives your business?' and 'Who is your audience?'. So I won't ask.

Finally – and more for the accountants out there – the last section shows how to do a much easier-to-understand balance sheet. And as a reminder for the accountants, here's where to look to improve other pages in your packs: staff numbers, page 97; provisions for liabilities and charges, page 120 (and the principles apply to the reconciliation of shareholders' funds too); debt ageing, page 118; cash flow, the text box on page 99; the pack's commentary schedule, page 256.

Variance analysis

Figure 8.1 is a typical nasty-looking page from the management accounts. It shows the contribution from four operating units, then deducts overheads to arrive at operating profit. For both monthly and year-to-date figures, it compares actual to budget.

I bet your packs are similar. OK, maybe you show sales and maybe you compare to 'last year' as well. Whatever. The layout is very popular: an ugly-looking table at the top and an uninviting commentary underneath it (or, even worse, on the next page).

And as is often the case, the first part of each variance commentary is redundant. Look at the Central commentary: '£0.1m ahead of monthly contribution target, and on budget for year to date contribution'. Yet all this is in the table above it, so why does the commentary need to repeat it?

The page has been redone in Figure 8.2. Study the broad layout – there's some extra stuff on it. There is a summary profit and loss account, then underneath are tables of variances, both for contribution and overheads. Also, there are columns down the left headed up 'excluding timing diffs' – more on this later.

FIGURE 8.1

ABC Group
6 months to June 2007
2.2 Contribution and variances

Contribution	Year to date			For month		
	Actual	Budget	Fav/ (adv)	Actual	Budget	Fav/ (adv)
	£'m	£'m	£'m	£'m	£'m	£'m
Central	12.0	12.0	0.0	2.2	2.1	0.1
North West	19.1	16.2	2.9	5.5	2.9	2.6
South East	15.8	14.0	1.8	2.3	2.3	0.0
West and Isles	16.9	17.8	(0.9)	2.3	3.1	(0.8)
Total	63.8	60.0	3.8	12.3	10.4	1.9
Overheads						
Salaries	(14.1)	(12.5)	(1.6)	(2.5)	(2.1)	(0.4)
IT	(4.1)	(6.5)	2.4	(0.3)	(1.1)	0.8
Property	(4.9)	(6.1)	1.2	(0.7)	(1.0)	0.3
Group	(7.2)	(5.8)	(1.4)	(1.7)	(1.0)	(0.7)
Legal	(10.5)	(5.5)	(5.0)	(5.9)	(0.9)	(5.0)
Depreciation	(4.2)	(4.3)	0.1	(0.7)	(0.7)	0.0
Other	(3.1)	(3.0)	(0.1)	(0.6)	(0.5)	(0.1)
T&E	(2.2)	(2.3)	0.1	(0.4)	(0.4)	0.0
Overheads	(50.3)	(46.0)	(4.3)	(12.8)	(7.7)	(5.1)
Operating Profit	13.5	14.0	(0.5)	(0.5)	2.7	(3.2)

CONTRIBUTION

Central: £0.1m ahead of monthly contribution target, and on budget for year to date contribution - some small wins, some small losses. Nothing material.

North West: reported a contribution of £2.6m up on budget for month and up £2.9m for year to date. Mostly due to two big new contracts booked this month - ABC (£1.5m) and DEC (£1.1.m). The extra £300k is small one-offs reported in prior months.

South East: reported a contribution on budget for this month, and up £1.8m for year to date. Favourable variance mainly due to £1.6m extension on Project Smith booked last quarter (+ £1.2m more due in Q4), plus a few smaller other new contracts.

West and Isles: reported a contribution down £0.9m for year to date, £0.8m in month. Month variance all due to delay of Contract Xanvier (£0.8m a month and due to start 1 June). Now expected to start 1 September.

OVERHEADS

Salaries: £1.6m over budget for year to date and £0.4m over budget for the month due to 2 unbudgeted changes. First, the new unbudgeted 'Solutions' department (40 staff - an extra £0.2m per month). Also in the last 2 months, higher than expected pay rises have added another £0.2m a month to salaries.

IT: £0.8m under budget for the month, £2.4m under budget for year to date. Both variances due to delay of Project MIS-Development. Costs previously expected to be incurred in Q1 and Q2 will now be spent in Q3 and Q4.

Property: £0.3 under budget for month, £1.2m under budget for year to date. Due to unbudgetted income of £0.3m a month from subletting the empty factory since March.

Group: £0.7m over budget for month and £1.4m over budget for year to date - due to Group Marketing campaign brought forward from Q3 to Q2. A timing difference.

Legal: £5m over budget for month and for year to date because of unbudgetted court fine for polluting local river.

FIGURE 8.2

ABC Group

Contribution, variances   **2.2**

6 months to June 2007

Excluding timing diffs (£m)

To date	To y/e								

Summary P&L

		Year to date			For month		
All £m		Actual	Budget	Fav/ (adv)	Actual	Budget	Fav/ (adv)
Contribution		63.8	60.0	**3.8**	12.3	10.4	**1.9**
Overheads		(50.3)	(46.0)	**(4.3)**	(12.8)	(7.7)	**(5.1)**
Operating profit		13.5	14.0	(0.5)	(0.5)	2.7	(3.2)

To date	To y/e
3.8	3.4
(5.4)	(6.0)
(1.6)	(2.6)

Items in bold are analysed below

Variances (£m)

Contribution

To date	To y/e		For yr	Month	
2.9	2.9	North West	2.9	2.6	Two new contracts booked this month – ABC (£1.5m), and DEC (£1.1m)
1.8	3.0	South East	1.8	-	Mainly due to £1.6m extension on Project Smith booked last quarter (+ £1.2m more due in Q4)
-	-	Central	-	0.1	On target - some small wins and losses. Nothing material
(0.9)	(2.5)	West and Isles	(0.9)	(0.8)	Contract Xanvier (£0.8m a month) delayed from 1 June start to 1 Sept
3.8	**3.4**	Total contribution	**3.8**	**1.9**	

Overheads

To date	To y/e		For yr	Month	
-	-	IT	2.4	0.8	Project MIS-Development delay from Q1/ Q2 to Q3/ Q4
1.2	3.0	Property	1.2	0.3	Sublet the empty factory on 1 March
-	-	Other, Deprec, T&E	0.1	(0.1)	Minor differences, none material
-	-	Group	(1.4)	(0.7)	Marketing campaign brought forward from Q3 to Q2
(1.6)	(4.0)	Salaries	(1.6)	(0.4)	New 'Solutions' department = 40 unbudgeted recruits for 6 months (£0.2m a month). Also, higher than budgeted pay rises (£0.2m a month for last 2 months)
(5.0)	(5.0)	Legal costs	(5.0)	(5.0)	Court fine for polluting local river
(5.4)	**(6.0)**	Total overheads	**(4.3)**	**(5.1)**	

Page 5 of 15

The page layout is much more inviting	It's no longer dauntingly ugly. It has 'C-R-A-P' (see Chapter 7) and the typographical changes are more than just cosmetic. Readers can navigate more easily around the information pack and find a particular page because we've put the page title, section number and page number on the right of the page, not in by the report binding.
The commentary is now in a table	The commentary was crying out to be 'WiT' (Chapter 1) – it had a repeating structure *and* was in brief sections. With 'WiT', the commentary is in narrower rows of text making it easier to read. Also, we waffle less because we have less room to waffle.
The variances are in the same table	Previously, readers' eyes constantly jumped between the table of numbers at the top and the commentary underneath. The redo makes it easier to compare numbers with their related comments. Also, we don't need all the repetitive stuff – 'the variance to date is £x under budget . . .'. Yes, with 'WiT' we have less room to say something – but by putting the numbers alongside the comments in the table, there's less we need to say.
We've grouped immaterial items	We've combined Other, Depreciation and T&E because none had any material variance for month or year to date.
We've put the rows in order	Each 'variance' table is in descending order of year-to-date variance – previously the operating units were in alphabetical order.

We've shown the results to date excluding timing differences (see far left column)	Readers want to know: 'What's the position to date if I ignore timing differences, given they will reverse anyway? Does our £xm positive variance to date transpire to be a £ym negative variance?' So they get out their calculators and add this back, then add that one back too – but not that one, and so on. The far left column does this for readers and shows the year-to-date variance, ignoring timing differences.
We've shown the 'run rate' (see second column from the left)	Management accounts often leave readers to work out the impact of variances on the expected year-end results. Let me explain. By the half-year, Legal costs are £5m over budget because of a £5m one-off fine, so we expect a £5m variance by the year-end. But Property has a £0.3m favourable variance every month because we've relet the empty factory – and if the half-year positive variance is £1.2m, the year-end variance should be about £3.0m.
	All this is in the second column from the left. We give a rough back-of-the-envelope idea of the year-end position. It isn't a full-blown bottom-up reforecast. *It does what management would do if the schedule hadn't.* And even if you can't do these estimates for income, do it for costs at the very least.
We've a summary P&L at the top	It gives management a quick overview of the numbers.

As well as these big changes, there are many small changes too. For example, we say '£m' just once. We've made gridlines faint. For numbers, we've vertically centre aligned them so they don't butt up to gridlines, we've put a '–' instead of a '0', and we've shunted numbers in brackets slightly to the right so as to align the smallest digits of the numbers. For page titles and table labels, we've got rid of underlines and horizontal centre alignment. And so on.

All in all, we've given management a far more inviting document. We've also given them far more insight into the numbers – we've stripped out timing differences, and we've shown how variances will affect the year-end position.

And even if you don't want those two columns on the left, take them out, *but then leave the rest of the page exactly as it is* – pages look really sharp if you keep the left half or third of them empty. Figure 8.3 is a mockup of 'Provisions for liabilities and charges'. It has a table at the top and the related commentary underneath – but the commentary stretches over only half the page. And the page looks really good. You never thought a table as dull as this one could look so darned cool. If this layout can make provisions look this cool, just think what it will do for a table of interesting figures.

FIGURE 8.3

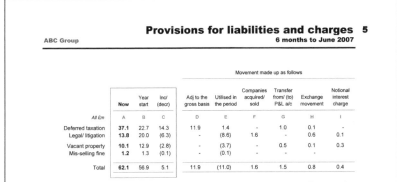

Provisions for liabilities and charges 5

ABC Group

6 months to June 2007

Movement made up as follows

All £m	Now	Year start	Inc/ (decr)	Adj to the gross basis	Utilised in the period	Companies acquired/ sold	Transfer from/ (to) P&L a/c	Exchange movement	Notional interest charge
	A	B	C	D	E	F	G	H	I
Deferred taxation	37.1	22.7	14.3	11.9	1.4	-	1.0	0.1	-
Legal/ litigation	13.8	20.0	(6.3)	-	(8.6)	1.6	-	0.6	0.1
Vacant property	10.1	12.9	(2.8)	-	(3.7)	-	0.5	0.1	0.3
Mis-selling fine	1.2	1.3	(0.1)	-	(0.1)	-	-	-	-
Total	62.1	56.9	5.1	11.9	(11.0)	1.6	1.5	0.8	0.4

Numbers rounded for clarity, small rounding differences may arise

Summary

Lorem ipsum est gloriatur expetendis an. Congue contentiones consequuntur et eos, autem vocibus in nam. Agam conceptam mel cu, eum et porro recteque interesset. Ex ius idque corrumpit democritum, ad sit ponderum sensibus. Ea fugit ullum assentior duo, euripidis repudiandae quo cu.

Next year's outlook

Eu sit cetero appareat accusata. Per et dicam tempor praesent, eripuit nonummy volumus cu sea. Per tantas altera praesent in, nam assum recteque disputationi ut. Te nominavi deserunt qui, eum choro blandit consectetuer ad. Summo copiosae mea ex, doctus eleifend in sea.

Mea ne elit iusto. Id corpora salutatus usu, eirmod animal eu est. No natum eripuit lobortis sit, vel lucilius expetendis cu, ei possit perseqeris mel. Eum luptatum contentiones cu, eu mei fabellas mediocritatem. Vivendo antiopam nec te, malis ullum epicuri pro cu.

Graeco virtute detracto sit ei, mea sonet dicant et. Mei adhuc fabulas et, qui ex zzril postea posidonium, nec eu dico reque docendi. Mei cu dolore volumus volutpat, illum tamquam sanctus ex est.

Eum ad sumo invenire, nec falli inimicus at, mel delenit conclusionemque et. Vidit corpora ad mea, in altera accusamus quo.

Page 5 of 15

FIGURE 8.4

Contribution, variances 2.2
6 months to June 2007

ABC Group

Excluding timing diffs (£m)

To date	To y/e
3.8	3.4
(5.4)	(6.0)
(1.6)	(2.6)

Summary P&L

All in £m	Year to date Actual	Budget	Fav/(adv)	For month Actual	Budget	Fav/(adv)
Contribution	63.8	60.0	3.8	12.3	10.4	1.9
Overheads	(50.3)	(46.0)	(4.3)	(12.8)	(7.7)	(5.1)
Operating profit	13.5	14.0	(0.5)	(0.5)	2.7	(3.2)

Items in bold are analysed below

Contribution

		Variances (£m) For yr	Month	
2.9	2.9	North West	2.9	2.6	Two big new contracts booked this month - ABC (£1.5m), and DEC (£1.1m).
1.8	3.0	South East	1.8	-	Mainly due to £1.6m extension on Project Smith booked last quarter (+ £1.2m more due in Q4)
-	-	Central	-	0.1	On target - some small wins and losses. Nothing material
(0.9)	(2.5)	West and Isles	(0.9)	(0.8)	Contract Xanvier (£0.8m a month) delayed from 1 June start to 1 Sept
3.8	3.4	Total contribution	3.8	1.9	

Overheads

		For yr	Month	
		IT	2.4	0.8	Project MIS-Development delay from Q1/ Q2 to Q3/ Q4
1.2	3.0	Property	1.2	0.3	Sublet the empty factory on 1 March
		Other, Deprec., T&E	0.1	(0.1)	Minor differences, none material
		Group	(1.4)	(0.7)	Marketing campaign brought forward from Q3 to Q2
(1.6)	(4.0)	Salaries	(1.6)	(0.4)	New 'Solutions' department = 40 unbudgeted recruits for 6 months (£0.2m a month). Also, higher than budgeted pay rises (£0.2m a month for last 2 months)
(5.0)	(5.0)	Legal costs	(5.0)	(5.0)	Court fine for polluting local river
(5.4)	(6.0)	Total overheads	(4.3)	(5.1)	

P&L: detail

All in £m	Year to date Actual	Budget	Fav/(adv)	For month Actual	Budget	Fav/(adv)
West and Isles	16.9	17.8	(0.9)	2.3	3.1	(0.8)
North West	19.1	16.2	2.9	5.5	2.9	2.6
South East	15.8	14.0	1.8	2.3	2.3	-
Central	12.0	12.0	-	2.2	2.1	0.1
Total	63.8	60.0	3.8	12.3	10.4	1.9
Salaries	14.1	12.5	(1.6)	2.5	2.1	(0.4)
Legal	10.5	5.5	(5.0)	5.9	0.9	(5.0)
Group	7.2	5.8	(1.4)	1.7	1.0	(0.7)
IT	4.1	6.5	2.4	0.3	1.1	0.8
Property	4.9	6.1	1.2	0.7	1.0	0.3
Depreciation	4.2	4.3	0.1	0.7	0.7	-
Other	3.1	3.0	(0.1)	0.6	0.5	(0.1)
T&E	2.2	2.3	0.1	0.4	0.4	-
Overheads	50.3	46.0	(4.3)	12.8	7.7	(5.1)
Operating profit	13.5	14.0	(0.5)	(0.5)	2.7	(3.2)

Summary

Lorem ipsum est gloriatur expetendis an. Congue contentiones consequuntur et eos, autem vocibus in nam. Agam conceptam mel cu, eum et porro recteque interesset. Ex ius idque corrumpit democritum, ad sit ponderum sensibus. Ea fugit ullum assentor duo, curipidis repudiandae quo cu.

Eu sit cetero appareat accusata. Per et dicam tempor praesent, eripuit nonummy volumus cu sea. Per tantas altera praesent in, nam assum recteque disputationi ut. Te nominavi deserunt qui, eum choro blandit consectetuer ad. Summo copiosae mea cu, doctus eleifend in.

Contribution, variances 2.2

Back to our 'variance' redo – it doesn't have everything. There's no overall summary comment for the page. And unlike the earlier version, it doesn't show detailed numbers – what is the North West contribution to date? We only see its variance from budget. These are two quite important omissions.

We could try adding these two items to the redone page. The summary comments could squeeze in at the top and the detailed P&L could go at the bottom. But it won't work – a portrait page of A4 isn't tall enough to cope (not without shrinking to font size 6 or so). Alternatively, you could spread the information over two pages, but it's not ideal. Readers would be flicking back and forth between pages.

So see the dummied up landscape version in Figure 8.4. To do it as shown, you need to be comfortable linking between Word and Excel – see the text box below. In the landscape redo, the detailed P&L account is in a smaller font to de-emphasise it a bit. Also, we've put the Latin 'Summary' comment in Times New Roman. Times New Roman is more readable than Arial and also makes the page look less visually the same. You may also want to replace the word '**Summary**' with a more informative lead-in title like '**Two big new clients, but a £5m court fine**' or something similar.

The page is dramatically better – go back and remind yourself just how bad the original was. Also, we are now giving much more information than before, yet it's still on just one page *and* has more white space. That's design for you.

The next section looks at a one-page 'flash' report – though you may know it by another name such as key performance indicator (KPI) or information dashboard or whatever.

Doing the landscape page on your computer: the IT bit

(If you've never linked Excel to Word, you may struggle with this.)

The underlying base to the redo is a landscape page in Word (Figure 8.5). To the page we add three separate bits. Firstly, do the 'P&L: detail' table in

FIGURE 8.5

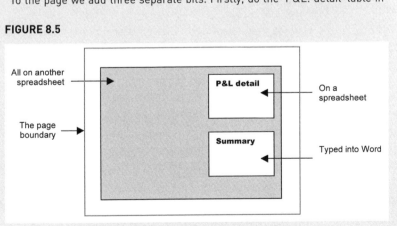

Excel and then copy it across. Secondly, type the 'Summary' words directly onto the landscape page in Word. Use the indent markers at the top of the Word screen to shunt your 'Summary' comments to the right of the landscape page and to align them neatly underneath the 'P&L: detail'. You could use a text box instead, but text boxes don't allow you to change line spacing, so you're stuck with single spacing when the optimum spacing is actually 1.2. If you do use text boxes, don't give them borders.

Finally, set up the rest of the page in another Excel spreadsheet – the variance commentary, the summary P&L, even the thick lines at the top and bottom, the page title, the page number, and so on. Then copy that across too. Move it around so it too is nicely aligned.

With the bits coming over from Excel, link or de-link as you see fit. It's probably best to link if it's a regular report. Also, lay them *behind* or in *front* of the text in Word ('Format Object', 'Layout', 'Behind Text'). Then move items to the back or front accordingly (right click, 'Order', then 'Send to back', etc.).

Finally, if you're wondering why I didn't do it all in Excel, it's because I wanted the row height of the 'P&L: detail' table to be much smaller than the row heights of the tables on the left hand side of the page. And on its own, Excel would struggle to give me them that way.

The one-page KPI and 'flashes'

Just after each month-end, many companies do a one-page summary of statistics to give management a quick 'heads-up' before the full information pack comes out a week later. The page might show summary financial results, maybe staff statistics and treasury figures, and so on. It may focus less on financial data and more on statistics for productivity or client retention or customer satisfaction. The page has many names: 'flash', KPIs, the dashboard, and so on.

Regardless of what they show and what they are called, these pages usually share something in common – their layouts can often be improved considerably. The one in Figure 8.6 certainly can (does it look familiar?).

In Figure 8.7 I've shown the same data but done it differently. Gone are the P&L figures that have six digits. Instead, the redo has a type of variable rounding in its P&L – the big numbers have no decimal places (e.g. turnover), the smaller numbers do (e.g. trading profit). Gone are the pointless graphs. Obviously not all KPI and 'flash' graphs are pointless, but these certainly are. Gone is the cell shading and text underlines. In comes smart, clean, clear layout. And in comes a document that management will want to look at, study and engage with. The difference is dramatic.

FIGURE 8.6

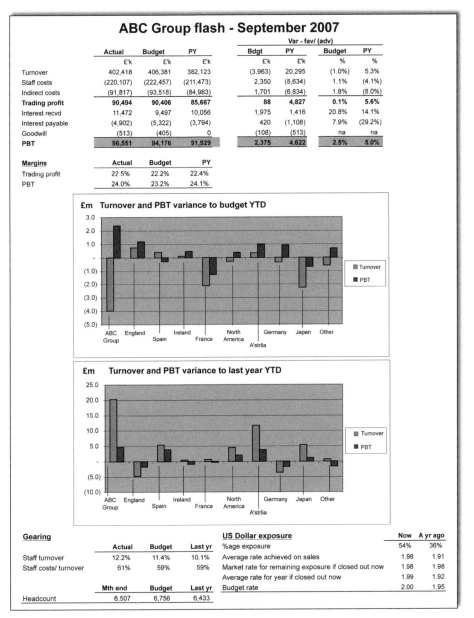

ABC Group flash - September 2007

	Actual	Budget	PY		Bdgt	PY		Budget	PY
	£'k	£'k	£'k		£'k	£'k		%	%
Turnover	402,418	406,381	382,123		(3,963)	20,295		(1.0%)	5.3%
Staff costs	(220,107)	(222,457)	(211,473)		2,350	(8,634)		1.1%	(4.1%)
Indirect costs	(91,817)	(93,518)	(84,983)		1,701	(6,834)		1.8%	(8.0%)
Trading profit	**90,494**	**90,406**	**85,667**		**88**	**4,827**		**0.1%**	**5.6%**
Interest recvd	11,472	9,497	10,056		1,975	1,416		20.8%	14.1%
Interest payable	(4,902)	(5,322)	(3,794)		420	(1,108)		7.9%	(29.2%)
Goodwill	(513)	(405)	0		(108)	(513)		na	na
PBT	**96,551**	**94,176**	**91,929**		**2,375**	**4,622**		**2.5%**	**5.0%**

Var - fav/ (adv)

Margins	Actual	Budget	PY
Trading profit	22.5%	22.2%	22.4%
PBT	24.0%	23.2%	24.1%

£m Turnover and PBT variance to budget YTD

£m Turnover and PBT variance to last year YTD

Gearing	Actual	Budget	Last yr
Staff turnover	12.2%	11.4%	10.1%
Staff costs/ turnover	61%	59%	59%

	Mth end	Budget	Last yr
Headcount	6,507	6,756	6,433

US Dollar exposure	Now	A yr ago
%age exposure	54%	36%
Average rate achieved on sales	1.98	1.91
Market rate for remaining exposure if closed out now	1.98	1.98
Average rate for year if closed out now	1.99	1.92
Budget rate	2.00	1.95

And management now know who to congratulate for this new schedule – the redo has a contact name and number on it (see bottom left). With all your work, be accountable. Put contact details so people know who to ring with a query. It also helps make corporate life seem just a bit more human.

FIGURE 8.7

ABC Group flash   **September 2007**

Group P&L to date

	Actual	Budget	Last yr	Budget	Last yr	Budget	Last yr
	£m	£m	£m	£m	£m	%	%
Turnover	402	406	382	(4.0)	20.3	(1%)	5%
Staff costs	(220)	(222)	(211)	2.3	(8.6)	1%	(4%)
Indirect costs	(92)	(94)	(85)	1.7	(6.8)	2%	(8%)
Trading profit	**90.5**	**90.4**	**85.7**	**0.1**	**4.8**	**0%**	**6%**
Interest recvd	11.5	9.5	10.1	2.0	1.4	21%	14%
Interest payable	(4.9)	(5.3)	(3.8)	0.4	(1.1)	8%	(29%)
Goodwill	(0.5)	(0.4)	-	(0.1)	(0.5)	na	na
PBT	**96.6**	**94.2**	**91.9**	**2.4**	**4.6**	**2.5%**	**5.0%**

Var - fav/ (adv)

Margins	Actual	Budget	Last yr
Trading profit	22%	22%	22%
PBT	24%	23%	24%

Variances to date by business unit

	Turnover		PBT	
All £m	Budget	Last yr	Budget	Last yr
Group to date	**(4.0)**	**20.3**	**2.4**	**4.6**
Split as follows:				
England	0.7	(4.7)	1.2	(1.7)
Spain	0.4	5.4	(0.3)	3.8
Australia	0.4	11.7	1.0	3.8
Ireland	0.1	0.4	0.5	(0.8)
North America	(0.3)	4.5	0.4	2.0
Germany	(0.3)	(3.6)	0.9	(1.7)
Other	(0.6)	0.7	0.7	(1.6)
France	(2.1)	0.6	(1.3)	(0.2)
Japan	(2.2)	5.4	(0.7)	1.1
Group	**(4.0)**	**20.3**	**2.4**	**4.6**

Staff statistics

	Actual	Budget	Last yr
Staff turnover	12%	11%	10%
Staff costs/ turnover	61%	59%	59%

	Mnth end	Budget	Last yr
Headcount (numbers)	6,507	6,756	6,433

US dollar exposure

	Now	A yr ago	
%age exposure	54%	36%	
Average rate achieved	1.98	1.91	on sales
Market rate	1.98	1.98	for remaining exposure if closed out now
Average rate for year	1.99	1.92	if closed out now
Budget rate	2.00	1.95	

David Smith, 0207 - 444 5555   **Page 1 of 1**

'The numbers don't align, though'

This is a detailed point you can skip on first reading if you want. It's about the numbers not aligning properly in Figure 8.7. Let me explain the problem. Study the £92m actual indirect costs (shown to no decimal place) and the £90.5m actual trading profit (shown to one decimal place). Typographically, the numbers are aligned – the smallest digit of £92m lines up with the smallest digit of £90.5m. But *financially they misalign* – the '2' of '92 is in millions, the 5 of 90.5 is in tenths of millions.

To correct this, we could financially align numbers, but they would then typographically misalign – and it does look odd. The 402, 220 and 92 figures that are above the 90.5 figure all get shunted quite a way to the left and we get two very distinct right margins to the column of numbers. It's quite distracting.

Anyway, the financial misalignment isn't actually a problem because *groups* of numbers still financially align. The group before the first subtotal financially align with each other. The group after the first subtotal financially align with each other too. And the gap and the line between the two groups helps 'disguise' the misalignment across the two different groups.

I've tried various alternative ways to align the numbers, and the way in Figure 8.7 seems to work best. It allows us to benefit from showing rounded numbers – income is much clearer as £402m than £402.4m.

If your page isn't just tables and graphs but words too, try the layout shown in Figure 8.8.

Notice how the big blocks of text create a strong source of vertical alignment both down the middle and down the right of the page. The blocks also give a strong source of horizontal alignment for the tops of the graphs and tables.

If your comments are briefer, i.e. maybe just one or two short sentences, try the layout in Figure 8.9. It's slightly different to Figure 8.8 because we no longer have big blocks of text creating strong sources of alignment. So this time I've had to create alignment whilst also ensuring I didn't accidentally create so-called 'trapped white space' (see page 199). So we now

FIGURE 8.8

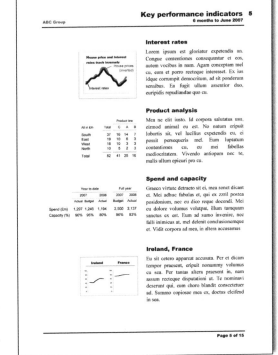

FIGURE 8.9

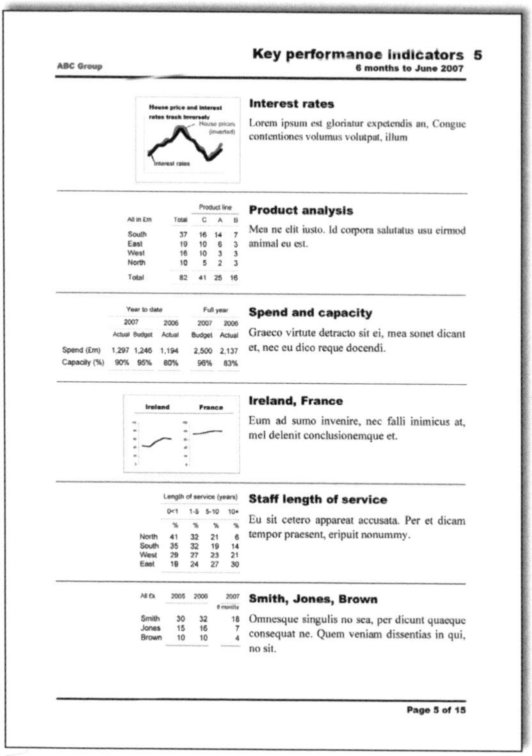

ABC Group

Key performanoe indicators 5
6 months to June 2007

Interest rates

Lorem ipsum est gloriatur expetendis an, Congue contentiones volumus volutpat, illum

All in £m	Total	Product line C	A	B
South	37	16	14	7
East	19	10	6	3
West	16	10	3	3
North	10	5	2	3
Total	82	41	25	16

Product analysis

Mea ne elit iusto. Id corpora salutatus usu eirmod animal eu est.

	Year to date 2007 Actual	Budget	2006 Actual	Full year 2007 Budget	2006 Actual
Spend (£m)	1,297	1,246	1,194	2,500	2,137
Capacity (%)	90%	95%	80%	96%	83%

Spend and capacity

Graeco virtute detracto sit ei, mea sonet dicant et, nec eu dico reque docendi.

Ireland, France

Eum ad sumo invenire, nec falli inimicus at, mel delenit conclusionemque et.

	Length of service (years) 0<1	1-5	5-10	10+
	%	%	%	%
North	41	32	21	6
South	35	32	19	14
West	29	27	23	21
East	19	24	27	30

Staff length of service

Eu sit cetero appareat accusata. Per et dicam tempor praesent, eripuit nonummy.

All £k	2005	2006	2007 6 months
Smith	30	32	18
Jones	15	16	7
Brown	10	10	4

Smith, Jones, Brown

Omnesque singulis no sea, per dicunt quaeque consequat ne. Quem veniam dissentias in qui, no sit.

Page 5 of 15

have a horizontal line between each section. Also, the top of each table or graph is horizontally aligned with the top of the *section heading* – compare this to Figure 8.8 where the top of the table or graph aligned with the top of the *comments*. These are small differences but they help make the page look elegant, not haphazard.

The layout looks clean and crisp with lots of effective white space. It puts words into columns, which makes them easier to read, and it encourages the author to be brief – there's not much room to waffle. Also, these examples are in portrait, though they can of course be just as effectively done in landscape.

When writing the comments for each graph or table, avoid these common mistakes:

Don't embed and hide lots of numbers in text	'West division grew 10% from £100m to £110m, whilst North went from £72m to £76m, an increase of 6%. Overall, group income went from £172m to £186m, up 8%.' *It's crying out to be in a table.*
Don't merely repeat what's in the table	'As seen from the table, West division grew 10% from £100m to £110m, North went from . . .'. *Say something that adds to the numbers in the table, not merely repeats them.*
Don't leave numbers isolated and out of context	'West got a score of 57% last month.' *Is that good or bad, though? Give context to your numbers.*

Finally, look for opportunities to develop templates. Reports often refer to similar points every month, be they quantitative (number of clients won this month) or qualitative (progress on departmental changes). If you spot this happening, try to develop an appropriate template – it helps both the writing and the reading. Try 'WiT', it's often a good starting point and a good end point too.

Next we look at a different way of doing a balance sheet. Your auditors won't like it for your statutory reports, but the board might like it for the management accounts.

Easier-to-understand balance sheets

Figure 8.10 shows how the balance sheet is often laid out in management accounts. It follows the statutory format, so isn't in numerical order. This means big and small numbers all compete equally for readers' attention. Also, everything is shown to the nearest £m – does the board need to know that 2007 debtors are £10,934m? Note also that the two biggest single items are 'Trade debtors' and 'Trade creditors', yet they aren't even separately shown on the balance sheet, they are lumped in with other items in 'Debtors' and 'Creditors'. And, for this balance sheet, trade debtors and trade creditors track each other, yet readers don't explicitly see how the two net down.

In Figure 8.11 we've redone the balance sheet. We've put the two biggest items at the very top and also shown how they net down. We've put other items in descending numerical order. We've variably rounded numbers. We've put minor items in a separate table and put a linking line between tables to help make the connection for readers. (The rounding formula for 'Sundry items' rounds to one digit if the original number is between £25m and minus £25m, if not then to two digits.)

We've variably rounded the balance sheet totals too, which means the balance sheet doesn't add up. The net assets for 2007 are £897m, yet Figure 8.11 shows it as £900m. Which is fine. But if you add up all the rounded items above it, they come to £880m, not £900m. *The balance sheet doesn't add up*. But it's far clearer. It's a trade-off. How do management want their information: confusingly and unnecessarily accurate? Or approximate and understandable? I know which I'd go for. All the same, cover yourself with a note at the bottom that says 'Numbers rounded for greater clarity; rounding differences occur'.

Some people argue that such a balance sheet makes it difficult to see a derived figure that might be of interest to a board, such as 'Net Current Assets' (NCA). If such a number is important, just put a row underneath the new-look balance sheet and show it there. Show all three figures for NCA – 2007, 2006 and Var – all rounded of course. Don't sacrifice the clarity of your entire balance sheet in order to show how a single number was derived.

FIGURE 8.10

All £m		
Fixed assets		
Intangible assets	291	298
Tangible assets	154	140
Investments in associates	41	37
Other investments	9	9
Employee benefit trusts	74	61
	569	546
Current assets		
Debtors	10,934	11,325
Investments and deposits	1,857	1,806
Cash	557	523
	13,349	13,654
Creditors	(12,519)	(13,195)
Net current assets	830	459
Creditors - due after one year	(32)	(61)
Provisions for liabilities etc	(441)	(204)
Minority interests	(30)	(20)
	897	720
Capital and reserves		
Called up share capital	57	56
Share premium	154	113
Profit and loss account	686	550
	897	720

Analysis on separate pages

Debtors		
Trade debtors	10,323	10,992
Other debtors	582	309
Sundry	30	24
	10,934	11,325
Creditors		
Bank and other loans	29	-
Unsecured loan notes	2	34
Trade creditors	11,809	12,582
Finance leases	2	3
Proposed dividends	125	106
Corporation tax	111	68
Social security etc	28	24
Other creditors	413	378
	12,519	13,195

FIGURE 8.11

	Reordered and rounded		
All £m	2007	2006	Var
Material items			
Trade debtors	10,300	11,000	(700)
Trade creditors	(11,800)	(12,600)	800
Net balance	(1,500)	(1,600)	100
Investments and deposits	1,860	1,810	50
Other debtors	580	310	270
Cash	560	520	40
Intangible assets	290	300	(10)
Tangible assets	150	140	10
Sundry items - see below	30	(10)	40
Corporation tax	(110)	(70)	(40)
Proposed dividends	(130)	(110)	(20)
Other creditors	(410)	(380)	(30)
Provisions for liabilities etc	(440)	(200)	(240)
	900	720	180
Capital and reserves			
Called up share capital	57	56	1
Share premium	150	110	40
Profit and loss account	690	550	140
	900	720	180
Sundry items			
Employee benefit trusts	70	60	10
Investments in associates	40	40	-
Sundry debtors	30	24	6
Other fixed asset investments	9	9	-
Unsecured loan notes	(2)	(30)	28
Finance lease creditor	(2)	(3)	1
Social security etc	(30)	(24)	(6)
Bank and other loans	(30)	-	(30)
Minority interests	(30)	(20)	(10)
Creditors - due after one year	(30)	(60)	30
	30	(10)	40

Rounding errors – the detail

Just so you know, every number in the variance column is a simple '2007 minus 2006' computation. There's no fancy rounding formula in it. Which means it adds across fine but adds down incorrectly. Add the variance figures from 'Net balance' down to 'Provisions for liabilities'. They come to £170m, but the total shows £180m. We could have changed the formula in the variance column so it added down correctly, i.e. so it showed £170m as the variance total. But then the total rows would not add across correctly – 900 less 720 is not 170. And this new rounding error would be annoyingly obvious. Lots of people would spot it and might get hot under the collar about it. By having the rounding error down the column, not across the rows, it's less obvious. How many of you had spotted the sum of the items was not £180m but £170m?

Final thoughts and recap

There's a lot more we could cover – one-page summaries are in vogue at the moment. Managers are tired of bulky management accounts packs and now want to shoehorn everything they need to know onto a single piece of paper. They and their staff devote much thought to the content of that page but then give little thought to its layout or design. But then again, so long as the information is on the page, it does the job, doesn't it?

Meanwhile, the IT companies rush into the vacuum and sell software that does groovy dashboards with pretty speedometers. You can guess my views on these.

If management are to engage with data, be it a single page or a 30-page pack, the information needs to be *designed*. And when it is, the difference can be staggering.

Recap

Do your variance commentaries as 'WiT', with the numerical variances sitting alongside the commentary. Maybe show the impact excluding timing differences. Maybe also show the estimated impact of variances by the year-end – the 'run rate'.

In your information packs, don't stretch your commentary across the entire width of the page. Keep text away from the left half or third of the page (though it's fine for tables to stretch over there – the provisions table did).

Remember document design tips: Arial Black for headings, Times New Roman for commentary. And contrast, repetition, alignment, proximity.

For internal management accounts, try doing your balance sheets in descending order and with variably rounded numbers.

Variances as 'WIT'

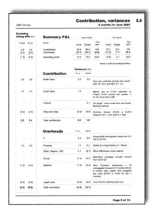

Page from management accounts

Flash report

KPIs – lots of words

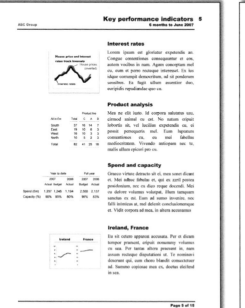

KPIs – not so many words

Chapter **9**

Organisation charts

How to provide greater richness and granularity to your charts

> Why most structure charts are poor
> A better way to show the structure of your organisation
> A pullout A3 page at the back for your index or your commentaries
> How to do the left-to-right chart in Excel

We tend to meet any new situation by reorganising (to create) the illusion of progress, while producing confusion, inefficiency and demoralisation.

Usually attributed to Roman Consul Petronius (AD 66) but apparently made up by a British Army Officer after the Second World War

This is not a long chapter, but if you do or review organisation charts, you'll see how to do a much better chart than the typical one in Figure 9.1.

FIGURE 9.1

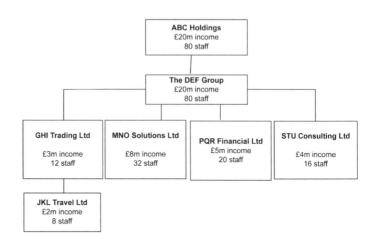

And the better way works a treat. I once used it to show 250 reporting units spread over six reporting levels on a single sheet of A3 paper. Its striking simplicity made it indispensable for the project team because people could see both detail and overview.

If the hierarchies had been shown using a 'conventional' chart, it would have taken ten pages to do it. I know that because someone in the project team did this before I did mine. He taped the ten pages together and, if he needed to show the group structure at a meeting, he would unfurl this monstrosity and lay it out on the table like a tablecloth. He also issued a report and put these ten pages in an appendix. It was impossible to get an understanding of the group's structure and interrelationships because readers had to constantly flick back and forth between pages ('Ah, this bit continues on page 8').

Firstly, let's quickly see why the conventional way doesn't work well.

The conventional organisation chart

A typical chart is shown in Figure 9.2. It shows the holding company (B&W Group Ltd), then various levels of subsidiary. It suffers from several problems, many of which you should be familiar with by now.

FIGURE 9.2

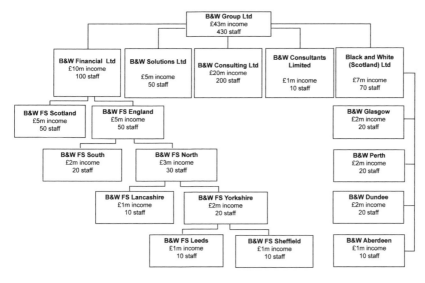

Firstly, there are the boxes around the names. They visually dominate. They isolate and fragment information, making it more difficult to scan and compare – readers' eyes have to constantly leap over black borders. And they look hierarchical and bureaucratic. Is that the impression you wish to create?

But even if you wanted to get rid of the borders, you can't – the words would run into each other. The second row would read 'B&W Financial Ltd B&W Solutions Ltd' without pause or break.

Secondly, the chart tries to show numbers such as income and staff but shows them badly. Study the second row of boxes, the one starting 'B&W Financial Ltd'. It's difficult to scan and compare numbers across divisions because comparable numbers are in rows not columns, and we find it more difficult to scan across rows (see page 117). Also, comparable numbers aren't aligned properly: income and staff numbers for the two entities on the right are a row lower than for the two entities to the left of them, and the numbers for the far left entity align with none of the others. (I deliberately misaligned numbers in this chart simply because it happens so often in organisation charts – poor attention to detail leaves charts looking a bit slapdash.)

Thirdly, you can't squeeze many business units on a single page – maybe 30 maximum – and as businesses get bigger and more complex, that is not enough.

Finally, it is poor at highlighting hierarchy. Look at the bottom left of the chart, and 'B&W FS Leeds' is five levels from the top. Now look at the bottom right – 'B&W Aberdeen' is just two from the top. Yet in the chart, they seem to be at the same level within the group simply because they are both on the bottom row. That's because we wanted to squeeze more units onto the one page, so we put the Scottish units down the page, not along a row.

The same bad layout applies to staff charts. I've seen non-executive directors shown like the chart in Figure 9.3. It suffers from the usual problems – black borders, poor use of space, and so on. It says the words 'non executive director' seven times. Also, its layout raises questions: why are Violet, Brown and White on the top row? And if you want to add further details (e.g. age, experience, other directorships), you don't have room; so much space has been taken up with the boxed-in names.

Why not just lay it out as in Figure 9.4? It's neat, logical, easy to scan. If you wish to give more details, such as each director's age or experience or other directorships, just create more columns to the right. And as we see next, the layout is similar to how we should show organisation charts.

FIGURE 9.3

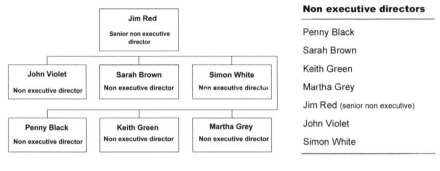

FIGURE 9.4

Non executive directors
Penny Black
Sarah Brown
Keith Green
Martha Grey
Jim Red (senior non executive)
John Violet
Simon White

A better way to show the structure

FIGURE 9.5

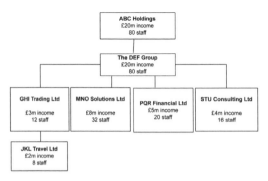

Figure 9.5 is the conventional structure chart we saw earlier. Figure 9.6 shows it laid out not top to bottom but *left* to *right*.

The hierarchy of the group is denoted by the short gridlines on the left – ABC Holdings has one subsidiary, DEF, which in turn has four subsidiaries, and so on. Company names no longer run into each other, so we don't need borders to separate

FIGURE 9.6

	Statistics			Directors					Notes	Activity
	Income	Gross profit	Staff	Dave Smith	Bill Brown	Sally Pink	Peter Black	David Grey		
	£m	£m	Nos							
ABC Holdings				✓	✓				Registered in the Isle of Man	Holding company
(100%) The DEF Group	20.0	2.0	80	✓	✓	✓			£5m goodwill	Group trading company
(100%) MNO Solutions Ltd	8.0	0.8	32	✓		✓			Halved in size last year	Global accounts
(80%) PQR Financial Ltd	5.0	0.5	20	✓		✓	✓		20% held by passive investor	Targets IFAs
(51%) STU Consulting Ltd	4.0	0.4	16	✓		✓			49% held by Chief Executive	Consulting - Wales only
(100%) GHI Trading Ltd	3.0	0.3	12	✓		✓	✓		Pension deficit of £10m	Broking
(X%) = shares held by Group										
(76%) JKL Travel Ltd	2.0	0.2	8	✓		✓	✓		50% of income from Ukraine	Travel insurance

them. We have room for more information – we show percentage holdings (e.g. STU Consulting is 51% owned). We show income, gross profit and staff numbers. We show the directors of each entity and we give notes on items of interest (e.g. MNO Solutions has halved in size). We also describe the activity of each company.

Try shoehorning all that into a conventional organisation chart.

There are even more benefits. Comparable numbers are in columns and hence are easier to scan. And we've avoided unnecessarily repeating labels – the word 'income' is said once, not seven times.

It offers a far greater *richness* than conventional charts. This level of detail might not be appropriate for a slide in a presentation, but it is great for reports. You can either take half a page to badly show the structure and a few numbers, or take the same space to elegantly show much more.

Maybe you don't need extra richness, maybe you just want to show hierarchy. In which case the left-to-right layout is still far superior.

Figure 9.7 shows both detail and overview for over 200 units spread over six reporting levels – and the layout still gives room for extra information as well. When I did the chart for the group with 250 subsidiaries, its management accounts pack was over 200 pages and a nightmare to navigate. So on the organisation chart, I wrote the relevant page number alongside each business unit's name (e.g. next to ABC's name on the chart, I put '184' in brackets, signalling that ABC's figures were on page 184 of the management accounts).

The schedule became the indispensable reference tool for the project team.

I've even done a reports' index as a 'left-to-right organisation chart', (Figure 9.8). The 'chart/ index' not only shows where to find items in the report (there's a page number in brackets after each name), but also shows

FIGURE 9.7

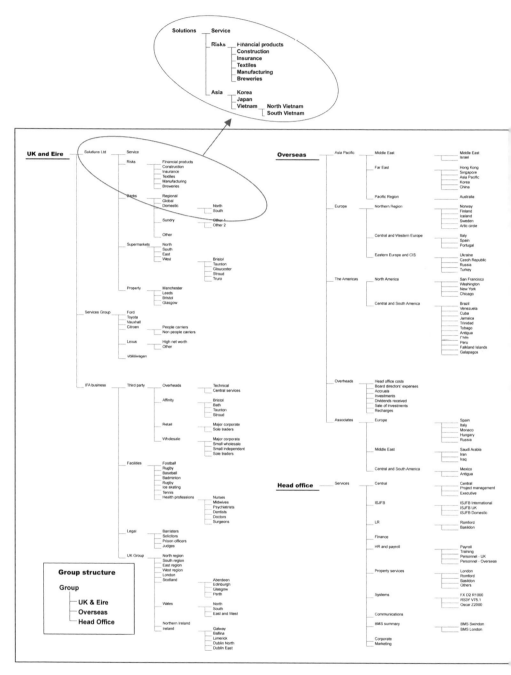

FIGURE 9.8

the group structure and describes each unit's line of business. Also, I've done something different to the 'chart/ index' – it's not at the front of the report but at the back on a folded A3 page (you can only really do this if the report is circulated not in soft-copy form but bound, then distributed). Readers can unfold the A3 page, then refer to it as they read and scan the report. The page helps them understand group structure *and* navigate the report.

For any accountants out there, this pullout A3 back page is great for commentary in your information packs (again, this assumes the pack isn't circulated in soft-copy form). Many finance departments can churn out page after page of tables or graphs with no manual intervention, but tables and graphs benefit from a lead-in comment. Rather than putting a comment on every page and having to cope with many manual interventions, just have one – put all comments on the right half of a pullout A3 back page (Figure 9.9). Readers can put the report on their desk, unfold the A3 page at the back, then refer to its comments as they go through the pack. Also, the comments will be better formatted – you can do them properly in Word rather than squeeze them into text boxes between spreadsheet tables. Notice that I've done the comments in 'WiT'.

Time to return to organisation charts. Despite all their faults, conventional charts are almost universal – but not quite. When I do Google image searches, about one chart in a hundred goes left to right. One entity laid out its organisation left to right and effortlessly showed 39 business units

FIGURE 9.9

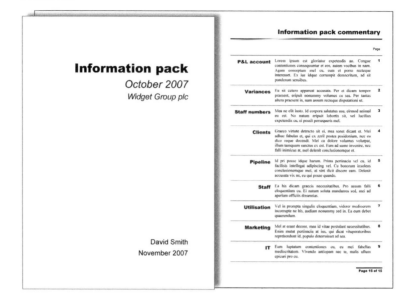

spread over five hierarchies on a single sheet of paper. Unfortunately, it snatched defeat from the jaws of victory by putting every business unit's name in a box. The chart was effortless – but inelegant.

A shame really, given that the box wasn't particularly needed.

One organisation got it spot-on: the Office of the Auditor General for Western Australia had a great organisation chart in its 2005 Annual Report. It showed its organisation chart left to right and found room to include directors' CVs and photos and team members. It is an elegant and thoughtfully designed chart (http://www.audit.wa.gov.au/reports/annualreport2005/organisation-chart.gif)

FIGURE 9.10

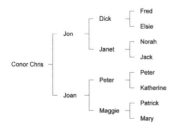

You may recognise the left-to-right layout, it is often done for genealogy, the charting of family trees (Figure 9.10). Family trees have been around a long time, so the custom and practice of charting them has survived the onslaught of new, 'better', modern ways of showing information.

Often family trees have more information on them, e.g. dates of births, deaths, marriages. And often they are elegantly laid out. Notice how the horizontal lines in Figure 9.10 are as short as possible so as not to visually detract from the names.

The final example is from Microsoft itself (Figure 9.11). Most of us regularly see this one, it is the file directory layout. It effortlessly shows hierarchy. Left to right really does work.

Next we briefly look at how to prepare these charts – and it isn't in PowerPoint.

FIGURE 9.11

```
Desktop
  My Documents
  My Computer
    Local Disk (C:)
      CanoScan
      Cartoon
      DELL
      DemoJava
      Documents and Settings
      DRIVERS
      Fonts
      I386
      My Documents
      MyFlashProjects
      MyJava
      mysql
      NFL2005
```

The technology bit

To do a left-to-right chart, use Excel. Fix the column widths and put in cell borders appropriately and you're there. Figure 9.12 shows part of an organisation table prepared in Excel. On the left we see the cells of the spreadsheet and see also the cells we've given borders to (the borders' thicknesses are exaggerated so you can see them). On the right is how it appears when printed.

FIGURE 9.12

When including extra information to the right, you can dispense with the gridlines that stretch across the page if you so wish. Instead, maybe try a very light shading running across the row (Figure 9.13). There are pros and cons of gridlines versus shading. I'm not a fan of shading but grids can hinder readers as they scan down a column of numbers.

FIGURE 9.13

	Statistics			Directors					Notes	Activity
	Income	Gross profit	Staff	Dave Smith	Bill Brown	Sally Pink	Peter Black	David Grey		
	£m	£m	Nos							
ABC Holdings				✓	✓				Registered in the Isle of Man	Holding company
(100%) The DEF Group	20.0	2.0	80	✓	✓	✓			£5m goodwill	Group trading company
(100%) MNO Solutions Ltd	8.0	0.8	20	✓			✓		Halved in size last year	Global accounts
(80%) PQR Financial Ltd	5.0	0.5	20	✓		✓	✓		20% held by passive investor	Targets IFAs
(51%) STU Consulting Ltd	4.0	0.4	20	✓			✓		49% held by Chief Executive	Consulting - Wales only
(100%) GHI Trading Ltd	3.0	0.3	20	✓			✓	✓	Pension deficit of £10m	Broking
(76%) JKL Travel Ltd	2.0	0.2	8	✓			✓	✓	50% of income from Ukraine	Travel insurance

Final thoughts and recap

We've seen a few organisation charts this chapter but haven't yet seen this horror (Figure 9.14). It's often seen in reports to prospective clients: 'The chart on the left shows our group structure'. Wow! And note that it took nine words to introduce the chart.

FIGURE 9.14

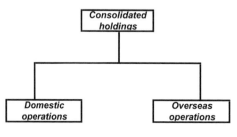

If explaining the structure to a nine-year-old, you'd say 'The group is split between domestic and overseas operations'. What a coincidence – nine words too. Nine words to explain the structure or nine words just to introduce a typographically bad chart of the structure.

If you must do a chart to explain the structure, then at least get rid of the box borders and keep connecting lines short and faint – like the family tree.

It gets even worse when there are just two boxes: holding company and subsidiary. Investment banks seem to like this one, they do it a lot. On that note, let's have the shortest recap in the whole book.

Recap

Do organisation charts left to right, not top to bottom. Use Excel to create them.

Try a pullout A3 back page as an index to help readers navigate reports whilst also understanding the group structure.

And if you're an accountant, try a pullout A3 back page for the commentaries in your information packs (assuming you distribute the report in hard copy).

And that's it.

Chapter **10**

Next steps

Rolling out these ideas to benefit even more from them

It's worse than it was before, if I hadn't seen such riches,
I could live with being poor.
James, 'Sit Down'

I once read an impenetrable 30-page report by an accountancy firm and had to fly a thousand miles so the firm could spend four hours explaining it to me. Yet on my return to the office, a colleague said we should send the 30 pages to our directors so they could read it too. It was a strange idea. He seemed to accept impenetrable reports as just being the way things are. Everyone's confused by them. Everyone expects to be confused by them. And no one minds if they are.

Now it's different. We've seen just how much better things can be and how to make them better. And clarity and impact are virtuous circles. With clear work, the more people see it, the more they want to see it. Once they've seen riches, they can no longer live with being poor.

If you apply the ideas in this book, your documents and slides will be clearer than you thought possible. It doesn't matter if they are year-end slides for the analysts, a written client sales pitch, a monthly management accounts pack, an industry circular, HR KPIs or just a one-page note, they will all benefit. I know they will because I've redone all of these for my clients using these principles.

Not only will the documents be better, but you will feel in *control* when preparing them. When you know you're doing the right thing, your work is more confident. And to help you do the right thing, below are ideas for rolling out these tips and principles among your colleagues:

Be more demanding of your colleagues' work	If confused, stand up and be counted. Don't rationalise away your confusion. Demand the information be improved. Remember the London Tube map – everyone thought it fine until Mr Beck did his iconic version.
Be more demanding of your own work	You know how to do things better, so think twice before printing off that table of numbers or lazily clicking on the Graph Wizard or blasting out slide after slide of bullet points. Be harsh on yourself – if you find yourself saying: 'What this report is meant to say . . .', it means the report doesn't clearly say it.
Be proactive about rolling out this book's tips in the organisation	Get your colleagues into clarity too – the clearer their work, the less time you spend wading through it. Don't let people defer your enthusiasm until after 'HR has done its annual Training Needs Analyses' (wow!). No one will say 'I want to learn how to do better bullet points', they don't realise there's a problem with them. And even if they did,

people think it more fun to sign up for a 'body language' course ('His report is bad but he sure can *sit* well').

So be proactive and help your colleagues to help you. And remember to check out 'Info Bingo' (www.jmoon.co.uk/downloads).

Involve end-users with changes to their reports	If changing the information pack you do every month, take time to involve the end-users. Talk through the differences between 'before' and 'after'. Good changes always look better when contrasted with the earlier bad version.
Look for chances that give you a mandate for change	A company restructure will alter reporting lines and comparative figures, maybe even the KPIs. So if those are changing, why not tweak the templates while you're about it? And watch out for confusion. If people ask questions that show they don't understand the documents they receive, is this an opportunity? Offer to redo the schedule to see if you can make it clearer for them.

And the learning doesn't end here. Build your awareness and knowledge. Study work done by consultants and colleagues, in newspapers and trade magazines. It helps develop your awareness and gives you ideas and inspiration. If confused or impressed by something, work out why and internalise the lesson. Build a library of the good and the bad. Try other books – but take care of advice on the Internet, there's some dodgy ideas out there ('Never have more than four numbers on a slide'). And let me know if you spot anything of interest or have observations to share.

A 'clarity' checklist – how clear is your information?

Check your monthly accounts and KPIs, your restructuring and investment proposals. Also review your client pitches – often their first impression is good but the rest is poor. If your documents don't stand up well to scrutiny, the analysis is probably poor too – incomplete, illogical, flawed. Flabby information is often a sign of flabby thinking.

Yet if you tighten one, you tighten the other. Clear information leads to clear thinking, and clear thinking leads to clear information.

▶

First impression	Is it inviting? Or intimidating, with numerous long numbers, endless bullet points and dense text?
Understanding	Can you digest it quickly? Or do you struggle? Do the authors have to talk you through it?
Good detail?	Do you know the point each graph makes? Or are they just there to break up dull text? Have you been told the message behind each table? Or do you have to guess it? Do you value the bullet points? Or merely endure them?
Recalling	Can you easily summarise the report? If yes, without referring back to the report, great. If yes, but only if referring back, not bad. But if a struggle even when referring back, there's a problem.

The benefits of clarity are numerous. You will prepare a more complete analysis – compare this to bullet points, which are a random collation of thoughts with no structure that ensures completeness. Your work is more likely to be read, it is more inviting and engaging for your readers. Your points will come across more clearly, readers will understand and absorb them faster, saving time and money. People will have more informed discussions because they can more easily refer back to the information. Better decisions are reached more quickly. Clear work gets *results*.

You really will never look at a table, bullet point, slide, graph, note, report or information pack in the same way. And with your heightened awareness of information design, I suspect you will never look at a road sign, a museum map or a poster in the same way either. The principles in the book are relevant for so many aspects of life.

For me, writing this book is the latest stage in a journey I started over 14 years ago. And it has been a wonderful journey, full of exploration, creativity and discovery. Whether your goal is to influence, inform, impress – whether it's clarity, elegance or impact – I really hope this book helps you on a similarly wonderful journey too.

Appendix

....

Computing

How to do some of the ideas in this book on your PC

- ➤ Doing some of the graphs in this book
- ➤ Excel versus Word for reports and information packs
- ➤ Formatting numbers, variably rounding, computing percentage variances

'To start press any key' . . . where's the 'any' key?
Homer Simpson

This appendix shows you how to get your computer to do some of the more unusual graphs we've seen in this book. Then we look at Excel versus Word for reports and how to link between them. Finally, we see how to format numbers, how to variably round and how to compute meaningful and correct percentage variances.

This appendix doesn't show you how to change line spacing or border thicknesses or any other routine IT queries. To find the answers to these, try the IT department, the person at the next desk, the 'Help' button or a Google search.

Remember also to check out the templates on www.pearson-books.com/impact or www.jmoon.co.uk/downloads.

Plotting some of the graphs in this book

Here's how I got Excel to do some of the graphs. For all I know, other graphical software packages might do them more easily, but I assume most readers do their graphs in Excel. Also, there may be better ways to do them in Excel than I describe – if you know a way, please drop me a line.

The logo chart
(page 58)

FIGURE A.1

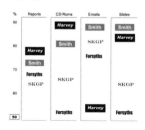

If wondering how Figure A.1 was plotted – it wasn't. I simply did a spreadsheet and put text boxes on the spreadsheet at the approximate place they needed to be. Not very scientific. Very steam driven. I suspect a lookup function might automate it and would put either a blank or a logo in a particular cell.

The UNICEF chart
FIGURE A.2 (page 60)

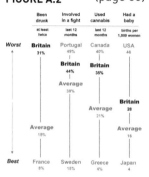

There are several steps to doing Figure A.2. Rebase numbers for all four *aspects* so that statistics for each aspect go from 0 to 1, e.g. for 'cannabis use', the report's statistics ranged from 40.4% to 4.2%, but when rebased they turn into the numbers in the right column of Figure A.3. If unsure how to do the maths for this rebasing, find someone who's into numbers and they'll do it in a jiffy. Alternatively, to rebase, say, '34.9', it's [(34.9/lowest number) – 1]/[(highest number/lowest number) –1].

FIGURE A.3

	Original	Rebased
Highest	40.4	1.00
Britain	34.9	0.85
Average	21.4	0.48
Lowest	4.2	0.00

FIGURE A.4

A	B	C
Lowest	1	0.00
Highest	1	1.00
Average	1	0.32
Britain	**1**	**1.00**
Lowest	2	0.00
Highest	2	1.00
Average	2	0.69
Britain	**2**	**0.86**
Lowest	3	0.00
Highest	3	1.00
Average	3	0.48
Britain	**3**	**0.85**
Lowest	4	0.00
Highest	4	1.00
Average	4	0.29
Britain	**4**	**0.57**

Then lay out the rebased numbers like columns B and C in Figure A.4 , i.e. repeating groups of 'lowest, highest, average, Britain'. Each group is for one of the four aspects. Put the groupings in descending order of 'Britain' score (see how the bold numbers decrease as you go down the table). Doing this ensures your graph's vertical lines are in order of Britain's 'badness'.

Then plot columns B and C as an 'x-y' plot – select the option that gives you just dots. Remove the x- and y-axes, and insert faint vertical gridlines. If too many vertical gridlines, make 'major unit' equal one, not 0.5.*

Insert text boxes for the words and individual statistics and give each text box a white fill and no border (i.e. no 'line'). The dots in the x–y graph tell you where to put the text boxes (though it's obvious where the highest and lowest text boxes go). Once all text boxes are in place, you can get rid of the dots on the graph, you no longer need them.

Head up each column with a text box that describes it. To help readers more intuitively understand the chart, put the arrow on the left, the one that says 'better' or 'worse'.

* If you find it easier to manipulate and align text boxes using PowerPoint, reach * above, copy the graph across into PowerPoint and then add the labels.

The graph of 2002 to 2006 income by territory (page 65)

FIGURE A.5

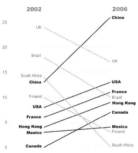

This one is a little bit fiddly (Figure A.5), but it's worth it if the report is important.

In Excel, put the 2002 figures in a column on the left and the 2006 figures in a column on the right. Don't bother with names or with the 100% total at the bottom. Then highlight the two columns and select the top left 'line' chart in Excel. Make sure you click on 'series in rows'. Remove background shading, lighten horizontal grids. Make upward-sloping lines dark and downward-sloping lines lighter.

Then put in two white boxes (with no borders) in order to hide the horizontal gridlines between

$x = 0$ and $x = 1$, and between $x = 2$ and $x = 2.5$. Then use text boxes to add the territory names on top of these white boxes. Use a text box to add the graph title.

The inverted graph – 'dollar weakens'
(page 74)
FIGURE A.6

The dollar weakens

I plotted not the exchange rate but 'minus the exchange rate' (Figure A.6). This gave a downward-sloping graph – but the axis runs from minus 1.6 down to minus 1.616. So format the numbers on the y-axis so they don't have a minus sign in front of them.

Excel versus Word and linking between them

This might sound obvious, but Excel is great for numbers and Word is great for words. Now you know. Word does much smarter text than text boxes in Excel – in Excel text boxes you can't change line spacing or do indents and so on. Also, in Excel a table's row heights are very much constrained by the row heights of other tables alongside it – and sometimes you don't want this. Sometimes you want one table to have a small font and hence a narrow row height, whilst the other one alongside it to have a larger font and hence a larger row height. We saw this on page 238.

So if doing something that you want to look smart, don't keep it in Excel with lots of text boxes splattered all over the place. Instead use Excel to do tables and graphs, then copy or link them to Word. Then type and format your words as you wish. See below for how to link between Excel and Word.

Tip: The default Excel colour palette has only four different shades of grey, the lightest shade being 'Grey 25%'. Which isn't that light. To get more shades, modify the default palette using 'Tools', 'Options', 'Colour', 'Modify'. You get the same wide range of colours as offered by Word and PowerPoint.

Putting Excel tables and graphs into Word

If you aren't bothered about keeping the link, shade the area in Excel to copy across, then hold down the 'upper case' button on the keyboard, and left-click on 'Edit' – select 'Copy Picture', then select 'As shown when printed'. Go into Word and then use 'Edit', 'Paste Special'. I always paste the 'Picture (Enhanced Metafile)', though there's no great reason or logic for why I do it. It just seems to work. Finally, select 'Paste', not 'Paste Link'.

If you want to keep the link between the spreadsheet and the Word document, it isn't a case of doing the procedures above and doing the end bit differently – if you select 'Paste Link', it doesn't work well. If you try resizing the linked object in Word, content disappears, formats change. It's weird. I'm sure there's a reason why, but I don't know it.

So to keep the link *and* the formats when copying across, use Ctrl-C over the area to be copied, then go into Word and Select 'Edit', 'Paste Special', 'Microsoft Excel Worksheet Object', 'Paste Link'.

Once you've got the item in Word, position and resize as you want. To get your text in Word to run down the side of the graph, right-click on the picture, select 'Format Picture' (or 'Format Object'), then select 'Layout'. 'Square' or 'In line with text' are pretty good ones to try. (All of this will make sense when you have a go.) If, however, you find the Excel picture moves around the page like it's got a life of its own (you will know what I mean if and when it happens to you), then go for 'Behind text' or 'In front of text'. Then fix the position of your words in Word so none get in the way of the Excel object.

Finally, it can sometimes be difficult to grab back hold of your Excel object if it is placed outside the text boundary or if it sits in a Word table (again, you will know what I mean when it happens). Here's a way around this. When in Excel and highlighting the area to copy, highlight a bit beyond the area you actually need (say one-third extra all the way round) – give it a bit of a boundary. The boundary will be blank so, when it's in Word, no one will see it anyway. But it means that when your graph is sitting in the margin of a Word document, its boundary stretches invisibly over the text area alongside it. You can now grab the graph by clicking on the text area nearby. The same applies when putting Excel graphs and tables in a Word table. Give the object a big boundary so a bit of it extends beyond the left or right of the Word table. Then to grab the object, click just outside the bit of the table where the object is.

Showing numbers in Excel

This section gets your computer to do three things we've looked at previously: a decent format for numbers, variable rounding, and meaningful and correct variances.

Formatting numbers

The Excel formula below puts a '–' for a zero, puts brackets around negative numbers, and shunts negative numbers slightly to the right so the brackets don't throw out of alignment the smallest digits of positive and negative numbers:

 #,##0_);(#,##0);-_);@

To get Word to shunt bracketed negative numbers, do this:

1   At the very top left of the ruler in Word, there is a small square with a dark 'L' in it. Use the mouse to move the cursor so it hovers over this box, then click on the box three times. You will then see an upside-down 'T' with a dot after it. This is the marker for aligning decimals.

2   With the 'inverted T and dot' showing, click in the ruler bar where you want to align your decimals.

3   Tab across to this and then type your numbers, putting brackets around negative numbers. These bracketed negative numbers will be shunted slightly right.

Also, use the 'inverted T and dot' in Word tables too.

Variable rounding in Excel

To get Excel to variably round is a bit contrived and needs two steps:

1   *First Excel has to round to two digits*, e.g. you need to get Excel to round £3,623m to £3,600m.

2   *Then Excel has to round certain numbers to three digits if big rounding errors arise*, e.g. if you have £1,156m and £1,244m, you want Excel to show them to three digits (£1,160m and £1,240m), not two. If Excel showed them both as £1,200m, the two numbers would look the same, even though they are 8% apart from each other.

Here's how to do each of the two steps. And remember to check out www.jmoon.co.uk/downloads – Figure A.7 is there as an Excel file, along with the rounding formulae. That should save you having to retype it all.

Step 1: Get Excel to round to two digits An actuary once sent me this – it's really rather clever:

=ROUND(A1,-MAX(0,IF(A1=0,0,INT(LOG10(ABS(A1))))-1))

It shows the number in cell A1 to two digits. To show to three digits, change the final number in the above formula from '1' to '2'. To show to one digit, change it to '0'. And so on. It works for both positive and negative numbers.

Excel 'Help' gives a different formula for rounding the number in 'A1' to two digits:

=ROUND(A1,2-LEN(INT(A1)))

(To round to three digits, replace the '2' with '3'.)

It rounds positive numbers correctly: 5,432 becomes 5,400. But it goes awry with negative numbers: –5,432 becomes –5,000. When Excel is deciding how many numbers to keep, it seems to be counting the minus sign as a number. Of course, a simple 'IF' function can correct this error. Alternatively, use the actuary's formula instead.

No matter which of the two you use, they need step 2 – a mechanism to round to an extra digit if big rounding errors arise.

Step 2: Round to an extra digit if big rounding errors arise This has always worked when I've used it, but I can't promise it works under all scenarios. To *variably* round a column of numbers, do the following.

In column A (Figure A.7), put the unrounded numbers. In column B, round them to two digits using the formula above. In column C, round them to three digits, again using the formula above but tweaked so as to deliver three digits, not two. In column D, compare each number in column A with the number above it and work out the percentage difference that exists between them. The somewhat weird boxed '9999' on row 1 is a spreadsheeting fix, done because the top row can't compare with a number above it – there isn't one. The '9999' ensures we get the answer we want for the top row.

Then column E works out if we need to show two or three digits. We choose the '2 digit' number if there is a reasonable difference between numbers on different rows. If numbers on different rows are close to each other, we need to retain an extra digit so we don't incorrectly show close numbers as the same. I decided the 'reasonable difference' was 10%. Column E checks out

FIGURE A.7

	No rounding	2 digits	3 digits	% diff between rows	Variably rounded numbers
	A	B	C	D	E
1	3,623	3,600	3,620	9999	3,600
2	1,092	1,100	1,090	232%	1,100
3	753	750	753	45%	750
4	297	300	297	153%	300
5	124	120	124	140%	124
6	116	120	116	7%	116
7	114	110	114	1%	114
8	103	100	103	11%	100
9	45	45	45	129%	45
10	23	23	23	97%	23

column D *and column D in the next row down the spreadsheet* – and if either is less than 10%, column E shows a number to three digits. If not, it shows a number to two digits. The italicised bit is to ensure we compare a number not just to the one above but to the one beneath too. Study the number in row 5. It's nowhere near the number in row 4 , but is close to the number in row 6. So we need to retain three digits.

And we're there. It's not the easiest of exercises. Alternatively, just do step 1 and then simply give the numbers a quick once-over to make sure big rounding errors haven't arisen – and if they have, make any adjustments manually. With just a few numbers, that should be fine. But if you have a lot of numbers that you wish to variably round automatically, it's worth doing step 2 too.

Percentage changes with negative numbers

Variances are often computed as [(This Year)/(Last Year) – 1]%. Chapter 7 showed how this can easily give wrong answers with negative numbers (e.g. a loss turning into a profit). Also, this formula gives numbers like +350%, and percentages greater than 100% start to confuse people.

To get decent variances, I use the following formula. It uses seven nested 'IF' functions in Excel, but I do have a sneaking suspicion a more elegant way exists (this formula is in my website's downloads too):

=IF(This_Year=0,"na",IF(Last_year=0,"na",IF (Difference/Last_year>1,IF(Last_year<0,"<(99%), ">99%"),IF(Difference/Last_year<1,IF(Last_year<0, ">99%","<(99%)),IF(Last_year<0, -Difference/Last_year,Difference/Last_year)))))

FIGURE A.8

	Last year	This year
	£'m	£'m
	A	B
1	5	5
2	5	4
3	5	6
4	5	(3)
5	5	(7)
6	5	12
7	(4)	(4)
8	(4)	(6)
9	(4)	(2)
10	(4)	2
11	(4)	6
12	(4)	(10)
13	-	(2)
14	-	2
15	(2)	-
16	-	-
17	1	-

'This_Year' is this year's profit, 'Last_Year' is last year's, 'Difference' is 'This_Year' less 'Last_Year'. Also, 'na', '>99%' and '<(99%)' are cross-references to cells that have this text in them.

Figure A.8 shows 17 different configurations of profits and losses for two consecutive years – profits staying the same and losses staying the same, losses becoming a profit, small changes in profit or loss and big changes in them too.

If you apply the normal variance formula, it gives decent answers only four times out of 17 (rows 1, 2, 3 and 7). For all the others, it gives the wrong sign or a number that is greater than 100% or less than minus 100% (which confuses people) or #DIV/0! (which is meaningless and visually distracting, especially if a lot of them are on the page).

If you apply the seven nested 'IF' functions, it shows a number with the right percentage sign or shows '<(99%)' or '>99%' or 'na' if appropriate. It gives correct, meaningful and understandable variances.

Do let me know if the formula can be replaced with something more elegant. Years ago, someone got one of my spreadsheets and replaced five nested 'IF' functions with simple 'MAX' and 'MIN' functions. I was both impressed and depressed. Maybe someone can replace the seven nested 'IF' functions with something elegant and simple.

Bibliography

These books all share something in common – they hardly mention computers. Find out what you *should* do before worrying about *how* to do it on a computer.

The list is not in any order of preference.

How to Lie with Statistics by Darrell Huff (1999, Penguin)
A quick, short, entertaining paperback that talks in lay terms about the tricks people play with numbers.

The Visual Display of Quantitative Information (2001, Graphics Press)
Envisioning Information (1990, Graphics Press)
The Cognitive Style of PowerPoint (2003, Graphics Press)
all by Edward Tufte

Two of Edward Tufte's books helped get me into the topic about 14 years ago, so I have a soft spot for them. Neither book is specifically about business information – but this makes the analyses, observations and principles seem even more all-embracing and important. Amazon describes *The Visual Display of Quantitative Information* as one of the top 100 books of the twentieth century. *Envisioning Information* was his follow-up book. *The Cognitive Style of PowerPoint* is a thought-provoking article on the humble bullet point and why both it and PowerPoint should be banned. For all these, visit www.edwardtufte.com. And while there, click on 'Ask ET' and have a browse, it's fascinating.

The Non-Designer's Design Book (2003, PeachPit Press)
The PC is not a Typewriter (1992, PeachPit Press)
both by Robin Williams

Of all the books I've read on design, two really worked for me, both by Robin Williams, the female American designer. In the mid 1990s she published *The Non-Designer's Design Book* which outlined her four design principles. Doubtless there are other 'principles' dreamt up by other designers, but Robin's are easy to understand and quickly make a big difference to documents – and are easy to remember. Also, her book is accessible with a great range of 'before' and 'after' versions, both social and business: party invites, business flyers, report covers, business cards, newsletters, and so on. It's all in black and white too, so you don't feel it's only for fancy designers with Apple Macs.

She also wrote *The PC is not a Typewriter*, a slightly different book. It is less visual with few of the 'before' and 'after's that peppered her other book, but instead has lots on fonts, capitals, quote marks, and so on. The book's quick and easy style again made it a winner for me. This one is more for the real enthusiast, though, not just the casually interested.

Mr Beck's Underground Map by Ken Garland (1994, Capital Transport Publishing)
A fascinating story of love and devotion to one of the world's most iconic images. Warning: it borders on the obsessive – but it's that attention to detail that's made the tube map so brilliant.

www.plainenglish.co.uk
This is the website for the Plain English Campaign. It's good fun and educational too. It has the annual Golden Bull Award for the worst gobbledegook. It has some great downloadable free guides on plain English, simple alternative words, and so on. It has also recently developed free downloadable software that will check your work for plain English – 'drivel defence'. I haven't tried it so can't vouch for it. But I highly recommend a visit to the website and a look at the guides.

Books I referenced in the book
The Economist Numbers Guide (1998, John Wiley & Sons)
Dynamics of Document Design by Karen Schriver (1997, John Wiley & Sons)
A Primer in Data Reduction by Andrew Ehrenberg (1982, John Wiley & Sons)
Managing the Multibusiness Company by Michael Goold and Katheen Sommers Luchs (1996, Routledge)

Index

accuracy 179, 184
  unnecessary 180–1
acronyms 113, 174
  slides 155
active voice 159, 169
alignment 102, 103
  centre alignment 123, 216, 218
  of continuous text 24–5, 216–18, 227
  design principle 198–9, 201–4, 205–10, 228
  horizontal alignment 203–4
  KPIs 243–4
  left alignment 217
  negative numbers in tables 109, 110
  numbers in flash reports 242, 243
  right alignment 123, 218
  vertical alignment 90, 202–3
alphabetical order 93
argument, sequential line of 23–6, 37
Arial 168, 196–7, 199–200
arithmetic score 133
arrows 157
audience 33, 119–20, 147
  making the audience listen 163–5, 174
  slide preparation and 172
  use of colour and 221–2
audit trail 187
Auditor General for Western Australia 256
average column/row 112–13, 126
axes 51–3, 73, 76

balance sheets 102, 245–7
bar charts, stacked 70, 83
black and white 222
Blackberries 31
blank (empty) rows 62–3, 90, 101–2, 122, 125
blank (white) space 198, 199, 206, 227
borders 27, 28, 50, 80, 219, 227, 251

Boston Consulting Group matrix 137
brackets
  negative numbers 52, 109, 192
  unnecessary 108–10, 125
brief sections 21–3, 32, 39, 242–3
Buffet, Warren 72
bullet points 38, 143, 154, 175, 264
  comparisons and 128–31, 147
  hierarchies and 26, 27
  problems with 2–3, 13–14
  slides 168–71, 175
  turning a bullet point list into 'WiT 6–11
  using well 166–71
  when they are acceptable 30, 32–3
business reports 31, 39, 213–14

cartoons 156–7, 174
cash flows 99
centre alignment 123, 216, 218
change, mandate for 263
chart/index 253–4, 256
Churchill, Winston 159
circulars 213–14
clarity 262–3
  checklist 263–4
client meeting note 207–10
client pitch 12–15, 36
clipart 156
cluster charts 137–40, 140–1, 161, 162, 166, 174
clustered column charts 55, 58, 59, 67, 70–1, 83
clustering 8–9, 12, 40, 167
clutter, typographical 220
colour 51
  design and 220–4, 229
  slides and 171, 221

colour blindness 221, 223
column charts 50, 55, 56–8, 61, 83
    multiple 55, 58, 59, 67, 70–1, 83
    paired 64–5, 83
    side-by-side 61, 70, 83
    time-series data 57, 63–4, 64–5
column headings 91, 92, 123, 126
    indecipherable 113–16
column labels 114, 123
columns 11, 167
    aligning tops of 203
    average columns 112–13, 126
    bullet points 7, 9
    ordering in tables 87, 92–100, 121, 125
        comparable columns adjacent to
            each other 93, 95–6
        most important column nearest
            labels 93, 94–5
        order for comparable columns 93, 96
    vs rows for data 117–20, 126
communication, principles of 154
compact tables 87, 100–3, 125
comparable numbers 118–19
comparisons 127–49
    cluster charts 137–40, 140–1
    decision trees 142–7
    graphs for 55–63
        few sets of data 58–61
        multiple data sets 61–3
        single data set 56–8
    grids 133–7, 147, 148, 149
    ranges 136, 137–9, 140–2
    tables of ticks and crosses 128–33, 136
competitors' income 181, 181–3
completeness 3, 130–1
    'WiT' and ensuring 12–14
complexity 73
compound interest computations 186
computing 265–73
    Excel vs Word 268
    linking between Excel and Word 269
    plotting graphs 266–8
    showing numbers in Excel 270–3
conclusion, starting with the 7–8, 167
confusion 262, 263
    numbers as source of 178–9, 187
consistency 130, 159, 223
    rounding numbers 185
    tables 116–17, 126
    typography 201

'WiT' and ensuring 19–21, 38
contact details 241
context, numbers and 190–1, 192, 244
continuous text 197
    alignment of 24–5, 216–18, 227
    line spacing 218
contrast 10, 159
    design principle 198–9, 199–200,
        205–10, 228
control checks 186
copier/printer 222
correlations 75
cumulative graphs 71–2, 83
currencies 74
curriculum vitae (CV) 19–20, 38, 206–7

data markers 51
dates 220
decision trees 142–7, 160–1, 174
decodifiers 114, 126
derived numbers 187
descending order 63, 93
design 5, 193–230
    applying the principles 205–10
    colour 220–4, 229
    fonts 196–7, 199–200, 227
    ideas for documents 210–14, 229–30
    principles 198–205, 228
        alignment 198–9, 201–4, 205–10, 228
        contrast 198–9, 199–200, 205–10, 228
        proximity 198–9, 204–5, 205–10, 228
        repetition 198–9, 200–1, 205–10, 228
    typographical tips 197–8, 215–20, 227
design department 194, 224
design templates 33, 225–6, 230
detail 76, 264
'difference' column 101
discount rules 143–4, 160, 161
document design see design

editing 5
effective digits 183
emails 31, 39
emphasis
    avoiding mistakes in document design
        215–16
    avoiding too much emphasis in tables
        87, 91–2, 124
empty rows 62–3, 90, 101–2, 122, 125
end-users, involving 263

errors
    hiding with rounding numbers 186
    rounding errors *see* rounding errors
European Union 178, 180
Excel 46, 50, 89
    changing how words wrap around in an
        Excel cell 115–16
    computing percentage changes 190
    default colour palette 224, 268
    linking to Word 269
        for landscape page 239–40
    plotting graphs 266–8
    showing numbers in 270–3
    using for left-to-right charts 257–8
    vs Word 268

faint gridlines 89
family trees 256
features and benefits table 12–14
findings of interest 6–11, 22, 35
flash reports 240–5, 248
flashes 213, 214, 229
flexibility 225–6
font size 91, 92, 199–200
    row height/font size ratio 102
fonts 196–7, 199–200, 227
formatting numbers 270
front cover 199, 211, 230
    logos on 230
full stops 203

genealogy 257
general impression 43
Gerstner, Louis 164–5
grammatical consistency 168
granularity 131, 141–2
graphs 41–84
    avoiding popular graphs for more than
        one set of data 69–72
    comparison graphs 55–63
    graphs unsuitable for clarity 83
    inverted 74–5, 77, 82, 268
    labels, words and axes 51–3
    overview and detail 76–7
    plotting 49–50, 80–1
    plotting with Excel 266–8
    in presentations 73–4, 84
    rebased 75–6
    'rules' for 79

sizing and positioning 53, 81
    time-series graphs 57, 63–9
    tips for smart graphs 48–55
    useful 81–2
    what makes a graph good 77–8, 80
    when to use 42–8, 80
grey 224
gridlines 49–50, 54, 80, 258
    removing unnecessary gridlines in
        tables 87, 88–90, 124
grids 133–7, 147, 148, 149, 160, 173

handouts 172–3, 175
haphazard layout 163
headings 197, 212
    breaks in 220, 227
    column headings *see* column headings
    line spacing 219
    unnecessary repetition in tables 111–13
    'WiT' 26–30, 37, 40
hierarchies
    highlighting in tables 103
    levels and 'WiT' 26–30, 37, 40
    organisation charts 251–2, 252–3
histograms, detailed 76, 82
horizontal alignment 203–4

ideas
    for documents 210–14, 229–30
        for any document 211–12
        for particular documents 212–14
    for slides 175
in–house design templates 33, 225–6, 230
income by overseas operation 64–6, 77,
        267–8
indenting 168
information packs 71–2, 232–40, 247, 248
    pullout A3 back page 255, 256, 259
insight 43–4
inverted graphs 74–5, 77, 82, 268
isobar graphs 50, 54, 73
italics 215

jargon 48
'jigsaw' slide 157
justified text 216, 217

key performance indicators (KPIs) 240–5,
        248
    'WiT' 15–17

labels 197
  graphs 51–3, 76, 81
  tables 91, 92
    alignment of labels 204
    labels for columns and rows 114–15, 123
    most important column next to labels 93, 94–5
    unnecessary repetition 111–13
landscape format 238, 239–40
  reports 212–13, 214, 230
lead-in titles 53, 169
  tables 87, 104–8, 125
left aligned text 217
left-to-right organisation charts 252–7
  using Excel 257–8
legends 51, 81
line of argument 23–6, 37
line graphs 63–4, 82, 83
  plotting 267–8
  time-series data 63–4, 65–9, 77, 267–8
line length 198, 227
line spacing 218–19, 227
lines
  between 'WiT' rows 34
  borders and 219, 227
list of issues 145–6
listening, encouraging in audience 163–5, 174
literal titles 53, 105
log graphs 50
logo chart 58–9, 60–1, 77, 82, 266
logos 226, 230
London Underground
  map 49, 262
  train timetable 76
long lines of text 198, 227

management accounts 232–48
  balance sheets 102, 245–7
  cash flows 99
  KPIs and flash reports 240–5, 248
  profit and loss see profit and loss account
  table of provisions for liabilities and charges 120–3, 237
  variance analysis 232–40, 247, 272–3
margin 198
mastertable 62–3, 81

McKinsey grid 137
memorability
  getting the message remembered 152–7, 174
  graphs and 44, 45
mental arithmetic 43, 93, 101, 179
message, memorability of 152–7, 174
metaphors 157, 175
Microsoft
  Excel see Excel
  file directory layout 257
  Word see Word
mini-graphs 67–9, 82
minimalism 152–4, 163–4
minutes of meetings 23, 207–10
mixing things up 171, 175
monthly update reports 4, 22–3, 35
Morgan, James 33
multiple column charts 55, 58, 59, 67, 70–1, 83
multiple data sets
  comparison graphs 61–3
  popular graphs to avoid 69–72
  time-series graphs 64–9
multiple pie charts 69, 72, 77, 83

narrative 17
negative numbers 52, 56, 192
  formatting 270
  percentage changes with 272–3
  tables 109, 110
numbering 167, 168
numbers 48, 154, 177–92
  alignment in flash reports 242, 243
  context and 190–1, 192, 244
  formatting and Excel 270
  graphs and 43–4
  gridlines butting up to 90
  KPIs 244
  negative see negative numbers
  organisation charts 251
  percentages 189–90, 192, 272–3
  rounding see rounding
  showing numbers in Excel 270–3
  showing in text 188, 192
  source of confusion 178–9, 187
  table for comparison 132–3
  in tables 110–11, 122
  vertical alignment 203
  see also graphs; tables

oddness, commenting on 106
Office of National Statistics (ONS) 106, 187
one-page summaries 240–5, 247, 248
ordering
    bullet points 167
    rows and columns in tables 87, 92–100,
        121, 125, 235
    'WiT' 8–9, 17, 40
organisation charts 249–59
    conventional 250–2
    left-to-right 252–7
    using Excel for left-to-right charts
        257–8
    overview 76
Oxford University rowing chart 45, 46

paired column charts 64–5, 83
paragraphs, starting at the end 10
percentages 189–90, 192
    big percentage changes 189
    computing percentage changes in Excel
        190
    percentage changes with negative
        numbers 272–3
pictograms 49
pidgin English 170
pie charts 44, 55, 56, 83
    multiple 69, 72, 77, 83
positioning
    graphs 53, 81
    mini-graphs 68–9
potential purchasers 137, 138, 140–2, 161,
        162
PowerPoint 36
    avoiding paraphernalia of 157, 175
    see also slides
presentations
    compiling at same time as report 136–7
    graphs in 73–4, 84
    tables in 107
    see also slides
printer/copier 222
profit and loss account 99, 109
    summary P&L 234, 236
proposal for client 26–30
pros and cons, table of 132
provisions for liabilities and charges
        120–3, 237
proximity 198–9, 204–5, 205–10, 228
pull quotes 25, 211, 229

pullout A3 back page 253–4, 256, 259
punctuation 170, 203

quantification 136
quote marks 203
quotes
    getting the message remembered
        155–6, 174
    pull quotes 25, 211, 229

RAG reports (Red, Amber, Green reports)
        17, 223
railway timetables 118, 220
random upper case 170, 215
ranges
    of data 136, 137–9, 140–2
    of numbers 188
reassurance of readers 18–19, 21, 38
rebased graphs 75–6
recall 152–7, 174, 264
reference tables 106
regulatory controls 137, 138
reordering tables 100
repeating patterns 21–3, 32, 39
repetition 130
    design principle 198–9, 200–1, 205–10,
        228
    unnecessary in tables 111–13
report index 18–19, 37
    left-to-right organisation charts 253–4,
        255
reports 31, 39, 213–14
reversing 216
right alignment 123, 218
rounding 180–7, 191–2
    balance sheets 245, 246–7
    KPIs 243
    reasons for not rounding 180
    variable 181–5, 191, 270–2
    when not to round 186–7, 192
    when to round big numbers more than
        small numbers 183–4
rounding errors 182, 183, 246–7
    rounding to an extra digit if big rounding
        errors arise 271–2
row height/font size ratio 102
row labels 114–15, 123
rowing chart (Oxford University) 45, 46
rows
    average 112–13, 126

rows (*continued*)
  vs columns for data 117–20, 126
  empty 62–3, 90, 101–2, 122, 125
  lines between 'WiT' rows 34
  ordering in tables 87, 92–100, 121, 125,
    235
    most important rows first 97–100
rules
  bending rules for slides 171–2
  breaking design rules 195
  for graphs 79

sans serif typefaces 52, 81, 168, 196–7, 227
script, presenter's 165–6
section headings 212
segmenting 8–9, 12, 40, 167
sequential line of argument 23–6, 37
serif typefaces 196–7, 227
shading 49–50, 54, 80, 102, 258
simplification 131
  graphs and 42–3, 73
Sims, John 75
single data set
  comparison graphs 56–8
  time-series graphs 63–4
sizing
  graphs 53, 81
  words and numbers on slides 152–4
slides 151–76
  alternatives to bullet points 158–62
  bending 'rules' for slides 171–2
  better bullet points 166–71, 175
  colour 171, 221
  design principles 205–6
  getting the audience to listen 163–5
  getting the message remembered
    152–7, 174
  graphs in 73–4, 84
  handouts 172–3, 175
  presenter's props 165–6
  tables in 108
  when to show nothing 163–4, 174
  'WiT' and 14–15, 30, 39, 158–9, 173
small differences, rounding and 186
spider graphs 83
squinting at small gaps 71–2
stacked bar charts 70, 83
staff charts 252
staff numbers table 87, 97–8, 101, 103,
    104, 105

staff utilisation graphs 46–7, 66–9, 78
standard of templates 225–6
starting at the end 7–8, 10, 167
strategic decisions 144–5
stripping out 8–9, 12, 167
style guides 33, 225–6, 230
subheadings 26–30, 37, 40, 197
summarising 11, 25, 40, 131
summary, starting with a 7–8, 167
summary tables 106

tables 85–126
  Big Five changes 87–108, 124–5
    compactness 87, 100–3, 125
    emphasis 87, 91–2, 124
    gridlines 87, 88–90, 124
    lead-in titles 87, 104–8, 125
    row and column order 87, 92–100,
      121, 125
  common mistakes 108–17
    inconsistencies that detract 116–17,
      126
    indecipherable column headings
      113–16
    numbers 110–11
    unnecessary repetition 111–13
    unnecessary zeros and brackets
      108–10, 125
  comparison 142
  constructing complex tables 125–6
  horizontal alignment of labels 204
  managers' dislike of 47–8
  rather than graphs for detailed num-
    bers 44, 46, 80
  redo of table of provisions for liabilities
    and charges 120–3
  rows vs columns 117–20, 126
  tables of ticks and crosses 128–33, 136,
    162, 174
  time-series data 66
  transposing 119
  vertical alignment of edges 202
  Words in Tables *see* 'WiT'
Telephone Directory 212
templates 159, 244–5
  in-house design templates 33, 225–6,
    230
text
  blocks of text in KPIs 243
  bullet points as dull text 3

line length 198, 227
positioning graphs in relation to 53
showing numbers in 188, 192
three-by-two grids 147, 148, 149
three-dimensional graphs 49, 80
tick marks 51, 52, 81
ticks and crosses, tables of 128–33, 136, 162, 174
time-series graphs 57, 63–9
more than one set of data 64–8
one set of data 63–4
Times New Roman 168, 196–7, 199–200
timing differences 234, 236
titles 197
graph 52, 53, 81
lead-in 53, 87, 104–8, 125, 169
literal 53, 105
'total' row 90
train timetables 118, 220
transposing a table 119
Tufte, Edward 171
two-by-two grids 133–7, 160, 173
typefaces
sans serif 52, 81, 168, 196–7, 227
serif 196–7, 227
tables 91, 92
typography 26–7, 122
bullet points 10
consistency 201
contrast 10, 159, 198–9, 199–200, 205–10, 228
document design 197–8, 215–20, 227
emphasis 87, 91–2, 124, 215–16
oddities to avoid in graphs 54–5
signals and comparisons 135, 140–1
trick to keep reader's eye on the page 25–6

underlining 215
UNICEF chart 59–61, 82, 266–7
updates on year-start plans 15–17, 36
upper case 215
random 170, 215
'Upside Down' maps 75

variable rounding 181–5, 191
in Excel 270–2
objections to 184–5
variance analysis 232–40, 247
percentage changes with negative numbers 272–3

Venn diagrams 139
vertical alignment 90, 202–3

waterfall graphs 78, 83
When Harry Met Sally 127, 146
Which? 133
white on black 216
white space 198, 199, 206, 227
Williams, Robin 195, 198
'WiT' (Words in Tables) 1–40, 212, 235, 245
advantage over bullet points 3–5
benefits of 21, 38
consistency in writing 19–21, 38
constructing 40
cutting out words 15–17
developing a line of argument 23–6, 37
ensuring completeness 12–14
gridlines 89
headings and subheadings 26–30, 37, 40
for particular formats 39
reassuring readers 18–19, 21, 38
slides 14–15, 30, 39, 158–9, 173
turning a bullet point list into 6–11
using to improve documents 35–8
variance analysis 235, 247
when not to leave lines between rows 34
when to use 21–3, 39
when you can have too much 'WiT' 30–1
Word 69, 100–1
Excel vs 268
linking Excel to 269
for landscape format 239–40
vertical alignment 202–3
words
changing how words wrap around in an Excel cell 115–16
cutting out unnecessary words 15–17
in graphs 51–3
vs graphs 43, 46, 80
unnecessary repetition in tables 111–13
writing, consistency in 19–21, 38

year-end position 234, 236

zeros
leading zero for numbers in text 188
unnecessary 108–10, 125